Crossroads Africa:
Perspectives on U.S.-China-Africa Security Affairs

Preface by
David H. Shinn

Foreword by
Theresa Whelan

Edited by
Robert R. Tomes
Angela Sapp Mancini
James T. Kirkhope

Council for Emerging National Security Affairs

Published in the United States of America
by the Council for Emerging National Security Affairs.

Copyright © 2009

Council for Emerging National Security Affairs
Cathedral Station, P.O. Box 534
New York, NY 10025
http://www.censa.net

Library of Congress Control Number: 2005934905

Library of Congress Cataloging-in-Publication Data
Crossroads Africa: Perspectives on U.S.-China-Africa Security Affairs
Edited by Robert R. Tomes, Angela Sapp Mancini and James T. Kirkhope
Includes biographical references
     ISBN10 0-9723858-4-3
     ISBN13 978-0-9723858-4-8

1. National Security. 2. Counterterrorism. I. Title. II. Robert R. Tomes

Printed and Bound in the United States of America

1 2 3 4 5 6 7 8 9

Cover Photo: 09/03/2006—Kenyan army soldiers walk back to their troop transport vehicle after a
fuel stop, as a U.S. military convoy prepares to resume travel toward Nginyang, Kenya, site of exercise
Natural Fire 2006 Aug. 2, 2006. The exercise, the largest held between East African Community nations and the United States, consists of military-to-military training as well as medical, veterinary,
and engineering civic affairs programs conducted in rural areas throughout the region. (U.S. Navy
photo by Mass Communication Specialist 2nd Class Roger S. Duncan) (Released)

CONTENTS

Section III: Security and Development Challenges

Section IV: AFRICOM and U.S. Military Strategy

Africa at the Crossroads

David H. Shinn

Former U.S. Ambassador to Burkina Faso and Ethiopia

Africa seems almost constantly to be at some kind of crossroads. Perhaps this goes with the territory for a continent that consists of fifty-three (fifty-four if you include the disputed Western Sahara) highly diverse countries, nearly all of which have been independent for less than fifty years. They have mixed records when it comes to economic success and political stability. A minority of these countries have been blessed with oil and/or mineral wealth, but most are among the world's poorest nations. They range in size geographically from Sudan, which is equivalent to the United States east of the Mississippi River, to tiny islands in the Atlantic and Indian oceans. Nigeria's population is 140 million while fourteen African countries have a population of two million or less. It is dangerous to generalize about Africa and impossible to understand the continent without first taking its diversity into account.

Historical Perspective, Pessimism, and Optimism

A comparative historical perspective is instructive. Where was the United States fifty years after independence? A quarter century after its first fifty years, the Civil War tore the U.S. apart before it could knit together again. A little patience may be in order when considering Africa today. There is a tendency by Americans to look at Africa in a negative context, largely due to media coverage that emphasizes bad news. The media are quick to report failures of leadership, civil and ethnic conflicts, border confrontations, famine, food shortages, terrorist attacks, acts of piracy, the HIV/AIDS pandemic, the scourge of malaria, and so forth. And it is true; all of these are serious problems and greater challenges than they should be.

Foreign Policy magazine's 2008 Failed States Index listed eleven African countries among the world's top twenty most endangered nations. At the same time, Africa's fifty-three countries are geographically more than three times the size of the United States and have a population that is about three times as large. With so many countries, so much land area, and a huge total population, there is considerable room for things to go wrong. Not everything is wrong with Africa. We just don't hear much about the success stories in countries such as Mauritius, Botswana, Ghana, South Africa, and Benin.

Analysts of Africa have long oscillated between Afro-pessimism and Afro-optimism. Afro-pessimists seem to have predominated in the United States, and perhaps Europe, in recent years while Afro-optimists prevailed and continue to predominate in newly emerging powers such as China, India, and Brazil. The difference in the way these two groups have approached Africa has been dramatic. When it comes to investment and non-oil trade, the United States and Europe have recently pursued a passive approach to the continent, whereas India, Brazil, and, especially, China have moved ahead aggressively and taken greater risks.

In July 2008, Edward N. Luttwak and Marian L. Tupy exemplified the pessimistic school *in extremis*. They argued that most African states function for the enrichment of political elites and have contempt for the African masses. There is an element of truth in their conclusion but also gross oversimplification of the problem. The remedy, according to Luttwak and Tupy, "might be to let Africa's failing neocolonial states disintegrate totally—so that organic African political structures can emerge." This is exactly what the international community did following the failed 1992–1995 nation-building effort in Somalia. Except for providing emergency food aid, it abandoned Somalia politically and economically and let the country fail totally.

With all due respect to Luttwak and Tupy, and I understand their frustration, this is not the remedy. Neither Africans nor the rest of the world needs a half dozen Somalias scattered around the continent with growing extremist movements and a higher terrorism potential.

U.S. Interests and Themes in Africa

United States' interests in Africa are modest but increasing. The U.S. imports about 20 percent of its oil from Africa and the figure is on the rise. American global security interests depend on African countries for aircraft overflight and landing privileges and access to ports for naval vessels. With more than a quarter of the membership in the United Nations General Assembly and proportional representation in other international forums, the U.S. must take African votes into account. Twelve percent of the U.S. population has its origins in Africa, and recently created African Diasporas are increasingly making their voices heard in the American political process. In addition, Africa's 950 million people are potentially an important market for American products and direct investment, especially as Africa becomes economically stronger. Its average GNP has increased 5 percent annually since 2004.

There are also some African developments of interest to the U.S. that Washington wants to prevent or mitigate. They include keeping international terrorism out of Africa, rolling back the HIV/AIDS pandemic and preventing the spread of highly infectious diseases, and preventing Africa from becoming an important link in international crime, money laundering, and drug trafficking. Finally, the U.S. wants Africa to become more stable politically and more democratic, with a higher level of economic development. Progress in these areas will reduce the need for American emergency and humanitarian aid. A surprising number of these U.S. interests overlap with China's interests in Africa.

There have been four broad themes in U.S. policy toward Africa since the end of World War II. First, until the end of the Cold War at the beginning of the 1990s, the containment of communism and especially the threat from the Soviet Union drove American policy toward Africa. China also played a key role in the Cold War competition for Africa. Second, Africa, especially sub-Saharan, has consistently been at the bottom of U.S. foreign policy priorities when measured against other major regions. Since the Bandung Conference in 1955, Africa has been a relatively higher priority for China. Third, with a few important exceptions, there has been a relative constancy of U.S. policy toward Africa by both Republican and Democratic administrations since the end of World War II. Fluctuations in Chinese policy toward Africa depended on internal policy decisions by the Communist Party of China, such as the impact of the Cultural Revolution. Fourth, the U.S. has always been the first country to provide the most assistance to Africa when there are humanitarian disasters such as droughts, floods, locusts, civil conflicts, and the HIV/AIDS pandemic. Only recently has China become an important contributor to African humanitarian disasters.

Future U.S.-Africa Relations: Several Assumptions

As power changes hands in Washington the assumption is usually made that Africa will once again be treated as a backwater. While Africa was not a major foreign policy issue during the campaign, we may be surprised at the attention it gets by a new administration. The Bush administration actually trebled the amount of financial assistance to Africa although it paid scant attention (Democratic Republic of the Congo) or late attention (Somalia) to some of the most intractable conflicts on the continent. Sudan was the major exception where it helped achieve a north-south peace agreement. Even today, there are only about forty American personnel assigned to Africa's seven U.N. peacekeeping operations. Neither Barack Obama nor John McCain said much about Africa during the 2008 presidential campaign. But based on the significant increase in resource commitments to Africa during the Bush years, the traditional pattern of minimal assistance increases from one administration to the next may have been broken.

The international community must accept as a given that there will be several conflict situations somewhere in Africa at any given time. Clearly, the U.S. and others need to do everything possible to prevent new crises and to mitigate ongoing ones, but, having said that, conflict will remain a fact of life. The international community, if unable to prevent or end any particular conflict, will have to work around the problem to the extent possible.

There are emerging regional powers outside Africa that now have far more influence in Africa than was the case just five years ago. Principal among them are China, India, and Brazil. Russia is beginning to reassert itself in

Africa. Some of the Gulf states and Iran are showing increasing interest. The European Union, always an important force on the continent, has taken note of these changes and may be emerging from its recent passivity. These new challenges from emerging countries seem to have caught the attention of Japan and possibly South Korea. The playing field in Africa has become much more crowded. The U.S. must adapt quickly and accordingly.

Future U.S.-Africa Relations: What to Do?

The Bush administration left a pipeline of about $10 billion in assistance to Africa. The pipeline aid will drop sharply by 2011 unless the new administration makes the case and Congress approves new funding. Because of the traditionally low foreign policy priority accorded Africa, the African affairs component of the U.S. bureaucracy has not been adequately staffed to do its job in recent years. The large amount of pipeline funding will exacerbate the staffing shortfall. The new administration will need to consider quickly how to staff the African affairs bureaucracy, especially in the State Department, in order to take maximum advantage of this funding. If it fails to do so, this will be an important missed opportunity.

The U.S. approach to counterterrorism in Africa needs to be restructured. It tends to rely heavily on direct support for African security organizations and U.S. or joint efforts to catch or kill bad guys. Five aerial attacks in Somalia against suspected terrorists since the beginning of 2007 are cases in point. Support for African security organizations is appropriate but not very useful if done largely in isolation. Catching or killing bad guys is only good if it works. Successful operations require nearly perfect intelligence. In those parts of Africa where terrorism has been a problem, American mastery of intelligence has often been inadequate. Obviously, it is important to improve American intelligence capacity in vulnerable areas.

Generally missing from this counterterrorism program have been discussions with Africans and other partners, including China, that deal with the root causes of terrorism and suggest solutions. It is long overdue to determine what is motivating Africans to support foreign terrorist operatives. I have one cautionary note: Some African countries try to convince the

U.S. to support counterterrorism programs to end terrorist attacks aimed at overthrowing them. The U.S. must avoid taking sides in these strictly internal conflicts.

Nearly everyone agrees that the Africa Growth and Opportunity Act (AGOA), born in the Clinton administration and carried forward by President Bush, is a good idea. Forty of sub-Saharan Africa's forty-eight countries are eligible for AGOA's duty-free benefits. AGOA has not, however, lived up to expectations. Two-way trade, excluding oil, between the U.S. and AGOA-eligible countries increased only 7 percent from 2005 to 2006. There was a sharp increase in U.S. oil purchases in Africa but it would have occurred with or without AGOA. In some cases, African countries do not know how to take full advantage of AGOA. In others, deficiencies in infrastructure and local capacity limit their ability to be competitive. The new administration should take a hard look at ways to make AGOA a more effective tool for improving African economies, especially the poorest ones. China has its own, more restrictive, duty-free entry program for certain products from the poorest African countries.

The Millennium Challenge Corporation (MCC), although slow out of the starting blocks, is now fully engaged in fighting poverty through economic growth in Africa. There is often a tendency by a new administration to dismiss the initiatives of the former administration. For whatever reason, there does not appear to be a strong domestic constituency for retaining the MCC. A change in administration is a good time to look at ways to improve or even restructure the MCC, but it would be unfortunate to eliminate the initiative just because it was the brainchild of the previous administration. The MCC deserves more time. It is the only American assistance program in Africa that is making a significant contribution to infrastructure, something the Africans desperately want and an area where China has responded enthusiastically.

I have been involved in African affairs dating back to the 1960s; it has always been difficult to convince the American private sector to invest in Africa. Oil is, of course, an important exception. Many administrations tried hard to encourage American companies to invest in Africa. The results have been discouraging. The Office of the U.S. Trade Representative estimated that by the end of 2005 U.S. direct investment in sub-Saharan Africa was about $15 billion. Chinese direct investment in sub-Saharan Africa almost certainly exceeds this amount today and is growing more rapidly than U.S. investment. Unless the new administration makes American investment in Africa a major priority, it will have no more success than previous efforts.

Increased American trade and especially private investment could do more than any other program, including aid, to strengthen African security and economies. As one South African analyst whimsically suggested, when the next American president visits Africa he should fill the plane with business people who are prepared to make deals and leave the bureaucrats in Washington. Even the Dow Jones Indexes launched in July 2008 a pan-African index that measures the stock performance of fifty companies that are headquartered in or generate the majority of their revenues in Africa. It follows markets in eleven African countries. African economies are moving; it is time for the American private sector, with a strong push from the new administration, to jump in.

The new American military command for Africa, AFRICOM, is a sound idea that had a terrible announcement party. It has been trying to recover ever since. So much effort was focused on making AFRICOM sound like a different kind of military command that the justification was not credible among Africans. Nor did it make any sense to put the headquarters with its large footprint in Africa, a decision that was implicit in the beginning. Many Africans concluded, inaccurately in my view, that AFRICOM was a U.S. response to China's growing role on the continent. Time will overcome these initial missteps.

AFRICOM is still struggling to define its mandate. The solution is not hard. It should operate much like other U.S. military commands. There should be an emphasis on training African security forces for peacekeeping operations and counterterror operations. AFRICOM should also provide assistance to African countries to improve maritime security, combat piracy, secure control over offshore fishing, and prevent attacks on offshore oil facilities. Any effort to replace the functions of USAID or nongovernmental organizations does not make sense. AFRICOM should do what the military does well and refrain from a new, exotic agenda.

A change of administration is a good time to reevaluate U.S. priorities for assistance to Africa. During the Bush administration, most of the funding has gone to HIV/AIDS. This program has considerable support in the U.S., and it is a virtual certainty that a future administration and Congress will continue to support HIV/AIDS funding. Although this may sound like heresy, it is time to shift more of this funding into other health programs. To some extent, the Bush administration began this process by providing money for combating malaria, addressing tropical disease, and training health workers. These efforts should increase even at the expense of reduced funding for HIV/AIDS.

The international community must also expand assistance for Africa's health care infrastructure. The health care systems in some of the poorest African countries are on life support. The brain drain has decimated much of their medical staff, equipment and medicine are in pathetically short supply, and physical structures are in disrepair. There is not much political support for providing assistance to health care infrastructure because the systems are part of a large government bureaucracy. But until these systems are improved, much of the money aimed at combating HIV/AIDS and other diseases will have a poor return.

Another health care program that requires urgent attention is family planning. In spite of all its medical challenges, Africa still has the highest population growth rate of any region in the world—on average almost 2.5 percent annually. Each year there are two million additional Ethiopians who require food. Ethiopia has had a structural food deficit since the 1960s and faces with increasing frequency additional food shortages due to drought, floods, and/or insects. Without a major family planning program, there is no reasonable prospect that Ethiopia will ever become food self-sufficient. Greater investment in agriculture could improve the situation across the continent. This should be another focus area for U.S. assistance. But in view of the marginal land in much of Africa, it is questionable whether even a green revolution can prevent the inevitable—a continent unable to feed itself—unless African countries and the donor community provide strong support for family planning.

There are several other sectors that merit increased assistance from the U.S. and the international community generally. The unemployment rate in many African countries is incomprehensibly high—for example 40 to 45 percent in economically powerful South Africa. Any aid programs aimed at creating jobs, especially for young people, will improve political stability and decrease the likelihood that Africans will be tempted to support external terrorist groups. Job creation is essential to economic growth.

There has also been deterioration in African higher education. Not only are graduates less skilled than in earlier decades but the most qualified graduates are the most likely to join the brain drain, either leaving for more advanced African countries or, more often, departing for Europe, North America, and the Gulf states. A significant investment in Africa's institutions of higher education would help to ameliorate this problem.

Finally, improving the environment has never been a high priority in most African countries or for donor assistance programs. There have simply been too many other higher priority problems. Global warming is having a more negative impact in the tropics than any other part of the world. The donor community should begin working with African governments now to counter these negative effects and not wait until most of the damage has already occurred.

Areas for providing assistance such as improving African higher education and confronting environmental degradation play to American strengths. Others cry out for cooperation with other partner countries, including China. Beijing offers, for example, appropriate agricultural technology and it has a strong record in sending grassroots medical teams to Africa. The United States should make every effort to work with China and others to improve these sectors in Africa.

This is an ambitious agenda. Availability of scarce resources will require prioritization and some hard choices. It is, however, in the interest of the United States and donor nations, including China, to encourage political, economic, and social progress in Africa.

Africa: A New Strategic Perspective

Theresa Whelan

Deputy Assistant Secretary of Defense for African Affairs

Introduction

Former Deputy Assistant Secretary of Defense (DASD) for African Affairs, James Woods, used to begin his annual presentation to U.S. Army Foreign Area Officers (FAOs) with a question: "Why is Africa important to the United States?" The answers would range from the practical (natural resources) to idealistic (people yearning to be free of dictators) to the altruistic (prevent disease and save lives from humanitarian disasters). According to Woods, while those were sound reasons, he wanted to draw the FAOs' thinking to the strategic level, so the answer was: "Because it's there."

That's a simplification, but Africa's place in the world cannot be overlooked. As the second-largest continent in the world—11,700,000 square miles (22 percent of the world's total land area) with an estimated population of 690 million people (roughly 14 percent of the world's population)—it's geographically and demographically important. It's economically important as well: By 2005 economic growth was averaging 5 percent and there were tens of thousands of U.S. jobs tied to the African market; Africa possesses an estimated 8 percent of the world's petroleum; and it is a major source of critical minerals, precious metals, and food commodities. It is also politically important: Of the ten elected members of the U.N. National Security Council, three are elected from the General Assembly by African nations.

Africa's strategic importance has been reflected historically in ways that have sometimes been less than a blessing for the continent. It sits astride millennia-old trade routes; the possession of its resources and even its people have been fought over by many nations both ancient and modern, a "fight" that continues to this day, albeit in less stark terms as that which occurred during the so-called "scramble for Africa" of the nineteenth century. The legacies of that colonialism continue to haunt the international community. There is perhaps a magazine or newspaper article written somewhere in the world every week that draws a parallel between what happened during the "scramble" and the alleged maneuvering between modern powers for access to African natural resources, be they oil, minerals, timber, or fish.

Africa remains a rich, vibrant, and diverse place with an ever-increasing strategic significance in today's global security environment. President Bush's 2007 decision to direct the reorganization of DoD Unified Command structure in order to add a new stand-alone Unified Command for Africa, AFRICOM, was a direct recognition of Africa's importance as well as a clear signal that the U.S. understands the need to work more regularly and consistently on developing, building, and expanding security partnerships with African states to help promote a more secure and stable global environment.

United States military engagement on the African continent is not new. For many years the U.S. military has undertaken joint military exercises and training programs to assist African nations in the professional development of their military forces. The DoD has also had a long history of working in support of other U.S. government agencies and international relief organizations in delivering humanitarian assistance and medical care and coordinating disaster relief. However, despite this long history of engagement on the continent, DoD has never focused on Africa with the same level of consistency with which it has focused on the other regions of the world. The intent of this new unified geographic command is to enable greater consistency of focus in a way that reflects post–Cold War and post–9/11 lessons learned. Those lessons learned highlighted the changing nature of the twenty-first-century threat environment, the consequent value of building security partnerships with like-minded nations throughout the world, and the importance of a holistic approach to security and stability issues.

Changing Paradigms

With the end of the Cold War the strategic paradigm the U.S. had used for nearly fifty years to understand and respond to the global security environment gradually became less and less relevant. No place was this more apparent than in Africa where Africa's strategic importance to the U.S. had been defined almost entirely in relation to U.S. Cold War security objectives. In the absence of the Cold War, U.S. national security policy makers in the 1990s struggled to understand exactly where and how Africa fit in the security context. The initial answer was that Africa's security challenges manifested no direct threat to the U.S., militarily or economically (given the assumption that the collapse of the bipolar division of the globe would now allow free market–based access to world commodities) and therefore were relevant to the U.S. primarily in a humanitarian context. However, the events of 9/11, combined with 20/20 hindsight made clear that Africa was integral, not peripheral, to global security in general, and U.S. security in particular, in the post–9/11 world.

This was a world in which catastrophic threats to a nation-state's security were not simply confined to rival nation-states with the capacity to build large, sophisticated, conventional militaries with the means to deliver WMD. Rather, such threats could come from anywhere in the world, including from among the poorest, least developed, and least secure countries on the planet. If a small group of terrorists operating out of an undeveloped country in Central Asia could inflict more damage on the U.S. in a few hours than the entire Japanese Imperial Navy did at Pearl Harbor, the U.S. could no longer afford to prioritize its security concerns using traditional, conventional, power-based criteria. To further complicate matters, it became clear that non-state actors could now be just as dangerous, if not more so, as an aggressive state-based power. In this post–9/11 world, African security issues could no longer be viewed as only a humanitarian concern. Cold, hard "realpolitik" dictated a U.S. national interest in promoting a secure and stable African continent.

Security and stability in Africa, however, are not merely functions of developing competent military and police forces. Experiences in Africa and the Balkans in the 1990s and in Afghanistan and Iraq over the last five years have made clear that those tools only provide security and stability on a temporary basis. Sustainable security and stability are dependent on good governance, the rule of law, and economic opportunity. Those elements of security, in turn, have a symbiotic relationship with such things as health and education. If a secure and stable Africa is in U.S. national interest, then the U.S. would need to take a holistic approach to addressing the challenge. Additionally, in the new, more volatile, fluid, and unpredictable global security environment, the old adage about an ounce of prevention being worth a pound of cure does not simply make sense from a resource perspective but also from a risk mitigation and management perspective.

The relevance of places like the African continent to global security is highlighted by the problem of ungoverned or under-governed space and its impact on security in the twenty-first century. Under-governed space can be either physical or nonphysical in nature. The common denominator is an area where there is an absence of state capacity or political will to exercise control. Africa is dominated by vast expanses of rugged and remote land area as well as large areas of ocean, lakes, and rivers where central state-based governments have difficulty even establishing physical presence let alone control.

This is hardly the least of the continent's problems but it is the one category of ungoverned space that is most directly addressed by expanding a country's security capacity. However, expanding a country's capacity to provide physical security addresses only part of the problem.

Beyond their inability to exercise control over physical space, numerous African governments still have difficulty exercising meaningful control over governing space. There are many cases in which African governments find themselves competing with outsiders for influence within their own country. Unable or, in some cases even unwilling, to exercise particular governing responsibilities they cede authority to non-state or even outside elements. For example, lack of government support for education can ultimately default this "space" to potential exploitation by extremists who set up madrasas that directly and indirectly spread religious intolerance and extremist hatred. This kind of ungoverned space can be as dangerous as the physical kind but it does not necessarily lend itself to a security fix. African governments are also subject to the exploitation of weak legal systems and to their inability to monitor business and money transactions as much as they are hamstrung by their inability to control their ports and airports. While improvements in security capacity may address some aspects of these nonphysical areas, they do not address all of them.

AFRICOM

It is in this context that former Secretary of Defense Rumsfeld asked his military and civilian staff to reexamine the merits and feasibility of establishing a stand-alone Unified Command focused exclusively on Africa. Africa's direct relevance to U.S. national security demanded that DoD rethink the Cold War–based structure that artificially divided the continent among three different commands that were frequently distracted by responsibilities in their primary geographic regions. Keeping Africa divided among three commands would mean that, at best, Africa would remain a secondary and sometimes even tertiary concern for those commands. As such, neither the commands, nor the military services that supported them with personnel, would deem it a priority to develop a large body of personnel with knowledge and expertise on Africa. Yet the complexities and subtleties of the security challenges in Africa require regional expertise to navigate. It also meant that the bureaucratic barriers created by the "seams" between the commands would continue to present challenges to coherent and efficient action in the areas where the seams met. The fact that the seams ran through key areas of conflict and instability on the continent made them even more problematic. Additionally, the establishment of the African Union (AU) and its ambitious program for a continent-wide multilateral security architecture created further complications for DoD's command seams, as the U.S. European Command (EUCOM) found itself working more and more in the U.S. Central Command (CENTCOM) backyard in Addis Ababa with the AU. Further, both CENTCOM and EUCOM struggled to deal with emerging African standby brigade structures that cut across their respective areas of responsibility.

Beyond simply mandating a relook at the way lines were drawn on the DoD map, the Secretary also directed that the effort involve members of the U.S. government interagency, in particular, the State Department and USAID, and that the team consider innovative organizational constructs as well as mission sets for a command dedicated solely to Africa. The former Secretary believed that if DoD was going to establish a command for Africa it needed to be a twenty-first century command, not a twentieth century command and it needed to be tailored to address the unique security challenges of the continent. Dealing with security challenges in Africa required not only an organizational restructuring in DoD but also new ways of doing business.

Secretary of Defense Gates has since embraced the effort, stressing that the command should "oversee security cooperation, building partnership capability, [and] defense support to nonmilitary missions" and expressing the importance of moving away from an "outdated arrangement left over from the Cold War."

The result of the interagency study team's work was a proposal for a Unified Command for Africa that would concentrate its efforts on prevention rather than reaction. Its primary objective would be to contribute DoD's expertise in the security arena in support of U.S. diplomacy and development efforts to "prevent problems from becoming crises, and crises from becoming catastrophes." In that context the command would help build the capacity of African countries to reduce conflict, improve security, deny terrorists sanctuary, and support crisis response. In order to do this, the traditional military J-code organization structure designed for combat operations would need to be fundamentally changed to incorporate an integrated civilian/military architecture that would emphasize and facilitate nonkinetic missions, such as military-capacity-building training, security-sector reform, and military professionalization, as well as support to the humanitarian assistance, disaster relief, and medical assistance efforts of other U.S. government (USG) agencies. The study team also recommended that the command not be developed in a U.S. vacuum but rather that the specifics of its mission, design, and even possible location be informed by consultation with international partners. Particular importance was placed on consultation with African partners to ensure that it would be appropriate to the African context. On 7 February 2007, President Bush publicly announced his direction to DoD to develop and stand up a Unified Command for Africa by the end of September 2008 based on the principles outlined by the interagency study team.

Taking the "Road Not Taken"

AFRICOM's mission statement succinctly articulates the tasks ahead: "*United States Africa Command, in concert with other U.S. Government agencies and international partners*, [author's emphasis] conducts sustained security engagement through military-to-military programs, military-sponsored activities, and other military operations as directed to promote a stable and secure African environment in support of U.S. foreign policy."

Significantly, this mission statement places emphasis on what the February 2006 DoD Quadrennial Defense Review (QDR), refers to as "anticipatory measures." In other words, AFRICOM's primary objective will be, as the QDR put it, to "prevent problems from becoming crises and crises from becoming catastrophes." Given AFRICOM's mission emphasis on prevention versus reaction, one of the most significant organizational structure innovations that had been developed for the command is the creation of a Deputy for Civil/Military Activities. This dramatically elevates the role and importance of security cooperation and assistance activities in the command, making them equivalent to more traditional military operational functions. Further, for the first time, DoD has a non-DoD civilian as a senior official in AFRICOM's chain of command. A State Department senior foreign service officer is the Deputy for Civil/Military Activities and serves as one of two deputies reporting directly to the AFRICOM commander.

Areas of focus will include security capabilities (both land and maritime); medical skills; command, control, and communications; disaster relief; and security sector reform/restructuring, such as what is being done in Sierra Leone, Liberia, and the Democratic Republic of the Congo (DRC).

In particular, AFRICOM leadership will seek to interface with the African Union on developing ways in which AFRICOM can provide effective training, advisory, and technical support to the development of the African Standby Force. AFRICOM has already placed a senior U.S. Army colonel in Addis Ababa to serve as liaison to the AU. The State Department's embedded personnel in AFRICOM will also enhance AFRICOM's ability to support such State Department–funded endeavors as the African Contingency Operations Training and Assistance (ACOTA) program, a mainstay of the U.S. effort to build peace support operations capacity in Africa. Additionally, the integrated approach of AFRICOM will allow DoD's various military exercise programs in Africa, such as the AFRICAN ENDEAVOR communications exercise, Joint Combined Exchange Training exercises, and MEDFLAG exercises, to be more effectively synchronized with African Standby Force development goals.

A senior development advisor from USAID along with USAID personnel embedded in the command will provide AFRICOM with the expertise and guidance it needs to manage more effectively its small humanitarian assistance and civic action projects as well as HIV/AIDS prevention programs with other U.S. government agencies that have the lead in the development and health sectors. This type of coordination/cooperation has already proven effective in the Horn of Africa, where Combined Joint Task Force—Horn of Africa has worked closely with USAID and regional African governments responding to flood emergencies and conducting civic action projects such as digging wells and building schools in places where development agencies have identified critical needs. AFRICOM will build on this success.

The Department of Defense, working through EUCOM, CENTCOM, and PACOM currently has existing programs in many areas. AFRICOM will continue to execute those programs and, over time, seek to use its leverage as a stand-alone Unified Command to gain additional resources to strengthen and expand them, as well as develop new ones to address emerging African security needs.

Importantly, AFRICOM's sustained engagement in Africa is the means by which the Department of Defense can more easily consult with friends on the continent, collaborate on important initiatives that promote security and stability, and learn from civilian and military African leaders about how they view their own challenges, opportunities, and remedies for helping the continent achieve its full potential.

Conclusion

As illustrated above, the United States presently enjoys thriving security, economic, and political relationships with most of the countries on the African continent. In a sense, the creation of Africa Command finally brings DoD in line with the rest of the U.S. government and U.S. policy toward Africa. DoD's development of an Africa Command to streamline its Cold War legacy organizational structures is a logical step in what has been, and will continue to be, a long journey for both the U.S. and Africa—a journey toward a more stable, peaceful, and prosperous world. The security challenges of the twenty-first century demand that Africa be an integral, not peripheral, element of that world in a security context, as well as in political and economic contexts. Consequently, African countries should be partners in the journey. The idea of partnership has characterized the U.S. approach to security challenges in other parts of the world, which is one reason the U.S. has had geographically focused commands for those other regions for some time. In that context some might argue an Africa Command is long overdue. Whether it's overdue or right on time, the Africa Command is a concrete manifestation of the U.S. commitment to establish a serious, long-term partnership with African nations to address the issues that present challenges to our mutual security interests in this new century.

Africa at the Crossroads of U.S. Security Affairs

Angela Sapp Mancini and Robert R. Tomes

African security and stability issues are increasingly interwoven with American national security interests. When many of our authors first studied African security issues the focus was Cold War politics. Africa was another contested space, with African affairs viewed through the lens of bipolarity and balance of power politics. U.S. security strategists did not consider Africa through an independent lens, but rather only prioritized African issues to the extent there was a direct relationship to the Soviet Union, the Middle East, strategic resources, or something specific on an administration's foreign policy agenda.

Much of this has changed. Rising interest in African oil and natural gas resources, China's expanding engagement on the continent, and fears that failed states will provide sanctuary for terrorists have renewed the United States' interest in Africa. By the early 2000s, African security issues were centered at the crossroads of U.S. national security policy. From terrorism to armed conflict to human security concerns, Africa has become the source of new case studies for a post–Cold War generation of policy analysts seeking a more diverse, globally-focused security policy agenda. Many of the most significant security issues cannot be seriously discussed without addressing African issues, and in critical areas Africa has emerged as a touchstone for twenty-first century security affairs. This has been reflected by a U.S. foreign policy increasingly designed to secure energy resources, promote peace and development, strengthen military cooperation on the continent, and address long-term human security challenges.

A key factor that cannot be ignored is China's rising engagement on the continent, which has political, economic, and military dimensions that directly link Sino-African relations to other regional and global issues. Some U.S. observers concentrate on the dynamics of competition associated with a "rising China" and the negative implications this has for U.S. commercial as well as political interests. But while the U.S. may voice concern over China's energy exploration and extraction efforts, and protest Chinese aloofness from Western anticorruption regimes and other "fair play" business practices, the fact is that the U.S. and China share many similar interests in Africa. These include bringing stability to African states, strengthening Africa as an export market, ensuring predictability of energy resources, and combating terrorism and infectious disease on the continent. Great powers have common interests and common aversions. National security is a discipline defined by interdependence, and any discussion of China requires a balanced view of U.S. security objectives.

The Obama administration assumed office with an exhaustive list of foreign policy and security problems in the midst of an economic crisis. Afghanistan, Iraq, the covert war in Pakistan, and other international crises eclipse African security challenges. It would be easy to put Africa toward the end of the long to-do list of the new administration. But unlike previous administrations, the Obama foreign policy and security team includes a number of appointees with a personal interest in African affairs and a historic opportunity to engage with African leaders. The administration knows Africa will be one of the issues that history will judge them on. The challenge is balancing near-term geo-strategic issues, including the problems inherited from the Bush administration that dominated the election, and long-term security challenges.

This volume addresses the nexus of U.S. foreign policy and security issues that involve Africa and China, including the emerging role of the U.S. Africa Command. Stability, security, and reconstruction policies and operations will likely be the focus of U.S. engagement in Africa and, increasingly, these activities will require the U.S. government to work with, if not partner with, nongovernmental regional and international organizations focused on specific issues. This volume aims to explore ways in which the new administration can prioritize what are often competing U.S. interests in Africa and explores policy options to achieve them. In doing so, the volume continues the founding mission of the Council for Emerging National Security Affairs (CENSA): to focus attention on current international security issues and to provide an opportunity for the new generation of security policy professionals to contribute to policy debates while engaging with academics and policy makers.

Since 1999, CENSA has built a strong reputation in the national security community by addressing emerging trends and offering thoughtful analysis and solutions from the mid-career practitioner's perspective. This volume brings together perspectives and expertise from mid-career professionals working on these issues from many angles to offer views on how the new administration might consider crafting and implementing policies related to U.S. engagement in Africa, particularly through the lens of China's rising activities on the continent. The chapters reflect the mid-career perspective of CENSA's membership, which is drawn from the military, academia, and the private and public sectors. Authors offer policy recommendations based upon their experience as government officials, active military personnel, professors of security studies, geographic experts, professional risk managers, and managers of nongovernmental organization (NGO) field operations. Rounding out the volume are chapters by current and former government leaders and by scholars whose own research on Africa, China, and development inform U.S. policy.

This volume is divided into four sections. The first, *Framing U.S. Security Policy Toward Africa*," takes stock of U.S. interests in Africa and discusses the recent developments in both security issues facing Africa and the U.S. policies employed to tackle those issues. Paul Williams argues that the U.S. should prioritize human security, rather than security of regimes, and notes the three primary threats on the continent are violence, health, and environmental issues, while Melissa Cox Bosse recommends a variety of governance and training areas the new administration should focus on as they develop a new security strategy for Africa. Sean Macrae and Shannon Beebe offer reflections on U.S. efforts toward democratization in Africa over the past fifty years, noting that "democratization in Africa is a marathon" and recommending that the U.S. support democratization through simultaneous advances in economic development, health, and education. Anthony McIvor suggests that Africa is at a "tipping point toward democracy and wider prosperity" and that the U.S. must realize security issues are comprised of more than just defense issues in this "New Africa," while Peter Clark provides an overview of the interests and activities that other major players—Russia, India, and the European Union—are undertaking in Africa.

The second section, *"Perspectives on China-Africa Security Issues,"* explores the nexus between U.S., Chinese, and African interests on various issues on the continent, and discusses in further detail China's interests on the continent, including access to resources and a strong export market, investment opportunities, and diplomatic support for the "One China" policy. John Paden describes Sino-American competition and collaboration in Africa, arguing that America's interest is rooted primarily in Egypt, Angola, and Nigeria and explores Chinese activities in Nigeria as a case study. He recommends that the Obama administration increase cooperation with China through trilateral dialogues, particularly with respect to ensuring security of energy supplies. Ian Taylor also calls for increased U.S. engagement with China on African issues, noting the complexities faced by both countries and the evolving nature of circumstances and policy approaches on both sides. Sean McFate argues that "China needs Africa more than Africa needs China" and notes that the striking point about China's ascendancy on the continent isn't the volume, but the velocity.

Michael Argosino discusses opportunities and constraints in China's policies, adding his voice to arguments for a balanced view of China's strategy of global engagement. Michael Radosh highlights the dichotomy of China's military engagement in Africa while support for regimes in Sudan and Zimbabwe are destabilizing, Chinese involvement in U.N. operations helps mitigate conflict and reinforces the role of international organizations in development. He recommends the U.S. use quiet diplomacy to outline why Sudan and Zimbabwe pose a threat to Chinese interests, while publicly encouraging stronger Chinese engagement in peacekeeping operations. Peng Claire Bai provides a thoughtful overview of the widely-discussed Chinese interest in Africa's energy resources, including a detailed outline of China's National Oil Company (NOC) activity on the continent, and cautions U.S. policy makers against assuming that Chinese NOCs necessarily act in concert with Beijing's interests. Also advocating engagement with China, Bai recommends the administration focus on common U.S.-China energy security interests; specifically, encouraging the private sector pursue joint projects on exploration and production while the government urges China to act as a responsible stakeholder on energy issues.

A third section, *"Security and Development Challenges,"* outlines specific challenges Africa faces. Angela Sapp Mancini provides an overview of the size and trajectory of development assistance flows each country is providing to Africa and contrasts the U.S. "good governance" approach with the "China model" of "no strings attached." She urges the Obama administration to retain strong aid flows into Africa, even though the U.S. faces severe budgetary pressures, and to work in closer concert with China on African development. Blair Sondker explores the economic and political risks both the U.S. and China face in operating in China, recommending that strong engagement with Africa is critical to stabilizing the continent and thus reducing risk. Joshua Aaron Vogel offers policy suggestions to stem transnational Islamic extremism in Africa, including helping individual countries control borders and enhance citizens' opportunities, while cautioning against self-fulfilling paradigms of linking local Islamic rebellions to worldwide insurgencies. Richard Mehring and Daniel Trapp discuss offshore oil production in Africa, explaining the large resources held by Nigeria and Angola, and the risks of bringing production onshore. They argue that while oil companies can support development, it is really governments that must combat corruption and take the lead in ensuring development for their people.

A final section discusses *"AFRICOM and U.S. Military Strategy."* One of the most discussed developments in U.S.-Africa security issues in recent years, AFRICOM brings capacity, presence, planning resources, the potential to act quickly, leverage with Allies and partners, and the promise of security assistance. But AFRICOM's status has already declined since its 2007 stand-up in terms of resources and focus, and some question its movement into civilian affairs that crosses into what has previously been the domain of USAID. The Obama administration inherits a fledgling Command with draft strategies and lots of enthusiasm across the interagency. It also inherits skepticism, an uncertain resource plan at a time of budget contraction, and fragmented agendas across the interagency community interested in African issues. Robert Tomes examines defense strategy and the need to integrate African security issues and case studies more deliberately into planning processes. Matthew Shabat outlines the challenges and opportunities of AFRICOM, concluding that AFRICOM is a positive development but must focus on strengthening the interagency process, offering various ways in which to achieve this goal. Derek Reveron outlines how the U.S. can utilize AFRICOM to fulfill diplomatic and development roles, and advocates AFRICOM's ability to export security through increased cooperation, particularly through maritime security initiatives such as the East Africa and Southwest Indian Ocean Initiative. He concludes by noting that AFRICOM and other initiatives "must be judged by their own criteria—which are improving stability and security in Africa."

One of the most common recurring themes in the recommendations offered by these mid-career practitioners is to engage China across the broad spectrum of issues where U.S. and Chinese interests overlap. Rather than embrace the argument that Chinese activities threaten the U.S., the authors of this volume suggest taking a more nuanced view. As Peng Claire Bai noted, "Cooperation instead of competition is the key to U.S.-China relations in Africa." From trilateral dialogues on security issues and joint energy projects, to closer cooperation on development assistance in Africa and encouragement for an expanded role for China in peacekeeping operations, it is clear that the majority of authors advocate open communication and engagement as the method by which U.S., Chinese, and African interests can best be advanced. Many authors also reflect the theme of supporting Africans in taking the lead in issues such as development, counterterrorism, and maritime security.

Finally, the authors reflect a joint consensus that the U.S. continue to engage in Africa, most critically in the areas of stability, security, and reconstruction, and that partnerships are a key way to improve African security and development conditions. U.S.-African security policies succeed when they are multilateral approaches tethered to strong bilateral relationships and cemented by unambiguous U.S. leadership and commitments. None of these three conditions have been historically strong suits of U.S. foreign policy concerning Africa. The U.S. brings enormous resources and capacity, especially when short-term actions are needed to forestall a crisis. As AFRICOM planning unfolds, additional attention should be paid to adapting the 1990s' "rapid reaction, rapid decisive operations" view of military doctrine and strategy to the longer-term focus of doctrine and strategy that will be needed for security and stabilization missions in the future. In doing so, attention must be given to balancing U.S. defense planning objectives and the allocation of U.S. military resources toward diplomatic, economic, and development priorities.

ANGELA SAPP MANCINI   ROBERT R. TOMES, PHD
CO-EDITOR   PROJECT DIRECTOR

SECTION I:

Framing U.S. Security Policy toward Africa

Africa's Challenges, America's Choices

Paul D. Williams

Although there is just one African continent its inhabitants experience many different realities and often conflicting threat agendas. There are two agendas that largely shape the realities of African security affairs: the human security agenda and the regime security agenda. This chapter largely focuses on the human security agenda, addressing key issues and challenges for U.S. policy makers.

Thinking about Africa's Challenges

By many indicators, the world judges Africa to be its most insecure region. This chapter provides an overview of the global context within which Africa's human security challenges have developed. It concludes by posing some questions that the next U.S. administration will face when devising its Africa policies.

The 2007 Failed States Index concludes that Africa contains eight of the world's ten most failing states (in order they are Sudan, Somalia, Zimbabwe, Chad, Côte d'Ivoire, Democratic Republic of the Congo [DRC], Guinea, and Central African Republic).[1] A similar picture is evident in Freedom House's conclusion that Africa is home to seven of the world's seventeen most repressive regimes (Chad, Equatorial Guinea, Eritrea, Libya, Somalia, Sudan, and Zimbabwe).[2] Furthermore, its analysis suggested that during 2007, fifteen countries in sub-Saharan Africa registered significant reversals in the political rights and civil liberties they afforded their people.

The U.N. Development Program (UNDP) data also suggests that Africa is home to thirty-five of the world's forty most underdeveloped states.[3] The daily realities behind these figures include the uncomfortable facts that half the continent's people live on less than one dollar a day, more than half lack access to hospitals or doctors, one-third suffer from malnutrition, one in six children die before their fifth birthday, and the average African's life expectancy is just forty-one years.

In such circumstances, many of Africa's people face a wide range of threats to their security. Chief among them are violence, including armed conflict, warlordism, and other forms of criminality; health challenges, notably from HIV/AIDS, malaria, and TB; and environmental degradation, including greater deforestation and desertification as well as water and food scarcity. Africa's governments, on the other hand, do not always share a similar threat agenda. Many of them remain preoccupied with preserving their regime's grip on power and show virtually no interest in addressing the human security concerns of their least fortunate citizens. For such governments, the security agenda is about preserving their access to resources, maintaining control of state institutions, and keeping their political opponents weak and divided.

In this sense, although there is just one African continent its inhabitants experience many different realities and often conflicting threat agendas. We might refer to the two realities described above as the human security agenda and the regime security agenda. Foreign governments engaged in Africa thus face a choice about which of these security agendas to support and how it relates to their own priorities. The policies pursued by the George W. Bush administration suggest that its African priorities have focused on alleviating the HIV/AIDS pandemic, countering the threat of anti-Western terrorism, and ensuring access to the continent's sources of energy.[4] These concerns share elements with both the human and regime security agendas but it has been rare for the Bush administration to prioritize the former over the latter.

Local and Global

Although often depicted as the marginalized continent that globalization forgot, Africa and Africans are not immune from the wider processes shaping world politics. The most important of these concern human activities in the three crucial areas of economic growth, population growth, and energy usage, each of which has important repercussions for Africa's security equation.[5] The economic story, especially since 1820, is one of exponential growth facilitated by industrialization, Fordism, and economic integration.

This period also experienced the final stages of the second great surge in human population history with most demographers expecting one more doubling to come.

In relation to energy consumption, the scale and intensity was delivered courtesy of the internal combustion engine and refined oil. This permitted human beings to deploy more energy since 1900 than in all of human history before that date. Taken together, J. R. McNeill concluded that during the twentieth century, "The human species has shattered the constraints and rough stability of the old economic, demographic, and energy regimes." In so doing, it had unintentionally "undertaken a gigantic uncontrolled experiment on the earth."[6]

Although Africa was not at the forefront of any of these revolutions it has been caught up in their wake and is now experiencing an intensification of pressures in all three areas. First of all, Africa is now faced with more and more people living in bigger urban areas. Between 1750 and 1996, Africa's population increased from an estimated 95 million to 732 million people.[7] By 2016, the population of sub-Saharan Africa alone is estimated to increase by more than another 200 million.[8] Among other things this has had huge repercussions for levels of food and water scarcity on the continent, especially in urban areas.

Whereas for about eight thousand years of human history cities constituted what McNeill called "demographic black holes," in recent times they have stopped checking population growth and started adding to it. While in 1890 approximately 5 percent of Africans resided in urban areas by 1990 the figure was 34 percent.[9] The number of mega-cities on the continent has also increased; from just one (Cairo) in 1900, by 2000 there were thirty-six cities with populations of between 1 to 10 million people and two (Cairo and Lagos) with populations of over 10 million.[10]

These cities have giant metabolisms: massive appetites for energy, water, and food consumption, and they spew out huge quantities of pollutants, garbage, and solid wastes. And around the urban cores shantytowns and slums have quickly mushroomed. In many respects, Africa's slums are the epitome of urbanized insecurity, with their residents generally lacking law enforcement, regular sources of employment, sanitation, water, electricity, and health care facilities. With the constant possibility of eviction, it makes little sense to devote much time or money to neighborhood improvements and hence the environment quickly decays.

Shantytowns are also among the most densely populated land in Africa. The sprawling urban slum of Kibera in Nairobi, for instance, is home to somewhere between 500,000 to 1 million people with about two to three thousand people per square hectare.[11] For more and more Africans, this environment—not international anarchy—best captures their primary urbanized security dilemma.

Africa has also been caught up in the global scramble for oil and other sources of energy. Older oil fields like those in Algeria and Libya have been supplemented by newer discoveries like those in the Niger Delta, Cabinda, and Sudan. The race is now well underway to find the next significant deposits, especially around the Gulf of Guinea, which some predict will be the world's number one source of oil outside OPEC by 2010.[12] With Africa accounting for approximately 9.4 percent of the world's proven oil reserves and sub-Saharan Africa alone accounting for 15 percent of the United States' imported oil by 2002, the continent's oil producing governments inherited substantial newfound wealth, although significant domestic discord usually came with it.

For the consumers of African oil, the political instability surrounding the major oil exporting regimes and the fact that Africa is poised to significantly increase its oil exports has already had important repercussions for their own national security and foreign aid policies. As part of its concerns about energy security and winning its "long war" on terror, the U.S. government, for instance, has stepped up its naval operations, military training and assistance programs, and the search for military bases in Africa, and has established a new Africa Command. Among the main concerns of such consumers are the endemic corruption involved in the political economy of African oil and the safety of the facilities and production personnel. Even without the conflict that has often accompanied oil wealth, the process of extraction has usually come at a terrible environmental cost. In 1992, for instance, the U.N. declared the Niger to be the world's most ecologically endangered delta.

Global trends related to economic growth, demographic change and energy usage have thus clearly impacted upon African politics. However, given the strikingly different development trajectories apparent across the post-colonial world, security analysts should also be curious about what might be termed global-local interactions; that is, how some specifically African factors have interacted with external processes to produce today's political realities.

One issue is the relationship between the continent's governance problems and its political geography, especially the longstanding difficulties involved in trying "to project authority over inhospitable territories that contain relatively low densities of people."[13] A second issue is the importance of the spirit world for the way many Africans think about power. Put bluntly, politics in Africa cannot be fully grasped without reference to religious ideas; that is, "a belief in the existence of an invisible world, distinct but not separate from the visible one, that is home to spiritual beings with effective powers over the material world."[14]

It is within the complex interrelationships between global processes (including those related to demography, urbanization, energy, and the environment) and local contexts (including inhospitable political geography and religious ideas and practices) that the main threats to Africa's human security and regime security agendas will emerge.

U.S. Policy and the Human Security Threat Agenda

Clearly, the status quo is not working for the vast majority of Africans. In such circumstances, responding to the human security agenda will require significant political change. But what type of political changes will help promote security, and for whom?

The current human security agenda in Africa is daunting, but three clusters of threats deserve particularly high priority because of the insecurity they generate across large swathes of Africa. They are violence, health challenges, and environmental degradation.

Violence: Too many Africans face the threat or use of violence on a daily basis, usually from their own government's soldiers, police, or other "security forces." Since the early 1990s, Africa has suffered three particularly devastating clusters of interconnected wars centered around West Africa (Liberia, Sierra Leone, Guinea, Côte d'Ivoire), the Greater Horn (Chad, Ethiopia, Eritrea, Somalia, Sudan), and the Great Lakes (Rwanda, Burundi, Zaire/DRC, Uganda). Most casualties of these conflicts have been women and children, usually killed by the effects of diseases and malnutrition intensified by displacement. Although the number of armed conflicts across Africa more than halved between 1999 and 2006, and the combat toll dropped by 98 percent, by any measure warfare remains a pressing problem.[15] In the DRC, for instance, the most authoritative recent assessment suggests the war has resulted in approximately 5.4 million excess deaths between August 1998 and April 2007, the vast majority through preventable and treatable diseases.[16] Similarly detailed estimates do not exist for the conflicts in Côte d'Ivoire, Sudan, and Somalia, amongst other places, but they have clearly exacted a terrible human toll.

The causes and dynamics of Africa's wars hold important clues for how security policies should be devised. Although often involving complex international webs of pacts between governments and foreign insurgents, the root causes of most of Africa's wars lie in domestic state-society relations. In other words, they are more commonly triggered by grievances against the incumbent regime than by external threats from expansionist neighbors.[17] As a result, the path to true security depends less on devising interstate confidence-building measures than on building stable, democratic societies that can resolve their conflicts without resorting to violence. This is particularly apparent in relation to Africa's ongoing struggles for self-determination, such as those in Cabinda, Western Sahara, Southern Sudan, and Somaliland. If the continent's states worked for their people there would be fewer demands to break from them. Until they do, policy makers must think through the conditions under which new states should be allowed to join the international society club.[18]

Health Challenges: A second cluster of threats stems from the number of Africans who lack access to adequate health facilities, especially those needed to combat the spread of infectious diseases such as HIV/AIDS and tuberculosis as well as the other big African killer, malaria, which kills some three thousand Africans (mainly children) every day. In addition, some diseases are making an unwelcome resurgence in parts of the continent. In 2005, for instance, West Africa experienced 63,000 cases of cholera leading to 1,000 deaths, while in early 2006 an epidemic was claiming 400 lives per month in Angola.[19]

In recent years the spotlight has fallen on HIV/AIDS, which is clearly one of the most deadly transnational challenges currently facing the African continent. In 2005, for instance, an estimated 38.6 million people world-wide were living with HIV, the majority of whom were unaware of their status. During that year it is estimated that 4.1 million people became newly infected and 2.8 million died of AIDS-related diseases. With almost 25 million of those infected with HIV living in Africa, the continent "remains the global epicenter of the AIDS pandemic."[20] These figures suggest a level of HIV prevalence among Africa's 15- to 49-year-olds of approximately 7.5 percent.[21] Within the continent, southern Africa remains the worst affected region. It is also notable that in this region the majority of people killed by AIDS-related diseases are between twenty and fifty years of age, the most important groups for a well-functioning economy, polity, and society.

After a very slow start, Africa's leaders eventually afforded HIV/AIDS the sort of official attention it deserved. Specifically, in 2001 they adopted the Abuja Declaration and the Abuja Framework for Action for the Fight against HIV/AIDS, Tuberculosis and Other Related Infectious Diseases in Africa. The Abuja Declaration stated that "Containing and reversing the HIV/AIDS epidemic ... should constitute our top priority for the first quarter of the 21st Century." Human security in Africa is thus inextricably related to access to effective health facilities.

Environmental Crisis: Given the shaky foundations of knowledge about African environments, the speed, extent, drivers, and political consequences of environmental change on the continent remain distinctly unclear and contested.[22] Nevertheless, environmental issues are increasingly being linked to the continent's human security agenda.[23]

The degradation of Africa's environment is not solely linked to warfare but at the intersection of war and repression an environmental crisis is likely. Take the case of Sudan. Run by one of the world's most oppressive regimes and the site of several ongoing armed conflicts, Sudan is experiencing an environmental crisis. Not only is it situated in a region where droughts are endemic, with significant events occurring every three to five years, but its local ecosystems are also collapsing under the interrelated impacts of land degradation, deforestation, and climate change.[24] According to the U.N. Environment Program (UNEP), while armed conflict has degraded Sudan's environment, environmental issues such as competition over oil and gas reserves, Nile waters, and timber as well as land (especially rangeland and rain-fed agriculture land), have also been contributing causes of conflict. The links between land degradation, desertification, and the conflict in Darfur are particularly strong. Of course, environmental changes on their own do not produce conflict let alone war; whether such changes stimulate greater cooperation or conflict is ultimately due to decisions taken by the political authorities. But where environmental degradation and bad governance mix, durable solutions to conflicts are unlikely until local ecosystems are repaired and local livelihoods rebuilt.

Sudan's massive, conflict-generated population displacement (now affecting over 5 million people) has also caused significant environmental damage, especially in areas around the larger displacement camps. According to records dating back to the 1930s, Sudan has also experienced increasing levels of desertification with an estimated 50 to 200 kilometer southward shift of the boundary between semi-desert and desert. Desertification brings with it reductions in food production and an increased threat of drought and floods. At the same time, pressures on resources in general and the rangelands in particular have been intensified by the country's rocketing number of livestock (from 28.6 million in 1961 to 134.6 million in 2004). The picture in relation to deforestation is also grim. Between 2000 and 2005 Sudan suffered the third largest annual net loss of forest area of any country worldwide, losing some 589,000 hectares per year.[25] This process is driven principally by energy needs and agricultural clearance. In Darfur, for instance, a third of the forest cover was lost between 1973 and 2006.

Similar patterns can be observed across Africa more generally as the level of environmental degradation and its relationship to demographic and economic trends has become a disturbingly serious source of human insecurity. Data concerning water scarcity is particularly alarming. By 2015, the UNDP estimates that sub-Saharan Africa alone will account for more than half the global clean water deficit and just under half of the sanitation deficit.[26] Although the continent is reasonably well-endowed with water, some of its major lakes are shrinking due to over-exploitation (e.g., Lakes Chad, Nakivale, and Nakuru), and its water sources are unevenly distributed. Since water is not easily transferable in bulk quantities what usually matters most is local availability. The DRC, for instance, has more than one-quarter of the continent's total while states like Kenya, Malawi, and South Africa are already below the water stress threshold.[27] Indeed, sub-Saharan Africa has the most water-stressed states of any of the world's regions. Ironically, while some African states are predicted to get more rain in the future they will actually lose more water overall through evaporation as temperatures rise as a result of global climate change.[28]

Where water is scarce, so is sanitation. By 2005, only one in three people in sub-Saharan Africa had access to sanitation. In Ethiopia, the figure was one in seven people.[29] In addition, many Africans have to share what domestic water sources are available with a growing number of animals. Across the Horn of Africa the picture has been especially grim with more than 20 million people being affected by drought in 2005 alone.[30] Droughts are now endemic across much of the Sahel, East Africa, and southern Africa. In East Africa, it is estimated that reductions in water availability may result in productivity losses of 33 percent for maize, more than 20 percent for sorghum, and 18 percent for millet.[31] This is particularly worrying because not only is most of sub-Saharan Africa's agriculture rain-fed rather than irrigated but between 1990 and 2004 the G8 has cut its aid to agriculture in the region by $590 million.[32] Water scarcity thus poses a significant and urgent set of security challenges. Indeed, put starkly, the UNDP estimates that in 2015 there would be 124,000 fewer child deaths in Africa if the water and sanitation targets of the Millennium Development Goals are met.[33]

Conclusion

The next U.S. administration faces a difficult set of choices about how to engage with Africa. Will it prioritize human or regime security? How important will democracy promotion be compared with energy extraction? How will it encourage governments preoccupied with preserving their regime's power to address the broader human security agenda? And how will it persuade Africans that AFRICOM really can contribute to the human security agenda?

In addressing these and other questions, violence needs to be understood as a broad category stretching from household incidents (such as physical abuse) to the nexus between criminality, warlordism, and more traditional notions of armed conflict. This means that violence poses a serious threat to many ordinary Africans during official times of "peace" as well as periods of "war."

Human security is not measured only in terms of violence. Without an environment capable of supporting human life all other discussions of security are moot. Of particular concern are the ongoing destruction of Africa's ecosystems and the inability of people (both foreigners and locals) to stop a variety of processes such as climate change, deforestation, desertification, land degradation (both cropland and pasture), as well as increasing water and food scarcity. Water resource management needs to become a focal point for regional cooperation across the continent's major river basins. The objective is constructing forms of political community that fulfill people's needs for recognition, representation, well-being, and security.

Notes

1 Fund for Peace, "The Failed States Index 2007," *Foreign Policy*, www.fundforpeace.org.

2 In all, Freedom House classifies eighteen African states as "not free." Freedom House, *The Worst of the Worst: The World's Most Repressive Societies 2008*, http://www.freedomhouse.org/uploads/special_report/62.pdf.

3 UNDP, *Human Development Index 2006*, http://hdr.undp.org/hdr2006/statistics.

4 Raymond W. Copson, *The United States in Africa* (London: Zed, 2007).

5 J. R. McNeill, *Something New Under the Sun: An Environmental History of the Twentieth-Century World* (New York: Norton, 2001).

6 Ibid., 16 and 4.

7 Ibid., 271.

8 UNDP, *Human Development Report 2006* (New York: UNDP, 2006), 55.

9 McNeill, *Something New Under the Sun*, 283.

10 Ibid., 285–6.

11 UNDP, *Human Development Report 2006*, 38.

12 Michael Klare and Daniel Volman, "The African 'Oil Rush' and US National Security," *Third World Quarterly*, 27:4 (2006), 610.

13 Jeffrey Herbst, *States and Power in Africa* (Princeton, NJ: Princeton University Press, 2000), 11.

14 Stephen Ellis and Gerrie ter Haar, "Religion and Politics: Taking African Epistemologies Seriously," *Journal of Modern African Studies*, 45:3 (2007), 387.

15 Simon Fraser University, 2008, *Human Security Brief 2007*, http://www.humansecuritybrief.info.

16 International Rescue Committee, 2008, *Mortality in the Democratic Republic of Congo*, http://www.theirc.org/resources/2007/2006-7_congomortalitysurvey.pdf.

17 See, for example, Morten Bøås and Kevin Dunn, eds., *African Guerrillas* (Boulder, CO: Lynne Rienner, 2007).

18 See Jeffrey Herbst, "Let Them Fail" in Robert I. Rotberg, ed., *When States Fail: Causes and Consequences* (Princeton, NJ: Princeton University Press, 2003), 302–18.

19 UNDP, *Human Development Report 2006*, 46.

20 UNAIDS 2006, *Report on the Global AIDS Epidemic: Executive Summary*, 6.

21 Nana K. Poku and Alan Whiteside, "25 Years of Living with HIV/AIDS: Challenges and Prospects," *International Affairs*, 82:2 (2006), 250.

22 See Melissa Leach and Robin Mearns, eds., *The Lie of the Land: Challenging Received Wisdom on the African Environment* (Oxford: James Currey, 1996).

23 For example, the AU Assembly Decision, January 29–30, 2007, Addis Ababa, Assembly/AU/December, 134 (VIII) and Ban Ki Moon, "A Climate Culprit in Darfur," *Washington Post*, June 16, 2007, A15.

24 See UNDP, *Human Development Report 2006*, 156; UNEP, *Sudan: Post-Conflict Environmental Assessment: Synthesis Report* (Kenya: UNEP, 2007).

25 Food and Agriculture Organization of the UN, *Global Forest Resources Assessment 2005* (Rome: FAO Forestry Paper 147, 2006), 21.

26 UNDP, *Human Development Report 2006*, 57.

27 Ibid., 135.

28 Ibid., 165.

29 Ibid., 12.

30 Ibid., 15.

31 Ibid., 15.

32 Ibid., 169.

33 Ibid., 58.

A Gathering at the Crossroads

Anthony D. McIvor

Africa is breaking with the patterns of the past and so must all those who wish to connect there. The New Africa, along with unwilling remnants of the Old, is being drawn more deeply into global politics. Once again, the continent's riches—not just its sorrows—are drawing much of the world there. Long-established relationships are shifting; new alliances are being vetted; interests and institutions eye each other warily while home office policy remains in play. This chapter frames the discussion of Africa at the crossroads by exploring key elements of African security policy.

The African continent is home to many distinct Africas. The fifty-three African states today represent almost three thousand culturally distinct groups, over two thousand living languages or dialects, and often inter-mixed Christian, Muslim, and animist religious communities. These states have singular histories, shaped by their distinctive experiences with their neighbors and with outside powers. Working across extraordinary differences, African statesmen are charting a new direction for the continent by redefining intra-African and external relationships. Their efforts will intersect and perhaps redirect the course of international affairs.

Cold War tensions and conflict in the Middle East long overshadowed the catalog of troubles that was Africa's post-colonial inheritance. With the fall of the Berlin Wall, African states were no longer useful as proxies in the intrigues of the superpowers. Ironically, the ensuing period of relative neglect prompted an era of optimism in Africa. Uganda's president

Museveni called for a "decade of awakening." Africans talked of a renaissance for their continent. And they set about making changes. The first objective was human security.

The violence, dysfunctional institutions, and criminal behavior still ravaging the continent, its populations, and their economies today are directly linked to deeply rooted deprivations that the African people suffer on a daily basis. Geofrey Mugumya describes the central pillar of Africa's philosophy on peace and security as the simple recognition of the need to enhance "per capita freedom," or a democratic space where human rights are secure and opportunities for self-development are unfettered. However imperfectly, African leaders began to address that space.

For defense or national security policy makers, a more nuanced understanding of global trends in political violence—and particularly the recent upsurge in international activism—could lead to reconsideration of the options in Africa. Forward-leaning African leaders already see the opportunity. And they are clear about the necessity of multiple and multipurpose partnerships to capitalize on it. They also share a sense that Africa may be in an historic moment—perhaps a tipping point toward democracy and wider prosperity for many states.

Africa is not alone at the crossroads. Once again, the continent's riches—not just its sorrows—are drawing much of the world there. Long-established relationships are shifting; new alliances are being vetted; interests and institutions eye each other warily while home office policy remains in play.

The Development Community

In addition to official state-sponsored development institutions such as the World Bank, International Monetary Fund, and United Nations, nearly every major development-oriented nongovernmental organization (NGO) and most private voluntary organizations (PVOs), including the large religious outreach organizations. has had, does have, or is planning a program somewhere in Africa. Why all this effort? In part because the problems have outrun the remedies and in part because we seem unable to get development right.

Not since Graham Hancock's *Lords of Poverty* in 1989 has the aid debate been so barbed and divisive. Hancock took aim at official aid agencies, not the voluntary sector, but today the critique ranges far and wide. Even the World Bank's traditional standard for measuring poverty—the one dollar a day—has come under attack from those who believe quality of life a better yardstick. Nobel Laureate Amartya Sen suggests that the criteria for poverty should not just be about food but "about what you want people to be able to do in life."

One of the development sector's most trenchant critics, New York University professor William Easterly, likens "development" to an ideology that promises a comprehensive, final answer to society's myriad problems from poverty and illiteracy to violence and ill governance. He chides the major development community institutions for their unthinking propensity to impose "globalization from above."

Easterly's argument for a reexamination of the entire development edifice—a *tour de force*—is laced with frustration and great sympathy for those who are getting "structurally adjusted" by bureaucrats in distant office towers. Easterly's impatience with these failures and the verbal foolishness that often accompanies them is salutary. But the alternatives are not so neatly obvious.

Another axis of contention dividing the development community is the newly U.N.-approved covenant, "the responsibility to protect." Marc Rieff writes eloquently about humanitarianism and human rights as the lodestars by which we "organize our moral imaginations." Perhaps. Rieff also wonders aloud whether humanitarian intervention can be, in any lasting sense, separated from regime change. By doing so, he drops the veil on the unspoken and highly risky assumption of sufficient political will. W h e n Rieff cautions us to think about the unintended consequences of acting in unfamiliar ways in unfamiliar places, it is sound counsel. And it is acutely relevant to the question of the limits to what might be done in Africa.

The nonprofit world is rethinking its relationship with the public sector and questioning its traditional rejection of government support. Offstage, new forms of collaboration are discussed in earnest. Relief workers can no longer assume even a thin shield of immunity from violence while in the field. It is clear that the aid community writ large is coming to a crossroads in Africa—as it is elsewhere—and awaits the leadership that will define new directions.

The U.S. Military in Africa

Development debates are further complicated by a new subject: the militarization of U.S. aid programs. Critics argue that increasing reliance on military solutions is skewing priorities and jeopardizing the resources vital to longer-term development projects. Officials at the Department of State and USAID are taking these concerns public, finding support from some unlikely allies in the Department of Defense.

Defense Secretary Robert Gates recently issued several warnings about "creeping militarization" and made a solid case for greater investment in non-DoD assistance vehicles. Secretary Gates is right about the imbalance between the instruments of civilian and military power. The numbers illustrate the issue. The Pentagon, which controlled 3 percent of official aid money a decade ago, now controls roughly 22 percent (with the difference bound up largely in military assistance and training programs) while USAID's share declined from 65 percent to 40 percent.

Correcting the balance will require more than a shift of dollars from one federal account to another. The Defense Secretary, in rare alignment with the Secretary of State, is beginning to outline a substantially different national security architecture. The nature of the civil-military relationship at its heart will be equally critical to the future of Africa. The U.S. military has long had a large footprint on the continent. Today, the Global Peace Operations Initiative (GPOI) is a multilateral, five-year program with planned U.S. contributions of nearly $600 million from 2005 to 2010. The GPOI incorporates several previous U.S. capability-building programs for Africa launched, with varying success, during the 1990s. Although the emphasis remains on Africa, GPOI now includes over forty partner nations and organizations throughout the world.

The African Contingency Operations Training and Assistance program (ACOTA), its predecessor, African Crisis Response Initiative (ACRI), and the Enhanced International Peacekeeping Capabilities program, are now subsumed under GPOI and implemented by the State Department's Africa Bureau. The impetus for GPOI came from DoD, especially from the Office of Special Operations and Low-Intensity Conflict. Military planners and advocates gave the program a significant boost and an unmistakable DoD cast.

GPOI has three core goals: to train roughly 75,000 troops in peacekeeping skills by 2010, again with an emphasis on Africa; to support Italy's initiative in training international constabulary forces; and to foster an international deployment and logistics system to deploy and sustain peacekeeping forces in the field. The African emphasis is real: of the 28,600 troops trained with GPOI funds by March 2007, 96 percent were from sub-Saharan Africa.

Africa's pronounced shift from *ad hoc* state-based security planning and execution to a pyramid of structured cooperation under the AU suggests that U.S. investments, such as GPOI, will earn higher returns in coming years. But in light of growing U.S. (and G8) interests in Africa—from energy to migration—the level of assistance on offer falls well short of the need. Even to maintain its present influence on the continent, the U.S. government as a whole will need to entertain significantly larger commitments. The answer is not likely to be found in the new U.S. combatant command, AFRICOM.

AFRICOM's promise comes from the pioneering of new methods of peacetime military engagement focused on war prevention, interagency cooperation, and development, rather than continuous rehearsal of traditional warfighting skills. But its roots are inseparable from the military-driven counterterror strikes following 9/11. With that, the strategic rationale for AFRICOM has not found a solid footing.

Scaling back ambitions and expectations for AFRICOM is prudent. So is backing away from the notion that the Command would be a full-blown interagency organization with military and nonmilitary elements. By emphasizing the value the Command could add to existing U.S. military programs already underway in Africa, AFRICOM's new commander is recasting the organization in that direction.

The apparent commonality between the military's "clear, hold, and build" and the aid community's "security, governance, and development" is deceptive. The right mix of military, interagency, and international forces and assets to contribute to Africa's own efforts has so far eluded the best of intentions. Understanding and acknowledging that conventional development challenges in Africa cannot be solved by the military is a fine first step.

Defense officials now admit the initial vision for AFRICOM will be a work in progress—for many years to come. Together with the GPOI and related military-to military training programs, AFRICOM stands at the crossroads.

China Arrives in Africa

China continues to refine and expand its direct aid to the continent. The *Christian Science Monitor* reports that just since 2000 China has cancelled more than $10 billion in debt for thirty-one African countries and given an additional $5.5 billion in new development funds. Beijing has now overtaken the World Bank in lending to Africa. The loans China offered Africa in 2006 were the equivalent of three times the aid given that year by rich countries in the Organization for Economic Cooperation and Development (OECD) and twenty-five times the total in loans and credits approved by the U.S. Export-Import Bank for sub-Saharan Africa. This largesse was highlighted by a succession of state visits—three in four years—by President Hu Jintao.

Between 2000 and 2005, Chinese trade with Africa tripled. China has at least forty (known) oil agreements with various African countries. China-Africa trade volume reached $70 billion in 2007. If, as expected, it tops $100 billion in 2010, Africa will have become China's single largest trading partner, surpassing the U.S. That milestone will change the content and likely the tone of the conversation on China's activity in Africa. But it is a mistake to view China's growing interests in Africa as unequivocally noxious or threatening to others.

The welcome mat is out for China partly because of fatigue with the bundle of Western development ideas known as the Washington Consensus:

privatization, low tariffs, free markets, and democracy. Across Africa—and much of the developing world—there is growing interest in the alternative demonstrated by China's explosive growth. Sidestepping direct confrontation, Chinese representatives emphasize innovation and growth through a social-market economy—with an unsubtle preference for noninterference in the internal affairs of other nations. Noninterference resonates, particularly with older Africans, as an echo of the founding principles of the postcolonial Organization of African States (OAS).

The "no questions asked" quality of China's loans and investments is attractive to governments seeking swifter, more efficient, and less intrusive solutions to development problems—without the often tiresome overhead Western lenders insist on. Beijing's state-owned firms can—in the short run—sustain losses in pursuit of long-term relationships without having to answer to stockholders at home. Not unreasonably, African leaders view China as an alternative to Western development funding and investment. In the short term, it is a painless way to diversify the supply chain for both direct aid and project financing.

China's approach also has an emotional appeal. The Chinese message is that it will not just protect its own interests, but "those of other developing countries" as well. In Africa, this sensitivity plays well. The unspoken but deeply felt subject of humiliation is never very far from the conference table or the parade ground. Western partners bear an inescapable risk of being perceived as aspiring neocolonial powers.

Assiduously working all of these levers, China has shouldered its way to a leading position at the crossroads. Its arrival signals both opportunity and risk, opening doors for Africans but also raising new questions about Africa's freedom to plot its own future.

African Solutions to African Problems?

There is an emerging alternative to the shopworn narrative of Africa as a land of ceaseless conflict, shady or incompetent government, and chronic underdevelopment. The working term for this story is the New Africa. Demagoguery is not dead, but its heyday in Africa may be over. African leaders know they cannot build the future they seek with clichés and rhetorical flourishes. They are working to transcend the moribund formalism of the past by creating a suite of institutions that match promises with performance. The flagship is the African Union (AU).

In 2002 the Organization of African Unity (OAU) gave way to the African Union—with a much different, much broader, and much more energetic mandate. The sacrosanct OAU principle of territorial inviolability, which protected a variety of odious regimes and not-so-thinly-disguised military dictatorships taking an enormous toll in human life, was finally weakened. With the establishment of the Peace and Security Council (PSC) two years later, the AU had a standing body to promote African initiatives for the prevention, management, and resolution of African conflicts.

The successful adoption of the principles in the Common African Defense and Security Policy and the subsequent Non-Aggression and Common Defense Pact (2005) provided the AU with fundamental guidelines for future operations. Reversing the OAS, these principles affirmed the right of the AU to intervene in member states—in circumstances sufficiently grave for human life—and declared that the integrity and security of any one state was the collective responsibility of all.

Independently and with scarce resources, the AU has drawn on the five regional brigades of the fledgling African Standby Force (ASF) to notch some impressive early achievements. Notable among these are the peace support missions in Burundi, Darfur, and the Comoros, as well as interventions on behalf of the democratic process in Togo and Sao Tome.

Of great significance for the long-term consolidation of these gains, the New Africa's driving principles of peace and security are infused with, and inseparable from, good governance and socioeconomic development. Weaving these ideas into concrete policies and programs is the responsibility of the New Partnership for Africa's Development (NEPAD) and the counterpart African Peer Review Mechanism (APRM). Animated by accountability, transparency, meritocracy, and professionalism, the cadres in these emerging institutions are already changing the rules for policy making and economic management.

NEPAD provides the context for developing and (more importantly) retaining the intellectual and human capital essential for competition in an increasingly knowledge-based global economy. ASF institutions, such as the Annan Centre in Ghana, the Rwanda Military Academy and Uganda's Senior Command and Staff College, are gradually earning respect at home and abroad. On the civilian side, the Institute for Security Studies (ISS) with offices in Pretoria, Nairobi, and Addis Abba, is building a reputation as a human security research institution with robust leadership training and publications program for senior cadres.

These advances have given rise to some unrealistic expectations of what African militaries are able to do. Time is required for a surer grasp of capabilities, doctrine, and unequivocal mandates. Scarce and subpar resources consistently undermine operational effectiveness. The seduction of expensive "glamour" equipment siphons precious resources from more mundane, but more urgent, security requirements. Weapons systems vendors—and governments that facilitate their sales with offset credits—do not always act in the best interests of their African clients.

Progress on civil-military relations remains tentative, with an uneasy relationship to internal security. The proliferation of inexpensive small arms and light weapons, notably in West Africa, assures that internal security will remain a high priority for the military as they strive to contain warlords, armed criminal gangs, and tribe-based bandits.

Aware of globalization's downside, African defense and security strategists are now working from a broad set of new definitions. Security is no longer seen purely in terms of state survival and protections from external aggression. Instead, defense issues are understood in terms of ecological and environmental degradation, endemic poverty, and access to food, medicine, transportation, and education: in short, protecting the ladder to a better life.

The AU leadership acknowledges that the ambitious peace and security agenda cannot and will not be realized soon. International partnerships remain indispensable. Rising fuel costs are changing the calculus of globalization—the "neighborhood effect" of higher transportation expense may yet damage Africa's ability to build more diversified economies. Even so, Africa's youth are eagerly harnessing new technologies, especially rapid communications and Web 2.0 social networks to create powerful currents for change.

The New Africa, along with unwilling remnants of the Old, will greet us at the crossroads. Along with shared interests, we will find some new priorities. And they will be unmistakably African.

Beyond the Crossroads

The crossroads theme captures the sense of pending change, of the need to take bearings, reflect, decide, and move on. But that image may be too static for the circumstances. All of the forces at work in Africa are actually in a kaleidoscopic moment, where each of the elements is shifting at once— altering not just their recognizable livery but their weight and measure relative to each other.

Africa is breaking with the patterns of the past and so must all those who wish to connect there. Writing in the RUSI *Journal*, Knox Chitiyo captured the African predicament in two succinct questions: 1) "how to reconcile the emotive power of the liberation war theology with the practical demands of post-nationalist governance?" and 2) "how to liberate the people from the *liberators*?" The answers are slowly emerging from the intertwined clash of ideologies and generations.

On the west side of the Atlantic, a default to purely military responses for all international challenges is no longer perceived as adequate. Neglected tools of statecraft are being reassessed. Unless derailed by a dramatic shock, the U.S. appears poised to undertake a root and branch restructuring of the national security institutions created in 1947. The outcome could redress the balance. But there will be no quick fix for long-broken machinery. Framed by a period of strained budgets and ballooning deficits, the coming battle will dwarf the fracas over reform of the nation's intelligence community.

In such circumstances, the key question may be whether U.S. policy makers, in all sectors, can match the creativity afoot in the New Africa, while still reckoning with the discrete qualities of the many Africans. Better, less cocooned mechanisms for mutual comprehension, and a renewed trust in the resulting insights, will surely have to be built. At present, there is promise in the fledgling Civilian Response Corps, and its deeper bench the Standby Response Corps, but it has yet to be tested.

The world is coming again to a crossroads in Africa. This time, Africans too will be active agents there. As the traffic is sorted out, the environment for joint, interagency, and coalition operations—of every stripe and purpose—with partners on the continent will change, perhaps beyond recognition. Are we in any sense ready for that?

AFRICOM: Recommendations for U.S. Security Strategy

Melissa Cox Bosse

The Obama administration inherits a broad slate of initiatives and programs that have fundamentally altered the course of U.S.-Africa engagement. This chapter reviews policy recommendations to build on current efforts in the areas of governance, economic and social development, and energy security; addresses key missions for AFRICOM; and recommends areas of concern the new administration will have to face in 2009.

African stability and development issues rarely rank among the top priorities in U.S. security planning or strategy documents. African security issues are unlikely to be on the top of the Obama administration's list of 2009 priorities. The wars in Iraq and Afghanistan, the economy, energy security, and other issues will continue to dominate the security policy agenda. Although there will likely be an "Africa agenda" announced as one of several regional strategies, it is likely that other issues will dominate the attention of top national security officials.

But unlike previous administrations, many appointees of the Obama administration have a demonstrated interest in African affairs, and many view this team as having a unique window of opportunity to engage with key African leaders. The power of the office of the president often works indirectly, through personalities and the elevation of expectations for innovation as appointees fill executive branch leadership positions. The appointments of Senator Hillary Clinton to lead the State Department and Susan Rice as ambassador to the United Nations will likely result in renewed commitment to Africa development objectives, new initiatives with African partners, and the affirmation of U.S. leadership in multilateral efforts to address security and stabilization challenges. To be successful, new initiatives must be defined and executed with meticulous detail, placing additional pressure on AFRICOM to mature as a combatant command charged with supporting interagency activities. Communication among African leadership and regional, sub-regional, civic organizations will become an imperative strategic objective for the success of AFRICOM. This chapter addresses key missions for AFRICOM and recommends areas of concern the new administration will have to address in 2009.

Professional Military Training for Africans and Americans
AFRICOM, in close coordination with the State Department, should work to expand the African Contingency Operations Training and Assistance (ACOTA) program, which provides training on peacekeeping support to the African Union. Professional military education remains an essential first step toward security and development. Many African nations have little experience with Western approaches to civil-military relations, where military leaders remain outside of politics. Professional military training should not only be offered to senior military but also civilian African leaders. Training should incorporate civilians in all aspects of contingency operations related to health, natural disaster response, and humanitarian aide. Other programs, such as International Military Education and Training (IMET) programs and the Africa Center for Strategic Studies (ACSS), should be closely integrated with AFRICOM's defense and security cooperation efforts.

Additionally, the U.S. must recognize the unique missions of AFRICOM and provide its own personnel the proper training to address Africa's needs. The military has traditionally focused on conflict operations but has slowly incorporate nontraditional pre- and post-conflict operations into its training. AFRICOM personnel and U.S. officials should have familiarity with Africa, its people, customs, languages, cultures, religions, and security aspects. The State Department should take the lead in this type of immersion training with its expertise in culture affairs and diplomacy operations in the region.

There are already plans to deploy more human terrain teams to Africa and to develop regional integration strategies. The priority should be on developing regional and local solutions that are perceived as African initiatives developed by African leaders, not U.S. programs.

Focus on Maritime Security and Training

Maritime security became a more important international security issue in 2008 with increased piracy, concerns over fisheries, and disruptions of oil supplies. The U.S. military has focused on regional maritime security initiatives, including naval cooperation efforts and new training programs. Among the issues requiring additional attention are piracy; fish poaching; trafficking of persons, arms, and narcotics; environmental concerns; and the stability of energy supplies.

Energy security is an area ripe for multilateral cooperation initiatives. The importance of offshore oil and gas production and of energy exports to the United States is well known: over 20 percent of U.S. energy imports derive today from the Gulf of Guinea, and that number is projected to climb. African governments are beginning to confront these maritime challenges, but the navies' and coast guards' capabilities still lack proper training for most African states. Many African states would welcome AFRICOM programs to help improve their maritime surveillance and enforcement capabilities. Joint exercises and training programs with other parties, including European, Chinese, and Japanese navies may provide an opportunity for U.S.-China confidence-building activities and security partnerships.

African governments have expressed willingness to support well-conceived plans reflecting U.S. policy commitment and resources. Providing seminars, training, and equipment will help support regional maritime security cooperation, whether that involves the AU, ECOWAS, Maritime Organization of West and Central Africa (MOWCA), the Gulf of Guinea Commission, or any others. AFRICOM should create programs that continue to support regional member states, as they make marine resources management a priority. This is an area where humility counts. AFRICOM should accept joint partnerships under African leadership or even consider new international agreements that recognize the interests of other powers.

AFRICOM Coordination with External Organizations

AFRICOM has an opportunity to reform military-NGO relationships and to reform U.S. government contracting processes. Defense planners are increasingly sensitive to the needs of NGOs and respectful of the capabilities NGOs provide. Often, the safety of NGO personnel depends on their neutrality in complicated political and ethnic environments. As Theresa Whelan, Deputy Assistant Secretary of Defense for African Affairs, acknowledged: "We recognize that their [NGOs'] safety depends upon their neutrality, and we are looking for mechanisms that allow us all to work together without undermining their mission." Working through mechanisms like the African Center for Strategic Studies and the U.S. Institute of Peace may function as neutral space between NGOs and government.

U.S. military programs should complement the U.S. Agency for International Development. For example, U.S. forces should continue to conduct de-mining activities and promote HIV/AIDS awareness programs in African militaries. Also utilizing NGO umbrella organizations, such Global Impact or Inter-Action, may help in jointly exploring partnership options. These types of organization represent multiple international charities and humanitarian organizations, which can serve as a model for AFRICOM in the future.[1]

Working with and through NGOs may be the most efficient route to achieving U.S. security and development objectives. Building capacity on the continent will also require contracting through and with external organizations, including NGOs and private firms. Dissatisfaction with Defense contracting practices in Iraq and Afghanistan is likely to impede AFRICOM attempts to win support in the Department of Defense and with congressional overseers. AFRICOM should create an independent advisory body and allocate inspector general billets to its contracting activities. In addition, AFRICOM should invest in contract officer training and education, making sure that contract officer duties are not given to already over-tasked staff officers as secondary duties. Ideally, this will be an interagency activity led by a USAID executive supported by personnel from Defense, Agriculture, and other departments.

Human Factor Investment in Education and Training

One of the most important areas for AFRICOM engagement with NGOs and private firms is education and training for African military and government personnel. The United States already invests in Defense education and training programs to encourage the professionalization of African militaries and to reduce government corruption. These efforts should be expanded and integrated with multilateral initiatives.

Another area where AFRICOM can provide supporting infrastructure is in assisting with regional development and project management efforts that employ Africans in safe, secure, and sustainable professions. Over time, this may reverse Africa's ongoing "brain drain," where talented, educated Africans seek employment elsewhere. This leaves African nations short of the skills and leadership qualities required to meet various security challenges. Highly educated and trained citizens often migrate to other countries in search of greater political stability, economic opportunity, and employment.

This loss of human capital contributes to the absence of legitimate leadership in areas of military, politics, science, academics, and technology. The United States can assist by providing additional student, cultural-exchange, and professional visa quotas. Visas such as the J-1 allow for foreign nationals to benefit from an American educational or professional experience, and then return to their home countries with the skills they have learned. J-1 visas are effective because they have an eighteen-month maximum duration; after the visa expires, the foreign national must return to his home country for a period of two years before being able to return to the United States.

Promote Private Infrastructure Development

Economic diversification is essential to economic growth and stability, especially in nations with faltering or failed indigenous production sectors that would become more viable with better government policies or investment planning. Development of industries outside the energy sector, for example, can mitigate declining oil prices and the long-term effects of government corruption. Additionally, industries related to agriculture can be resurrected to create jobs and reduce dependency on imports.

Job creation is essential for African populations to reduce their dependence on government-run social programs. These programs inevitably fall short of addressing public needs when funds are scarce. The United States cannot shoulder the burden alone but can be a leading proponent for the development of Africa's infrastructure through foreign aid and private grants. However, this has the potential to create a situation where African countries will continually rely on U.S. subsidies for development assistance, rather than becoming independent and self-reliant. Therefore, the U.S. would be better served using its influence to help these countries establish the necessary conditions to promote the development of infrastructure by private industry.

Greater Responsibility for Oil Companies in Economic Development

The twenty-first century is destined to see another scramble for Africa's natural resources. African oil development and exploration will continue to play a major role in future U.S. energy policy. The Obama administration must make its commitment and interests in the development and well-being of Africa unequivocally clear. U.S. economic policy toward Africa must reflect a long-term economic and humanitarian commitment without impairing the ability for American firms to compete for contracts and energy exploration rights. It is essential for the American oil companies involved in African oil exploration and production to develop strategies and methods for economic development, but they cannot shoulder the burden alone. In addition to leading efforts to secure energy supplies, AFRICOM should develop multilateral initiatives to create energy security zones in which African states are provided foreign assistance to monitor, safeguard, patrol, and secure energy exploration and extraction activities.

This will require redistribution of energy wealth within Africa to prevent additional conflicts over natural resources. This will also require programs enticing African leaders to account for revenue and provide additional transparency on contracts and state income. Plans that automatically funnel oil revenues into human development programs (health care, schools, and infrastructure) in return for international assistance securing energy zones, water resources, and other natural resources might promote African development and foster more accountable energy security policies.

As the U.S. diversifies its oil supply to minimize dependency on Persian Gulf sources, AFRICOM should pursue energy security and development programs that link regime stability to regional resource security planning.

Conclusion

AFRICOM's main mission is to act as a preventive structure that will identify hot-button issues before an actual conflict may ensue. Intimate knowledge of both the civic and government levels of society will be imperative. Realistically though, military planners must consider potential contingency and operational planning. AFRICOM should be a fully functional combatant command capable of committing U.S. troops to combat on the continent.

With that said, gaining legitimacy for those types of actions is a challenge. AFRICOM should link its operations closely with the United Nation's peacekeeping in Africa. The U.N. remains the most visible security force provider throughout the continent with more than 120,000 peacekeeping forces. But the U.N.'s credibility with African governments and degree of popular support within African societies are mixed. Regional peacekeeping forces are becoming more valued, with U.N. forces augmenting regional forces that have been trained, have professional officer corps, and are combined with international observers and resources providers.

AFRICOM activities and missions should be closely coordinated with regional and international organizations, including the U.N. operations. To the extent that AFRICOM is perceived as supportive of U.N. decisions and programs and of regional peacekeeping missions, international acceptance of AFRICOM will grow.[2] This will require working with China to promote security and stabilization.

AFRICOM will have to prove that it can expand beyond the traditional roles and responsibilities of combatant commands. In addition to developing as a defense department command it will have to facilitate an integrated set of diplomatic, development, and other activities. The Departments of Defense and State must work hard to streamline tasks and AFRICOM's involvement throughout Africa. Civilian agencies that provide humanitarian relief or development programs will likely resist close integration with AFRICOM staff unless they are assured they can continue to conduct their work independently with only *requested* support of AFRICOM personnel.

Additionally, U.S. official will have to work hard to coordinate with and address the concerns of African leadership in organizations such as the African Union (AU). To date, the vision of AFRICOM has been somewhat unclear and confusing to many Africans. The AU acts as an important security institution, most notably the Peace and Security Council, which is charged with monitoring and preventing conflicts around the continent. AFRICOM has a contribution to make in helping Africa achieve these objectives, but if so, this must be adequately explained by American officials.

Notes

1   Guideline for Relations between U.S. Armed Forces and Non-Governmental Humanitarian Agencies, http: //www.usip.org/pubs/guidelines_panplets.pdf (accessed May 2, 2008).

2   Mark Bellamy, Kathleen Hicks, and J. Stephen Morrison, "Strengthening AFRICOM's Case," Center for Strategic and International Studies, March 5, 2008, http://www.csis.org/component/option,com_csis_progj/task,view/ id,1160 (accessed April 23, 2008).

Realigning National Interests with African Needs: U.S. Democratization Initiatives in Africa

Sean T. Macrae and Shannon D. Beebe

Given today's changing political landscape one trend is clear—
Africa is factoring ever more greatly in United States' interests.
The United States is a relative newcomer to Africa, and our
foreign policy objectives forwarding African democracies have
not been without challenges. However, the overall outlook
is positive and should be carried forward—democracy is on
the rise and autocratic regimes, although not going quietly,
are declining. The U.S., although not perfect in execution,
undoubtedly facilitated a significant amount of democratic
advancement across the continent during the last several
decades. As we look across the African continent today there
exist many challenges to the democratization process. From
Zimbabwe and Nigeria to Kenya and the Sudan, institutions,
inflation, corruption, and ill-intentioned leaders are but a small
amount of the obstacles to freedom. The U.S. must remain
engaged with a consistent narrative, using lessons learned from
our fifty years working on the continent, founded on the idea
of human security, which espouses human rights, democratic
ideals, and transparency. This must be accompanied by
reinforcing programs targeting economic development at the
grassroots level and simultaneously focusing on accountability at
the macro level.

Africa has witnessed a flurry of newfound interest over the past year. From concerns of a new scramble for Africa led by the Chinese to the unveiling of the U.S. unified military command, Africa Command (AFRICOM), one thing is certain: Africa is factoring ever more greatly in United States' interests. With Africa now having a greatly varied choice of partners and still known as the richest continent below ground and poorest above, the question remains of which path African nations will choose—one of short-term prosperity led by "kleptocratic" regimes or one of a longer term, sustainable future replete with the challenges of democratic transition and consolidation. Although U.S. democratization efforts on the continent have a spotted past, the current trends are positive and should be reinforced through a whole of government approach.

The United States is a relative newcomer to Africa, and our foreign policy objectives forwarding African democracies have not been without challenges. As such, the United States has exercised a realpolitik brand of self-interest that often times runs counter to an end state goal of democracy. With all the shortcomings, however, our paradigm evolved with greater effectiveness over the years. This evolution might best be described in the following phases: Anything but Communism; Not Communism but Not Necessarily Democracy; and More Democracy than Not.

Anything but Communism: U.S. Efforts from 1950 to 1970

Despite the growing frequency of discussions today, Africa has traditionally been of interest to the United States as a backyard, buffer, or vis-à-vis allied interests. Prior to 1957, when the majority of the continent remained under colonial rule, Africa saw little direct U.S. attention.[1] It was not until August 20, 1958 that the U.S. created the Bureau of African Affairs on the heels of independence in the Republic of Ghana and on the cusp of thirty colonies declaring independence within the next five years.[2]

George B. N. Ayittey, author of *Africa Betrayed*, outlines the U.S.'s approach to sub-Saharan Africa at the end of the Eisenhower administration, stating: "The policy was based on three chief premises. First, the United States would limit the presence of the Soviet bloc in Africa to the minimal extent possible. Second, the United States would continue to keep the level of physical and human resources committed to Africa low relative to levels committed to other countries. Finally, the United States would continue to adjust its African policy in deference to European positions on African issues."[3] This is not to say there were not strategic U.S. concerns in Africa. The U.S. maintained some presence on the continent in the form of space tracking stations, intelligence gathering bases, and commercial mineral interests in the late 1950s and 1960s.[4] Yet, this activity was simply to reinforce other interests, and our policy maintained an outward focus on other factors rather than Africa of its own right. The Eisenhower policy translated to support for anti-Marxists regardless of their stance on human rights or democracy. President Kennedy continued this policy as demonstrated through U.S. endorsement of a military leader, Colonel Mobutu, in Congo during October 1962. The U.S. funded and resourced this military ruler until he was able to seize control of the Congolese government, overthrowing then President Joseph Kasavubu. Many of the Congo's problems today can be traced directly to this policy. Facilitating and maintaining strong political leaders, versus stable, grounded governments, demonstrates the anti-Soviet U.S. policy.[5]

The takeaway message was clear: the U.S. fostered a message that as long as African states maintained an anti-Soviet posture and were *not communist*, then U.S. objectives were met. Sacrificing the principles of democratic governance for more selfish national interest would be a theme for U.S. policy toward Africa. Arguably this theme can still be seen today as resource rich countries, such as Equatorial Guinea, receive preferential treatment and a blind eye is turned toward their human rights records.

Not Communism but Not Necessarily Democracy: 1970–1990
The Nixon and Ford administrations evolved the U.S. paradigm toward Africa; however, they did not entirely change it. With the acknowledgment of corruption and inefficiencies within the African regimes, yet still requiring allies to bolster the continent against communism, both administrations focused on providing services to the end recipient (farmer, mother, etc.) while

trying to avoid providing monies to regimes.[6] Jennifer Seymour Whitaker points to a talk given by Secretary of State Henry Kissinger as one example. In a speech delivered at Lusaka, Zambia, on April 29, 1976, Mr. Kissinger noted that the United States was firmly committed to a policy of "majority rule" in Rhodesia and Namibia, and would seek to end "institutionalized separation of races" in South Africa.[7] The Carter and Reagan administrations—although taking rather different approaches—followed suit, focusing on high profile, deep-seated African issues to include majority rule in South Africa and Rhodesia, as well as Cuban troop presence in Angola.[8]

More Democracy Than Not: The 1990s

The 1990s ushered in a time of tremendous change in global politics and U.S. policy. With the ultimate demise of communism as a competing paradigm, the U.S. faced significant uncertainty of unquestioned international hegemony while attempting to formulate foreign policy without a polar opposite. At this point, another evolution in U.S. foreign policy toward Africa occurred. A key input into the U.S. foreign policy equation soon became rule of law, good governance, and tailoring U.S. aid to supporting emerging democracies. Ayittey summarizes this adjustment from countering communism to facilitating democracy stating that "In May 1990 the U.S. Congress and the White House attempted to reshape the U.S. foreign aid program in light of global political changes and reordered priorities. President Bush [41] sought new flexibility to boost aid to emerging democracies … [therefore] Assistant Secretary of State for Africa Herman J. Cohen announced in May 1990 that, along with economic adjustment and the observance of human rights, democratization will soon be included as the third prerequisite for U.S. development aid."[9] The transformation seen today in U.S. policy, a strategic promise to support freedom and democracy globally, has its genesis in this 1990 shift.

As globalization began to take root, the push for democracy made logical sense in a quest for free markets around the world. President Bush focused his policy and programs in Africa on resolving armed conflict, "intervening diplomatically in seven civil wars—Ethiopia, Angola, Mozambique, Sudan,

Liberia, Somalia, and Rwanda. By the time [George Herbert Walker] Bush left office in January 1993, Ethiopia and Mozambique were in post-conflict transition, thanks substantially to U.S. diplomacy."[10] This continued with the Clinton administration, which expanded U.S. efforts to inculcate democratic ideals on the continent. However, inconsistencies continued to plague U.S. efforts. After the Somalia ordeal in 1993, the U.S. strongly resisted a U.N. intervention in Rwanda while failing to acknowledge genocide as it unfolded. Again, inconsistency or incoherence of message plagued U.S. democratization efforts. Cohen concludes that "Bill Clinton's presidency was notable for two major initiatives in Africa, one military [the African Crisis Response Initiative, now known as the African Contingency Operations Training and Assistance (ACOTA) program] and one economic [the African Growth and Opportunity Act (AGOA)]."[11] Despite the negative perception surrounding Rwanda, the 1990s brought a surge in the democratic initiatives.

The Twenty-first Century—the George W. Bush Administration in Africa
The George W. Bush administration deserves tremendous credit for its work on the African continent. Once again, U.S. foreign policy evolved in its understanding that democracy cannot occur in a vacuum. The Bush administration began the attempt to join governance with supporting advances in economics and health. This role incorporates both positive incentives for those successful states making legitimate reformative efforts to withholding assistance while openly discussing the shortcomings of other states. One of the two great successes this administration had is the Millennium Challenge Corporation (MCC). Through the MCC, the U.S. currently facilitates over $2 billion in assistance programs to Benin, Cape Verde, Ghana, Mali, and Madagascar—all of whom continue to make significant reforms in a quest for institutional democracies. Many other countries—i.e., Burkina Faso, Kenya, Malawi, Tanzania, Uganda, and Zambia—signed threshold agreements through the MCC acknowledging a continued need for reform but generally heading in a positive direction.[12] The second great success the administration had is the President's Emergency Plan for AIDS Relief (PEPFAR)—a $15 billion plan over five years to battle global HIV/AIDS. PEPFAR had and

continues to have a significant impact on sub-Saharan Africa.

While difficult to measure, U.S. democratic initiatives on the continent continue to advance the American ideals. Michael E. Hess, U.S. Agency for International Development (USAID) Assistant Administrator for the Bureau for Democracy, Conflict, and Humanitarian Assistance, testified before the Senate that recent research shows "Every $10 million of USAID democracy assistance generated a five-fold increase in the rate of democratization in a given country, in any given year, over the period from 1990 to 2003."[13] In an environment with tremendous uncertainty, externalities beyond U.S. control, and significant unknown variables, this should be seen as a success.

Current Trends in African Democratization: More Positive Than You Might Think

In broad terms U.S. foreign policy changed significantly over the past fifty years. Within a half century we witnessed a transformation of Goldwater's conservatism vehemently opposed to offering democracy as a substitute for communism, to President Reagan's rhetoric clearly offering democracy as communism's substitute, to President Bush's worldwide drive for democracy. There is an undeniable increase in the emphasis and visibility of such causes in the twenty-first century. But how successful has democracy development been in Africa?

Freedom House's Annual Survey of Political Rights and Civil Liberties provides evidence of a dramatic change in the African political landscape between 1988 and 2008. Of the forty-eight sub-Saharan countries, the number of autocracies decreased from thirty-nine to fifteen, the number of democracies increased from two to eleven, and the number of partly free countries was twenty-two in 2008, compared to seven in 1988. Although strongly positive and laudable, 40 percent of African governments remain autocratic today. The Polity IV Democracy Index provides further analysis in that there have only been three years (1989, 1997, 1998) where the number of retractions outnumbered the number of democratic advances in the last twenty years. Understanding the volatility of the democratization process,

Dr. Joseph Siegle, a senior advisor at DAI, outlines how most "backtracking" occurs within the first six years. Specifically 45 percent of all African democratizers backtracked for one period of time and 65 percent of this group experienced this atmosphere within the first six years. The good news is that two-thirds of those experiencing a regression in this six-year period recover within a three-year period.[14]

When one looks for other variables that influence this phenomena, data provides further refinement that 90 percent of all backtracking is associated with *economic* hardship. In fact, 40 percent of new democracies in Africa conduct their political transition within a negative economic environment. Further, African countries make their transition from autocratic regimes to democracy against a backdrop of armed conflict—eight of seventeen democratizers were in conflict in the last ten years.[15] This again points to what the U.S. has slowly learned in executing its foreign policy: Democracy is an end state and cannot be executed in isolation.

Today there exist numerous vibrant, multiparty democracies throughout the continent that go well beyond simply high profile free and fair elections. Assistant Secretary of State Barry F. Lowenkron (Bureau of Democracy, Human Rights, and Labor) summarized these democracies by stating they represent "models for the continent by virtue of their free and fair elections, their robust civil societies, and their respect for the rule of law." However, there are undoubtedly African states on the other end of the spectrum, such as Sudan, Zimbabwe, and Eritrea, that do not protect their citizens' human rights and fail to provide for basic human needs.[16] The schism between government capabilities and intentions represents one of the underlying African complexities that will challenge the foreign policy of the next administration. To meet this challenge U.S. foreign policy must include a coherent and continuous level of engagement, shifting from a U.S. perception of "right" to more focus on what Africans see as "relevant." Equally important is the understanding that the U.S. cannot take its eye off the ball by taking African democracy for granted.

Backsliding, an Occasional Unfortunate Reality, Does Not Equal Failure
Could U.S. diplomatic intervention have averted the Kenyan electoral farce
in December 2007? No one is certain. However, given the time required
to raise a generation fully versed in democratic ideals and principles void
of firsthand experience with corruption in all facets of their democratic
institutions, it is important to understand and recognize the challenges
and tendencies for selfish behavior. Another significant challenge is dealing
with the perception of democracy and the instant expectation for successful
economic conditions. Cyril Obi, contributor to *No Choice, But Democracy:
Prising the People out of Politics in Africa?*, provides insight that "Although
the people vote for political parties, the experience in Africa is that they do
not have a say in the economic policies of elected governments."[17] With the
statistics well known and clear, poor economic uncertainties significantly
increase the possibilities of a democratic backslide. The U.S. cannot be expected to magically facilitate immediate economic prosperity and stability.
However, we must recognize the important link between democratization
and economic stability.

America's Africa Perestroika Moment
The next U.S. administration has the opportunity to demonstrate America's
support for African democratization. This can occur only by shifting from
what historically America saw as right for self-interests to what is relevant
for African interests. Which is to say, the United States can easily create a
"positive sum game" foreign policy through engagement of the core drivers
currently preventing sustainable democratic developments. As mentioned
in the previous section, there is a growing understanding that democracy
can only occur with concurrent advances in economic development, improving health, and education. In short, the United States has the opportunity to take the mantle of international leadership in targeting the sources of
instability denying democracy's effort to take root. By shifting the strategic
paradigm to focus on human security issues afflicting the African continent,
the United States can facilitate leadership that matters.

Conclusion

As we look across the African continent today there exist many challenges to the democratization process. From Zimbabwe and Nigeria to Kenya and the Sudan, institutions, inflation, corruption, and ill-intentioned leaders are but a small amount of the obstacles to freedom. Democratization in Africa is a marathon. It is a process, not a short-term product. The U.S. must remain engaged with a consistent narrative based on human security that espouses human rights, democratic ideals, and transparency. This must be accompanied by reinforcing programs targeting economic development at the grassroots level and simultaneously focusing on accountability at the macro level. The Millennium Challenge Corporation is but one of many programs the U.S. utilizes to shape the democratization process. Consistency of message across the African spectrum develops U.S. relevance. At present, contradictions in the U.S. message remain. Akwe Amosu expressed this concern before the Senate in 2007, elaborating on the exceptions allotted to oil rich countries—i.e., Equatorial Guinea—which "has long been associated with some of the worst governance abuses in Africa, so notorious that the United States had cause in the 1990s to close its Embassy there"; however, the U.S. continues its business ventures with the country because of the high priority established for oil.[18] These inconsistencies unfortunately can and do overshadow the overwhelmingly positive programs on the continent and must be corrected.

The overall outlook is positive and should be carried forward—democracy is on the rise and autocratic regimes, although not going quietly, are declining. The U.S., while not perfect in execution, undoubtedly facilitated a significant amount of democratic advancement across the continent. As we face the dawn of a new administration three lessons learned from the past are essential to carry into the future to facilitate the continued upward movement of democratic ideals. First, adjust the U.S. strategic narrative away from crisis *de jour* engagement perceived through an American lens of right to one focused on the underlying human security issues impacting sustainable democratic transition and consolidation relevant to African needs. Second, facilitate sustainable democracy as an end state grounded in economic, health, and education development at a grassroots level while simultaneously increasing accountability at the top. Finally, demonstrate strategic patience through a consistent/coherent strategic narrative while building democratic pillars generationally rather than through a short-term process of "free and fair election" ruses. The application of a synchronized, coordinated, consistent U.S. policy, utilizing all elements of national power, will facilitate significant advances across the continent toward the desired democratic end state.

Notes

1   Guy Arnold, *Africa: A Modern History* (London: Atlantic Books, 2005), 114.

2   Herman J. Cohen, "A Mixed Record: 50 Years of U.S.-Africa Relations," *Foreign Service Journal*, May 2008, 17–18.

3   George B. N. Ayittey, *Africa Betrayed* (New York: St. Martin's Press, 1992), 268.

4   Ibid., 267.

5   Henry F. Jackson, *From the Congo to Soweto* (New York: William Morrow & Co., Inc., 1982), 40–42.

6   Herman J. Cohen, 19–20.

7   Jennifer Seymour Whitaker, ed., *Africa and the United States Vital Interests* (New York: New York University Press, 1978), 3.

8   Herman J. Cohen, 19–20.

9   George B. N. Ayittey, 350.

10   Herman J. Cohen, 22.

11   Ibid.

12   Barry F. Lowenkron, prepared statement before the Senate Subcommittee on African Affairs of the Committee on Foreign Relations (Washington: U.S. Government Printing Office, July 17, 2007), 10.

13   Michael E. Hess, prepared statement before the Senate Subcommittee on African Affairs of the Committee on Foreign Relations (Washington: U.S. Government Printing Office, July 17, 2007), 23.

14   Joseph Siegle, forum facilitated by Shannon Beebe, *Has Democracy in Africa Plateaued*, The Africa Discussion Series, April 30, 2008.

15   Ibid.

16   Barry F. Lowenkron, 8.

17   Cyril Obi, *No Choice, But Democracy: Prising the People out of Politics in Africa?* ed. Thomas Ohlson (Sweden: Universitetstryckeriet, Uppsala, 2008), 10.

18   Akwe Amosu, prepared statement before the Senate Subcommittee on African Affairs of the Committee on Foreign Relations (Washington: U.S. Government Printing Office, July 17, 2007), 55.

Scrambling in the Shadows: India, Russia, and the EU in Africa

Peter Clark

Amid growing concern over access to limited resources and a shifting global calculus, discussions of Africa's reemergence onto the world stage have centered on the roles of China and the United States. But beyond this focus lies a myriad of growing links being forged with Africa by other states. India, Russia, and the European Union in particular have pursued varied strategies in their interactions with Africa. Building on historical patterns, India has taken a path designed to cast it as a softer China as it seeks to secure resources as well as develop markets for its own goods. Russia for its part struggles to find a role outside of that of a resource exploiter akin to China at the same time as it tries to strengthen its global reach. And for much of the European Union, relations with Africa remain overshadowed by colonial remorse that shapes ineffective and inconsistent policy toward the continent.

Scrambling in the Shadows: India, Russia, and the EU in Africa
With Africa's reemergence onto the world stage, much of the attention given to the continent has focused on China's seemingly unending quest for resources or on the renewed strategic interest placed on the region by the United States. Lost at times are the increasing roles of other actors including India, Russia, and the EU. Often operating outside of the lime-light, these players are expanding trade and investment linkages at a frantic pace, forging new ties, and contributing to the rewriting of Africa's global relationships.

In contrast to China's relatively recent foray into Africa, Russia, India, and Europe's former colonial powers can each point to a significantly longer historical experience with the region. Russia's involvement during the Cold War is dwarfed by that of the colonial powers and India, whose informal links predate the Christian world. The ties and patterns put in place during those earlier interactions continue to shape—and in the case of Europe almost dominate—relations.

The "scramble for resources" certainly plays a role in these states' interactions with Africa; however, it is too simplistic, although tempting, to paint India as an industrializing giant bent on securing access to the oil and gas its economy needs. Likewise, observations about Russia require equal effort to go beyond the energy explanation. This article looks to shed some light on these actors and to offer a broad overview of their roles in Africa with a focus on economic interactions.

India

India's relationship with Africa reflects in large part its history with the region. As early as the sixteenth century, colonial ties have linked India with Africa—first through the Portuguese use of Mozambique as a staging post for its presence in Goa and later through the British India–based administration of Kenya and Uganda.[1] Following the end of European rule in Africa, a significant expat Indian community remained in the states along the Indian Ocean rim. This Diaspora, now firmly entrenched in the social and business communities, has formed the vanguard of Indian participation in Africa by providing a network of relationships and managers familiar with the culture.

In contrast to other nations, India's foreign direct investment (FDI) focus has been on small and medium-sized enterprises, as funding has flowed to Indian-owned firms already in Africa to help expand and enlarge their operations. Investment and trade from India have been significantly more varied than that of China and Russia and have seen significant activity outside of oil and minerals.[2] India has also had success selling goods into Africa. In particular, lower priced generic pharmaceuticals from Ranbaxy and Cipla have helped expand India's business reach, as they also offer an image boost for New Delhi.[3] Indian firms have been quick to recognize the similarities between their own markets and those of Africa, seeing the same strong demand for low-cost technology that exists at home. It is not surprising that Tata Motors has identified the region as a production base for its $2,000 Nano ultra compact car.[4]

By stressing capacity-building and recognizing Africa as a potential trading partner and market for Indian goods, India's policy toward Africa aims to tread the middle ground between what is often seen by African states as Europe's condescending approach and the "neocolonialism" associated with China.

This policy has emerged slowly and only recently. Faced with a string of defeats to Chinese firms—culminating in the Oil and Natural Gas Corporation (ONGC) failure to secure a 50 percent share in Angolan oil fields,[5] India's view of Africa has shifted from indifference to alarm as New Delhi has recognized the tremendous inroads China is making into the region's natural resource sectors. In response, the Singh government has sought to develop a coherent policy that backs the private sector with targeted development assistance and aid.

India has looked to broaden its influence outside of its historical beachhead in eastern and southern Africa through initiatives designed to build ties with the resource-rich states of western Africa. At the forefront of this effort is the 2004 Techno-Economic Approach for Africa-India Movement (TEAM-9)[6] that is intended to exchange Indian infrastructure investment and low-cost technology for access to resources in eight western African states—all under the umbrella of building mutually beneficial long-term economic linkages.[7]

Regional efforts such as TEAM-9 have been supplemented by larger continent-wide ones, mirroring the strategies of China, Brazil, and others. In April 2008 New Delhi's first India-Africa Summit attracted fourteen African heads of state and representatives from twenty other nations. The meetings saw India hand out offers of $5.4 billion in credit together with $500 million for development projects, as well as the formation of a duty-free regime for imports from thirty-four of the continent's least developed states.[8]

The summit also provided a spotlight for New Delhi to showcase its softer approach and play up its historical and cultural links to Africa. This promoting of India as a kinder, gentler alternative to China has become an important part of New Delhi's strategy. By stressing those factors India and Africa have in common and the desire for long-term relationships, the hope is that some of the attraction of Beijing's deep pockets will dissipate.[9]

India's role in Africa's security realm has also undergone a marked shift in the last five years. With a significant portion of its trade traversing the Indian Ocean, New Delhi's maritime policy in the region has become a focal point of its relations with Africa. China's growing influence in the Indian Ocean and the chaotic state of the waters off Somalia and Yemen have prompted a more active Indian naval presence. This effort to exert influence has included holding joint naval exercises and increasing training with a number of Indian Ocean rim states.[10]

India has tremendous strengths to call upon in dealing with Africa: a common experience with imperialism, a depth of expertise promoting and handling rapid development, a long history of support for African independence, a significant Diaspora, and a de facto common language. The question is whether it will be able to leverage these advantages in the face of China's aggressive tactics.

Russia

Despite the billions of dollars poured into pro-Marxist states by the Soviet Union during the Cold War, Russia can point to few sources of support on the African continent, and those ties that do remain are for the most part either outside of resource-rich states or perpetuate because of the abundance of Soviet bloc small arms in which much of the region is awash. Russian President Vladimir Putin has voiced his belief that the end of the Cold War wiped the East-West slate in Africa clean, putting the continent in play as a new Russian "field of operations."[11] Under Putin, Russia has spent considerable effort to promote relations with Africa, including making the first trip by a Russian leader to South Africa in 2006. Russia has also aggressively forgiven debt, including $11 billion written off in 2007. It should be noted that the bulk of this debt is related to arms purchases made by African states from the Soviet Union.

On the surface, Russian FDI in Africa mirrors that of China in that its primary focus has been on sourcing and exporting resources with minimal value added along the way. Yet despite these similarities, Russia's approach remains quite different. In contrast to China's strategy of securing access at almost any cost, Russia's energy deals are primarily motivated by profit. The distinction is in large part a result of China's focus on using state run energy firms to forge deals, where the private sector has taken the lead for Russian investment—with the obvious exception of Gazprom.

The need to be profitable has resulted in Russian firms actively seeking out opportunities that allow them to leverage their expertise and to extend Russia's control over supply and pricing. Gazprom's efforts to gain concessions in Algeria and Libya's natural gas fields provide a vivid example of this as the energy giant's motivation appears a desire to further limit Europe's choice of suppliers.

Russian firms have also been willing to participate in deals that Western competitors have found less palatable because of risk or political concerns. Gazprom's decision to enter into agreement with Nigeria to take over Royal Dutch/Shell's abandoned oil production facilities in Ogoniland provides an example of how ready Russian firms are to take risk in the name of opportunity. Abandoned in 1995 after a surge in violence and international condemnation of Shell's cooperation with the Nigerian government, the Ogoniland fields are located in the midst of Nigeria's troubled Niger Delta.[12]

In large part because of its overwhelming focus on oil, gas, and metals, Russia struggles with an image problem as an exploiter in Africa akin to China. While significant Russian FDI flows into Africa, it is almost entirely in capital intensive extraction industries that provide few jobs for Africans and little chance for transfer of technical skills and expertise. Likewise, trade is almost nonexistent outside of resources exports and is very much a one-way relationship.

The European Union

European relations with Africa at the state and EU level continue to be clouded by the vestiges of colonial remorse at the same time as private investment struggles to compete with more aggressive and nimble challengers. The EU operates in an environment where an Africa reinvigorated by its burgeoning geopolitical importance is willing to say "no thank you."

The December 2007 AU-EU Lisbon Summit provided a vivid illustration of this newfound confidence. Intended as a relatively straight forward EU-Africa gathering, the meetings instead became a platform for African states to condemn Europe for what they saw as a trade policy firmly rooted in the colonial past.[13] At the heart of the conflict lay the terms of new trade agreements needed to replace those hammered out at Lomé in 1975 and Cotonou in 2002 that run afoul of WTO rules by discriminating against developing countries outside of the Africa, Caribbean, and Pacific (ACP) group of nations.[14] The European Commission's decision to accelerate removing tariff protection for African exports and to insist that any preferential treatment given to non-EU countries (read China) had to be extended to Europe rankled many African states as moving too quickly and as an effort to play catch up with China.[15]

Combined with a growing credibility issue faced by the West over its dismal progress making good on the G8 Gleneagles promise to double annual aid to Africa to $50 billion by 2010, the rebukes at the Lisbon Summit serve as reminders of the problems facing EU-Africa relations.[16] European aid to Africa remains largely mired in a donor-recipient framework rather than the more strategic giving favored by others, including China and India.

Among Europe's former colonial powers, the changing geopolitical framework has led some to rethink the nature of ties with Africa. France under President Nicolas Sarkozy has been at the forefront of this reappraisal. In February 2008, Sarkozy announced France's intention to revamp its Africa policy in an effort to produce a relationship founded on transparency and mutual benefit.[17]

With growing domestic opposition to France's policy in West and Central Africa, Sarkozy's desire to build a "healthier relationship" with Africa,[18] together with his intent to focus foreign policy closer to home, suggests a significant shift away from the region is likely.[19] Sarkozy comments also amplified France's desire to reduce its military commitments to the region, which since its tragic experiences in Rwanda have seen a preference toward multilateral operations over unilateral ones.[20] The tricky part may be the presences of significant numbers of French citizens throughout Francophone Africa and their safety and security in a region not known for stability. To some observers, Sarkozy's desire to limit the military's role in Africa eerily echoes France's 1997 "hands-off Africa" policy that lasted a little over five years before Paris ordered troops into the Ivory Coast in early 2003.[21]

Conclusion

India, Russia, and the EU are each likely to play continuing roles in Africa in the coming years as they seek to capitalize on their existing positions and maneuver to take advantages of opportunities that present themselves.

India in particular has the potential to build on its synergies with Africa to form mutually beneficial relationships both economically and strategically. It is this last piece and the resulting need for New Delhi to establish control over the Indian Ocean that may result in India being the most interesting of the secondary actors in Africa to watch.

For its part Russia is likely to remain a resource extractor in Africa, viewing the continent as a tool in its overall energy policy. Moscow's limited ability to project power outside of its immediate sphere makes any greater Russian aspirations difficult in the short term.

EU policy toward Africa remains caught between a desire to make good on the types of promises coming out of the G8 Summit in Gleneagles and the EC's need to preserve what it sees as economic sensibility. In the absence of a consistent policy, private sector involvement will likely continue to grow all the same.

Perhaps the greatest challenge for Africa itself is to avoid the "resource curse" and instead find the means to leverage its newfound position into meaningful development and progress. With 50 percent of all FDI flowing into resource-related industries it is likely to be a hard feat.[22]

Notes

1   Alex Vines and Bereni Oruitemeka, "India's Engagement with Africa's Indian Ocean Rim States," *Africa Programme/Asia Programme Briefing Paper*, Chatham House AFP P 1/08, April 2008, 2.

2   Sushant K. Singh, "India and West Africa: A Burgeoning Relationship," *Africa Programme/Asia Programme Briefing Paper*, Chatham House AFP/ASP BP 07/01, April 2007, 9.

3   Vibhuti Haté, "India in Africa: Moving Beyond Oil," *South Asia Monitor*, no. 119, Center for Strategic & International Studies, June 10, 2008.

4   "Tata Motors' Nano Heads for South Africa," *The Economic Times*, April 10, 2008, http://economictimes.indiatimes.com.

5   China is believed to have offered Angola $2 billion in aid to secure the deal. See Tim Cocks, "Resource-hungry India Seeks to Increase Its Economic Ties with Africa," *International Herald Tribune*, April 3, 2008, http://www.iht.com.

6   TEAM-9 is made up of India and Burkina Faso, Chad, Equatorial Guinea, Ghana, Guinea-Bissau, Ivory Coast, Mali, and Senegal.

7   Singh, 6.

8   Randeep Ramesh, "India Joins Queue for Africa's Resources," *The Guardian*, April 9, 2008, http://guardian.co.uk.

9   Siddharth Srivastava, "India Loads Up Presents for African Safari," *Asia Times Online*, April 12, 2008, http://www.atimes.com.

10 Naval exercises have included joint training with South Africa, the Seychelles and Mozambique. In addition, India has reached agreements with the Seychelles (2003) and Mozambique (2006) to allow for the Indian Navy to patrol territorial waters of their coasts. See Vines and Oruitemeka, 12.

11 Michael Wines, "Putin Visits South Africa, Seeking Good Will and Trade," *New York Times*, September 6, 2007, http://www.nytimes.com.

12 "Nigeria: Gazprom in Ogoniland," *Stratfor Today*, July 8, 2008, http://stratfor.com.

13 Anver Versi, "Africa Stands Firm," *African Business*, no. 338, January 2008:12–18.

14 Neil Ford, "Why Africa Rejected 'Divide & Rule' EU Trade Deal," *African Business*, no. 339, February 2008, 42.

15   Ibid.

16   Patrick Wintour and Larry Elliott, "G8 Summit: West Told to Fulfill Its African Aid Pledge," *The Guardian*, July 7, 2008, http://guardian.co.uk.

17   "France to Overhaul Policies towards Africa," *International Herald Tribune*, February 28, 2008, http://www.iht.com.

18   Ibid.

19   "Sarkozy and Changing Relations with Africa," *Stratfor Today*, June 21 2007, http://www.stratfor.com.

20   Andrew Hansen, "Backgrounder: The French Military in Africa," *New York Times*, February 9, 2007, http://www.nytimes.com.

21   Keith B. Richburg, "France Abandons Hands-off Policy on Africa Conflicts: Some Fear Ivory Coast Quagmire," *The Washington Post*, January 4, 2003, http://www.washingtonpost.com.

22   UN World Investment Report, http://www.unctad.org/.

SECTION II:

Perspectives on China-Africa Security Issues

Strategic Engagement in Africa: The China Factor and U.S. Policy

John N. Paden

China's penetration into African political, economic, and military affairs has reinforced a superficial East versus West trope in national security affairs. From votes in the United Nations on Taiwan's independence to competition over natural resources to the opening of new markets for Chinese products, Africa is widely perceived as another focal point for conflict between a rising China and the United States. Lost in the hyperbole, however, are the political and economic realities of China's engagement on the continent and what it means for American security policy. This chapter reviews the evolution of China's engagement in Africa, assesses the political and economic policy implications of Sino-African relations, and considers the long-term viability of China's Africa strategy from the perspective of U.S. foreign policy, which has really focused on just a handful of countries, primarily Egypt, South Africa, and Nigeria.

China's penetration into African political, economic, and military affairs has reinforced a superficial East versus West trope in national security affairs. From votes in the United Nations on Taiwan's independence to competition over natural resources to the opening of new markets for Chinese products, Africa is widely perceived as another focal point for conflict between a rising China and the United States. Indeed, China's engagement in Africa is hard for many to perceive outside of a narrow lens highlighting China's growing military power. Lost in the hyperbole, however, are the political and economic realities of China's engagement on the continent and what it means for American security policy.

Meanwhile, U.S. engagement in Africa tends to be seen through a different lens altogether. Historic ties to countries such as Liberia and democratic initiatives in countries such as Mali or Mozambique suggest, for some, that the U.S. has long-held, deeply entrenched political and economic interests on the continent. For sure, energy security needs in the Gulf of Guinea and terrorism concerns in North Africa, East Africa, and the Horn are important. But even the creation of the U.S. Africa Command has been perceived as less of a military organization than a coordinator to bolster political and economic engagement across Africa. Although the new Command is intended to engage with all fifty-four African countries, American security interests are historically focused on just three: Egypt, South Africa, and Nigeria.

Egypt has been a part of African continental organizations since the 1960s, when most African states gained independence. Because of its weight in Middle Eastern affairs, it is sometimes underestimated in terms of its African connections. It is the only African country that does not fall under the domain of AFRICOM. Its historic connection to the Nile river countries ties it closely to Sudan, Uganda, Ethiopia, and others in that area. Of the Arabic speaking countries in Africa, it is by far the demographic and cultural center of gravity.

South Africa economics and demographics dominate the southern African region. It is also a major source of political and business connectivity. Nigeria is the demographic giant of Africa, with a population of around 150 million. It also straddles a major religious divide and is the largest country in the world with about equal portions of Muslim and Christian adherents. Finally, it is one of the major oil producers in the world.

How do these African countries fit into the strategic visions of the many stakeholders in a globalizing world? This larger picture is complicated by the fact that economic ties between countries are often cross-cut by transnational ownership, management, and supply chains. In the case of these three countries, it is useful to explore the current and likely axes of Sino-American competition and whether this competition remains political and economic in nature.

The recent appearance of China on the modern African scene raises questions about its impact within Africa and abroad. There is a sense in Africa that China has done an about-face in its economic development, through market reforms and a general opening up to the world. Thus, a China that plays by WTO rules is quite different from a China that was on a permanent quest for revolution.

This chapter reviews the evolution of China's engagement in Africa, assesses the political and economic policy implications of Sino-African relations, and considers the long-term viability of China's Africa strategy from the perspective of U.S. foreign policy, which has really focused on a handful of countries.

China's Early Engagement in Africa

China's approach to Africa has evolved significantly over the last three decades. Throughout the 1960s and 1970s, China's Africa policy was guided largely by ideological concerns, which impelled occasional support for guerrilla movements in South Africa. China engaged in infrastructure development on the continent, a tradition that continues. The most notable project was China's Tanzania-Zambia (Tanzam) railway, which established the long-standing practice of importing large numbers of Chinese workers into Africa, keeping them more or less secluded from indigenous populations. In China, efforts to bring African students to study in Beijing often backfired, in part because of the social backlash from Chinese women dating African students but also because of restrictions on student life.

Deng Xiaoping's "Opening" reforms marked the critical turning point in Sino-African relations. Beginning in 1978 and accelerating in the 1980s, Deng's reforms encouraged the international community to forge ties with China's new Africanists. The Ford Foundation helped sponsor a U.S.-China African Studies Exchange Committee between 1981 and 1996.[1] Many of the Chinese scholars in this program studied at U.S. universities and had extensive contact with African scholars at those universities. A number of the Chinese scholars from this program were active in the Trilateral Dialogues of 2006–07.[2] The exchange program ended in 1996, with a conference on South Africa in Beijing, and with the participation of a number of African scholars. One legacy of the program was the maturation of Chinese scholars with insight into African development and economic issues.

China's interests in Africa matured and diversified throughout the late twentieth century. China's nongovernmental interest in Africa expanded apace with the Chinese economy. Initially, China's private sector engagement with Africa originated in Hong Kong and often involved light manufacturing industries, including pots and pans, and textiles. By the millennium, there was hardly a major African city without an array of Chinese restaurants and China's engagement had become more expansive and diverse.

Recent Development in Sino-African Relations
According to a 2007 Center for Strategic and International Studies (CSIS) report, "While China has maintained good bilateral diplomatic relations with African nations since the 1950s, and provided substantial development aid and infrastructural assistance to partners on the continent, it was not until 2000 that Beijing launched a more comprehensive and ambitious effort to court Africa as a whole. This new, more activist approach is best seen in the activities and aims of the multilateral Forum on China and Africa Cooperation (FOCAC) process."[3] By the time of China's entry into the WTO in December 2001, a much more diverse range of private sector small- and medium-sized traders and business entrepreneurs had migrated to Africa with little involvement by or supervision from the Chinese government.

When the third FOCAC convened in Beijing in November 2006, forty-eight African countries were represented, forty-three of them by African heads of state. Never before had so many African leaders attended such a conference. For observers in the West, it was clear that China's presence in Africa and expanded engagement with African countries had grown significantly in the political, economic, and nongovernmental dimensions.

Politically, China has full diplomatic representation in Africa with the exception of five small states that maintain diplomatic relations with Taiwan: Burkina Faso, Gambia, Malawi, Sao Tome and Principe, and Swaziland.[4] China's influence at the United Nations, through its "permanent five" role, can usually count on widespread African support in the General Assembly. The World Trade Organization (WTO), which China joined in December 2001, provides a framework for trade relations, rule of law, and dispute settlement mechanisms in Africa and globally.[5]

At the political level, Chinese relations have been good with leaders of African states in part because of the Chinese policy of noninterference in the internal affairs of such countries. The 2006 FOCAC illustrated that a "state-centric approach to Africa will build strategically on Beijing's core strengths and align with the stated preferences of African countries."[6] China has played to the interests of African elites by helping build showcase projects such as stadiums and presidential palaces.

In the economic domain, China's interests have been mainly in resource extraction, which have often entailed infrastructure development. According to the *Wall Street Journal*, "Chinese contractors have stitched together a road network that reaches Ethiopia's northern border with Sudan to the eastern seaport of Djibouti to the southern border area with Kenya. China Road secured most of its contracts through public tenders."[7]

Clearly, the Chinese economy is hungry for the natural resources of Africa. Energy supplies from Africa remain critical to the Chinese economy. Three major sources are Sudan, Angola, and Nigeria. Regarding Sudan, according to *The New Republic*, Beijing has "a 40 percent stake in a refinery pumping more than 300,000 barrels a day and a 1500-kilometer pipeline from Sudan to the Red Sea."[8] China is also involved in copper extraction in Congo; oil and timber in Equatorial Guinea; natural gas in Algeria; gold, tin, and tungsten in Rwanda; cobalt and copper in Zambia; timber in Gabon; manganese, platinum, and chromium in South Africa; and platinum in Zimbabwe.

Regarding Angola, "The former Portuguese colony has become China's second-largest commercial partner in Africa and exports 25 percent of its oil production to China."[9] In 2006, Angola replaced Saudi Arabia as China's major source of imported oil.[10] The major producer of oil in Africa is Nigeria. China has been investing billions of dollars in exploration in the Niger Delta and offshore. (To be discussed in the next section.)

At the same time, China is both selling textiles to Africa and investing in textile factories in Africa to produce goods that may then be shipped duty free to the U.S. China is also purchasing African agricultural products, including virtually all of Zimbabwe's tobacco crops.

The fact that most of the above-mentioned commercial arrangements are negotiated by African officials, often without much transparency, lends credibility to charges of corruption and mismanagement. While this pattern may appease African elites, it may also produce a backlash at the popular level.

Finally, the emigration patterns from China to Africa are obvious, but under-reported and under-researched. Chinese overseas networks are a global phenomenon. It is often difficult to tell whether overseas Chinese are originally from the mainland, from Hong Kong, from Taiwan, from southeast Asia, or from North America. What is apparent is that the manufacturing boom in China has created a class of middlemen who use their connections to facilitate trade—both legal and illegal—in Africa.

A Case Study: China's Relationship with Nigeria

Given the diversity of Africa, at the state and sub-state levels, it is important to focus on critical cases to get a better sense of Chinese activities and African responses. Nigeria is such a critical case. The first visit by a Chinese leader to Nigeria was by President Jiang Zemin in April 2002, who emphasized the need for strong bilateral relations in general. He emphasized cooperation on regional and international issues.

In April 2006, President Hu Jintao visited Abuja and discussed a range of commercial projects with then Nigerian President Olusegun Obasanjo, including those dealing with the oil industry. The Abuja summit resulted in Nigeria establishing direct air links with China and a grant to Henan Province to develop a special free trade zone at the Lagos International Trade Fair.[11] Subsequently, the Nigerian president and at least forty high-ranking Nigerian cabinet officials attended the 2006 FOCAC.

Chinese companies invested in local projects that may have a political appeal to Nigerian leaders. In June 2005 Chinese companies announced investments in Ogun State to establish a furniture village. (President Obasanjo was from Ogun State.)

Chinese economic links with Nigeria range from low-level textile and furniture investments to high tech investments in oil and commercial links in satellite communications.[12] In the domain of textiles, the legal and illegal importation of Chinese textiles into Nigeria has basically put the Nigerian textile industry out of business in places like Kaduna. In fall 2007 the major textile factory in Kaduna closed, laying off four thousand workers. In fields such as satellite technology, Nigeria is working with the Chinese, not with the United States or with Europe. In May 2007 China built, launched, and placed into orbit a Nigerian satellite.[13]

Meanwhile, at a grassroots level in Nigerian cities, from Lagos in the south to Kano and Kaduna in the north, the number of Chinese entrepreneurs has increased exponentially in recent years. This reflects the demand for goods and services in the oil wealth economy, and the opportunities afforded immigrant communities with links to the global economy, especially in "Greater China."[14]

Implications of China-Africa Engagement for the U.S.

On December 5–6, 2007, a CSIS conference was held on U.S. and Chinese Engagement in Africa: Prospects for Improving U.S.-China-Africa Cooperation. Among other things, three case studies by African scholars had been commissioned on Nigeria, Kenya, and Angola.[15] All seemed to indicate the Chinese initiatives in their respective domains were welcomed by government and, to a large extent, by scholars and ordinary people.

The CSIS conference focused largely on trilateral forms of cooperation. Almost everyone speaking at the conference—Americans, Chinese, and Africans—seemed to perceive no basic conflict between U.S. and Chinese endeavors in Africa. To some extent, contemporary U.S. general perceptions of China influence U.S. perceptions of China's role in Africa. While China-U.S. relations have been described by former president George H. W. Bush as the most important bilateral relationship in the world, clearly, they are fragile and require careful handling. Furthermore, most U.S. expert observers are aware of the variations between different sectors in China, ranging from the military, to the foreign ministry, to the business community, to the academics.

U.S. political campaigns on all sides have attacked trade agreements, and China had become a political issue ranging from matters of currency pegs, to possible WTO violations. In February 2007, the U.S. took China to the WTO dispute settlement mechanism in Geneva on grounds of violating the Subsidies Agreement and National Treatment Principle. (The U.S. argued that tax rebates constituted an export subsidy.) In April 2007, the U.S. filed two more WTO cases: one on intellectual property rights, and the second on distribution restrictions on films and audiovisual products.[16] Yet, the fact that such trade issues were brought for consultation and, in some cases, arbitration to the WTO panels, is itself a form of conflict mitigation and management, which may have a demonstration effect in Africa.

At a popular level in the U.S., criticisms of China's noninterference policy in Sudan has infuriated many NGO Darfur coalitions, to the point that some called for a boycott of the Beijing Olympics. China's close links with the government in Zimbabwe seem to undermine efforts at a democratic transition in that country, which some in the U.S. regard as essential even on humanitarian grounds. Also, China's environmental record attracts criticism by NGOs in the U.S.

Yet, there seems to be a consensus in U.S. political, economic, and diplomatic establishment circles that see China's rise as natural, and linked to larger issues of worldwide peace and prosperity. Many see the challenge as keeping channels of communication open among U.S., Chinese, and African constituencies. Three Trilateral Dialogue conferences are important steps in this direction.

What are the main elements of agreement in such efforts? The most important is that "there is no strategic conflict between the U.S. and China in Africa, and there is no zero-sum dynamic between the two countries."[17] In addition, "All delegations agreed that peace and security are prerequisites for stability and economic development."[18]

While some in Africa may see the U.S. and China as strategic competitors at the international level, most African elites see the arrival of China on the world stage as an inspiration. Within one generation, China has lifted more than 400 million people out of poverty. Given the Cold War cooperation of China and the U.S. in Africa versus the Soviets, there is a presumed legacy of strategic congruence.

The "China model" does entail a heavy role for the state, much as Japan's rise did at one time. The implications for a single party system—as previously in Japan—raise questions about democratic transitions. Yet, with the exception of Sudan and Zimbabwe, which are special cases, most Africans have made the strategic decision that democratic systems are suitable to their current environment. The question of transparency and accountability in African governments is an ongoing challenge in the fight against corruption. Clearly, the U.S. feels that democratic procedures are the most effective way of achieving this end.

African opinion leaders do not see a new big-power rivalry emerging between China and the U.S. If anything, the rivalry is seen as between the newcomers (i.e., the U.S. and China) versus the former European colonial powers (especially U.K. and France). Yet, all are now interlinked in the global economy, in which national units may be less relevant than other socioeconomic ties.

Conclusion

The emergence of China on the African scene did not occur in 2000. The earlier legacy went through a Maoist phase, and then morphed into a strategic alliance with the U.S. during the Cold War. The reform transitions in China during the 1990s with its "opening" to Africa, included a retooling of intellectual and political capital, in which U.S. academics played a significant part.

The implications of "Crossroads Africa: U.S. perspectives on U.S.-China-Africa Security Affairs," especially economic relations, are a major challenge for the Obama administration. The new administration must take account not only of bilateral relations with China, or with African countries, but also manage creatively the cross-linked realities of globalization, in which economic cooperation ties national interests together.

The recent advent of China's economic and political initiatives in Africa can be turned into a win-win situation through trilateral dialogue and taking a larger view of the costs and benefits of various strategic options for U.S. engagement. While China is in many ways a competitor in Africa, it has also shown that it is willing to cooperate with the international community on basic issues of security and development.

In the period after 2001, marked by China's entry into the WTO, as well as the beginnings of the global war on terrorism—with its concurrent instability in the Middle Eastern oil producing areas—China's role in Africa has dramatically increased. The trilateral effort has emerged to create channels of communication and avoid unnecessary misunderstandings. Yet, Africa is not simply the African Union at a continental level. Each of the fifty-four African states has unique qualities. The challenge of managing the array of U.S.-China relationships in Africa requires attention at all levels, from continental, to regional, to national, to sub-national. This is a diplomatic challenge for the U.S. at a time when there are many other urgent priorities.

Many of these indicators of engagement between China and Africa are natural and should not be greeted with alarm in the West. The linkage of Chinese and African studies should be a natural development for American universities, given the predisposition for adaptability and flexibility in the U.S. system. The larger challenge will be to continue trilateral cooperation in the educational, political, and economic domains, which could well provide a breakthrough in African growth and development. The next step for China seems to be an extensive campaign in the educational domain, to bring young Africans to China to learn languages and other skills. China has made the transition to emphasizing African languages in its universities and in media broadcasts overseas.

The global rise of China, however, will continue and will be a challenge to the Western tendency to compartmentalize knowledge fields by regional areas. In March 2008, The Aspen Institute held a Congressional Program conference on U.S.-China Relations that covered such topics as "Core economic issues in U.S.-China relations: currency, the trade deficit, investment and finance, food and product safety," and "The nexus of energy, global warming, and environmental concerns" along with discussion of issues of political reform, and military modernization in China. The conference included U.S. congressmen and senators, but also academics and participants from China.

In June 2008, U.S. Treasury Secretary Henry Paulson, Jr. articulated his agenda under the U.S.-China Strategic Economic Dialogue (SED), emphasizing energy and the environment. Ongoing issues include managing financial and economic cycles, developing human capital, the benefits of trade and open markets, enhancing investment, as well as advancing joint opportunities for cooperation in energy and the environment.

Indeed, perhaps the most critical U.S.-China-Africa trilateral issue for the U.S. is energy security. China's energy needs have bid up the price of crude oil, and Chinese relations with Nigeria, Angola, and Sudan have challenged the older multinational oil companies. Yet, this also creates a situation in which China has every reason to support "security" measures in the Gulf of Guinea and elsewhere. If local violence prevails, the oil lifting process is shut down. There is a clear congruence of U.S. and Chinese strategic interests on this matter, which the Obama administration might consider as a key part of its own trilateral dialogue.

Notes

1   The Committee consisted of seven senior U.S. Africanists: Robert Cummings (Howard University), William Foltz (Yale University), Michael Lofchie (UCLA), John Paden (George Mason University), Carl Rosberg (UC, Berkeley) Crawford Young (University of Wisconsin), and George T. Yu (University of Illinois, Urbana.) Conferences were held in China and the U.S., with the first Beijing conference in 1984. (For an example of publications from such conferences see George T. Yu, *Contemporary African Economic and Political Development*, Urbana, Illinois, January 11–15, 1991.) Chinese scholars came to the U.S. universities for advanced studies. The leader of our group, George Yu,

is currently retired and living in San Francisco. The Ford Foundation director of this exchange program was Peter F. Geithner, currently Advisor, Asia Center, Harvard University.

2   Professor Xu Weizhong is currently Director, Department of African Studies, CICIR, and Deputy Secretary-General, China Association of African Studies.

3   Bates Gill, Chin-hao Huang, and J. Stephen Morrison, *China's Expanding Role in Africa: Implications for the United States,* Center for Strategic and International Studies, January 2007, p. 5. For an elaboration of these points, see CSIS, *Africa-China-U.S. Trilateral Dialogue: Summary Report,* December 2007. The lead organization in China for the dialogues is the Institute of West-Asian and African Studies (IWAAS), Chinese Academy of Social Sciences.

4   In addition, Taiwan maintains four quasi-official missions in Africa: one in Nigeria (Abuja) and three in South Africa (Pretoria, Cape Town, and Johannesburg).

5   See John N. Paden, "The World Trade Organization and Rule of Law in China: A First Year Assessment," *Virginia Lawyer,* April 2003, vol. 51, no. 9.

6   Gill, et al, *China's Expanding Role in Africa.*

7   Karby Leggett, "Staking a Claim China Flexes Economic Muscle Throughout Burgeoning Africa," *Wall Street Journal,* March 29, 2005.

8   Stephanie Giry, "China's Africa Strategy. Out of Beijing," *The New Republic,* November 15, 2004.

9   Jean-Christophe Servant, "China's Trade Safari in Africa," *Le Monde Diplomatique,* May 2005.

10 For a fuller elaboration, see the studies by Indira Campos and Alex Vines, of Chatham House, London.

11 See "Nigeria to Establish Air Link with Argentina, China," *This Day,* April 28, 2006.

12 For a detailed summary of Nigerian-Chinese economic and diplomatic relations, plus comments on the politics of the Lagos "China Town" and some of the cross-currents of Nigerian opinion regarding China, see Layi Adeloye and Sulaimon Adenekan, "Chinese Incursion to Nigeria: In Whose Interests?" *Punch,* December 30, 2007 (seven pages).

13 "China Builds and Launches a Satellite for Nigeria," *Washington Post,* May 14, 2007; "Snubbed by U.S., China Finds Its Own Space Partners," *New York Times,* May 24, 2007.

14 The term "Greater China" is used by the World Bank to indicate the economies of China, Hong Kong, Taiwan, Singapore, and other parts of Chinese-speaking southeast Asia, linked by networks of Chinese business entrepreneurs. This is consistent with the Asia Pacific Economic Cooperation (APEC) forum's emphasis on "economies" rather than sovereign political units. Thus, China, Hong Kong, Taiwan, and Singapore are all members of APEC.

15 The three papers included the following. Professor Pat Utomi, Lagos Business School, did not have a written paper, but focused on the emerging "China Town" in Lagos. Dr. Michael Chege, Advisor on Kenya and the Peer Review Mechanism (NEPAD), Kenyan Ministry of Planning and National Development, "From Disputes on Making Revolution to Agreement on Making Money: Economic Relations Between Kenya and China, 1963–2007." Alex Vines, Director, Chatham House Africa program, and Indira Campos, Research Assistant, Chatham House Africa Program, "Angola and China: A Pragmatic Partnership."

16 For a discussion of U.S.-China trade relations, see Stuart S. Malawer, "United States–China Trade Litigation in the WTO," International Practice Section, *The Virginia Lawyer*, December 2007. For background, see Stuart S. Malawer, *WTO Law, Litigation and Policy*, (William S. Hein & Co., 2007).

17 *Africa-China-U.S. Trilateral Dialogue*, 2007, 6.

18 Ibid.

Engaging Chinese Expansionism in Africa: Policy Implications for Washington

Ian Taylor

Much is said and written about Sino-African affairs and the expansion of Chinese activities on the continent. U.S. responses to Chinese foreign policy and commercial activities are mixed. But China's role in Africa is, like all other external actors, diverse, and its effect in the continent varies widely depending on local economic and political circumstances. This chapter argues for a more balanced appraisal of China's engagement in Africa, and a U.S. policy that recognizes the complicated multiplicity of China's activities in Africa and constructively engages China where possible.

The expansion of Chinese involvement in Africa is arguably the most momentous development on the continent since the end of the Cold War. The People's Republic of China (PRC) is now Africa's third most important trading partner, behind the United States and France, but ahead of the United Kingdom, with Sino-African trade hitting approximately $74 billion in 2007.[1] Compared to the $5 billion worth of official trade China was doing with Africa in 1997, one can quickly appreciate the rapidity of this development.[2] Most of this expansion in trade is driven by a desire to obtain sources of raw materials and energy for China's ongoing economic growth and for new export markets. In turn, this has provoked a variety of external reactions. Responses within the United States to the new dynamics of Sino-African ties have been mixed, although in general coverage has been negative.

Whilst Chinese actors are agreeable to expand economic and political relations with poor and frequently volatile African states anxious for foreign direct investment (FDI), the methods used in securing ties has meant that at times such strategies are at odds with expressed American policies regarding governance and development policies. An energetic sourcing of energy supplies, particularly oil, in Africa has also raised concerns within the Beltway.

It has to be said that in relative terms, the exponential increase in Chinese trade with sub-Saharan Africa (SSA) from the start of this century means that we are in the very early stages of a solidified Sino-African relationship. Thus far the repercussions of this sustained and in-depth political and economic involvement by the Chinese for broad-based development in Africa and/or American interests has yet to be ascertained. At present the picture appears mixed—there are instances where the Chinese role in Africa is clearly positive and appreciated. Equally, there are issues where Beijing is, at present at least, playing an equivocal role that arguably threatens to unravel some of the progress made in Africa in recent times on issues of good governance and accountability. It is here that concern over the effect of Chinese involvement in Africa for American policy is most felt. However, it does need to be stated that Beijing's role in Africa is, like all other external actors, diverse, and its effect in the continent varies widely depending on local economic and political circumstance. A balanced appraisal on China's engagement in Africa and how Washington should respond is thus needed.

A Revisionist Power?
One of the critiques aimed at Beijing in Africa is that it is threatening to overturn accepted practices related to governance in its quest for energy supplies. Whilst Chinese state-owned corporations do indeed pursue policies different from privately-owned American companies, Chinese interests in fact require a peaceful international environment. This is central to Beijing's current diplomacy, fitting with the strategy to "go global," which encourages Chinese corporations to invest overseas and play a role in

international capital markets.³ Globalization actually forces countries such as China, who are competing for foreign investment, to maintain peaceful, stable markets. Within Beijing there is a growing awareness regarding the interconnectedness of the international and domestic settings—this has been sloganized as "linking up with the international track" (*yu guoji jiegui*).⁴ American policy makers would be well advised to encourage such thinking rather than be tempted to a nationalistic zero-sum approach to China's expansion into Africa.

Equally, when accusations about China being a revisionist power in Africa are raised, analysts need to be very careful as to what they are talking about. In Chinese foreign policy making, central government ministries, provincial and municipal or local government bureaucrats all have an input, whilst state-owned enterprises (SOEs) now have to be sensitive both to general government policies and proclamations as well as the profit motive. Whilst the central state may have an Africa policy, this has to be mediated via the economic interests of separate corporations and the political motivations and aspirations of local state officials who, with growing autonomy, may or may not share the enunciated central vision. A form of "fragmented authoritarianism," where policy made at the center becomes ever more malleable to the parochial organizational and political goals of the different agencies and regions entrusted with enforcing policy, is a reality in contemporary China and complicates American engagement with Beijing over such issues. The willingness by Chinese actors to perform activities willy-nilly at the behest of Beijing cannot be assumed, and American policy needs to recognize this.

For instance, Beijing has as yet been incapable of enforcing a geographical division of labor on the main national oil companies (NOCs), namely the China National Petroleum Corporation (CNPC) and the China National Offshore Oil Company (CNOOC). The result is competition and overlap between and among China's NOCs, even though these are ostensibly central to Beijing's energy security policies.

These corporations possess subsidiary companies and have independent seats on their executive boards, meaning that various agendas are often pursued. There is little in the way of a joined up strategy to secure an entrée into specific oil and gas fields and it has been the case that two different NOCs have bid against each other—as when CNPC and China Petroleum & Chemical Corporation (Sinopec) vied against each other for a pipeline project in Sudan. Indeed, "The [NOCs] view one another as rivals, competing not only for oil and gas assets, but also for political advantage. The more high-quality assets a company acquires, the more likely it is to obtain diplomatic and financial support from the Chinese government for its subsequent investments. This is especially true for CNOOC, which does not have as much political clout as CNPC and Sinopec."[5]

This inter-firm competition is normal in the capitalist West, obviously, but puts a different take on "China, Inc."[6] and its oil strategy in Africa. Indeed, the idea of the strategic use of economic relations by Beijing as a means of achieving power politics objectives[7] needs to be treated with caution. It is imperative not to overestimate the degree to which the Chinese state has been able to wholly control and direct the evolution of its international economic relations.

In fact, it is important to recognize that there now exists "a more pluralistic range of Chinese decision makers whose diverse interests are reflected in foreign policy and behavior." Such decision makers "represent a variety of government, party, and military bureaucracies, government-affiliated and nongovernmental think tanks, and provincial and local governments."[8] Competition and compromise in policy formulation within China is now the norm at all levels of government as the policy process is becoming relatively more open, facilitating greater input in a proactive fashion rather than the reactive manner that formerly characterized policy input from various agencies. Although the role of the paramount leader continues to be significant, the general policy direction is increasingly open to advice from academics and business associations. These new channels of communication open up possibilities for Washington to engage in the policy-making process in Beijing, albeit not directly at such a level. The encouragement of knowledgeable Western academics to connect with the plethora of Chinese think tanks should be developed by Washington as one means to access policy formulation in Beijing. A greater receptivity to new ideas within China needs nurturing if Washington seeks to influence Sino-African relations.

Human Rights in Sino-African Ties

One of the recurring criticisms aimed at Chinese activities in Africa is the effect policies are deemed to have on the human rights and governance situation in a number of states where Chinese actors are present. American foreign policy needs to be cognizant of this, but also be realistic in its approach to the issue. China's leadership is intensely suspicious of American promotion of human rights and regards such calls as a Trojan horse through which Washington might undermine Beijing. Importantly, the perceived American strategy of "peaceful evolution" (*heping yanbian*) being exercised on Beijing's political security has been cast—not unreasonably—as being analogous to regime change.[9] Chinese policy in this regard has then been to consistently cast talk of liberal democracy and liberal conceptions of human rights (and, occasionally, the environment) as a tool of neo-imperialism being practiced toward both China and the developing world. This falls on many receptive ears in Africa at the elite level and China's policy makers are not unaware of this.

It does need to be pointed out, however, that Beijing's noninterference policies are not particular to Africa but are a central element of Chinese foreign policy *in toto*. Whilst there is justifiable disquiet that aspects of Chinese engagement in parts of Africa may undermine political and economic reform, the reasons for much of Africa's current predicament are complex, and erecting a potential scapegoat to blame makes little sense. Here, the charge of hypocrisy can be leveled against Washington in this regard. As Burstein and De Keijzer point out, "While the human rights situation in China is not good by American standards, it is not unlike that in Indonesia, India, or Saudi Arabia, for instance. Yet in most of these cases, the United States is able to have normal and even close relationships that are not overwhelmed by the human rights agenda."[10]

Furthermore, "European and North American leaders in general, and French politicians in particular, tend to give their African counterparts lessons on democracy, respect for human rights, and governmental transparency—even if such lessons are also exercises in Western hypocrisy. France, for instance, maintains privileged relations with the corrupt regimes of oil-rich Gabon, ruled since 1968 by Omar Bongo, and of Congo-Brazzaville (Republic of the Congo). And the United States has been wooing African dictators such as Teodoro Obiang and Eduardo dos Santos, who rule oil-rich, poverty-ridden Equatorial Guinea and Angola, respectively, both since 1979."[11] Such double standards feeds into the Chinese suspicion that "forces do not like to see a strong China with a rapid growing economy. Because they perceive China as their potential rival, they will use all possible means including the Taiwan, Tibet, and human rights issues to contain China's development.[12] It is naïve not to recognize this.

By focusing significantly on Beijing's human rights stance in Africa, to the detriment of other features of the relationship, there is an implicit delegitimization of China and, by extension, what "the Chinese" are doing in Africa. This does not mean that Beijing can or should be above criticism, only that context is required at all times when discussing such issues as a means to avoid the exoticization, if not demonization, of China and its engagements in Africa. It should be stressed that before critiquing aspects of Chinese involvement in SSA where it impacts upon governance and human rights, analysts need to understand both the Chinese human rights discourse and the nature of most African states. Beijing stresses social unity and development before individual rights as per the Western liberal definition. And African states, many of them little more than kleptocratic quasi-states, are the real problem for governance and human rights standards, not China per se. Obviously, if whilst adhering to the principle of noninterference, Chinese activities actually make things worse for some in Africa, then Beijing needs engaging with. But demonization will never work.

Having said the above, it is important for policy makers to recognize that China is changing and conceptions of human rights are evolving and changing. As with a variety of aspects of Chinese engagement in Africa, Chinese official policy is developing and maturing. One of the reasons why Beijing finds itself in such positions as it does with regimes such as Zimbabwe or

Sudan is that as relative late-comers to Africa, Chinese actors go to places on the continent where other actors and corporations cannot (as in Sudan) or will not go (as in Zimbabwe). As a result, Beijing at times arguably ends up in places impulsively and before the political environment is settled.

Equally, relations with regimes in places such as Sudan or Zimbabwe are not typical of Sino-African engagement, anymore than Washington's relations with Equatorial Guinea are emblematic of American policy toward Africa. What is interesting is the growing realization amongst policy makers in Beijing that attempts to separate politics and business do not generally succeed, particularly in many of the African countries that Chinese actors find themselves. It is this development in thinking and the maturation of Beijing's foreign policies—even if only spurred by pragmatic considerations—that opens up space for policy makers to engage with Beijing. Like all investors in Africa, security and stability is required by Chinese actors, as is economic rationality. In places where human rights abuses so destabilize a country's polity, Chinese interests become threatened. Working with Beijing on such issues is surely the way forward.

Conclusion

A stable international order based on economic and political cooperation is key to facilitating a supportive environment for the goal of developing China. Much of this is "seen as contingent on economic reform and friendly relationships with the West."[13] Given that Beijing is eager to be seen as an unthreatening, responsible power, there is also concern about the way China is perceived abroad and a palpable feeling in both government and business that a bad national image is damaging to broad Chinese interests. Thus anything that might undermine a stable environment or undercut Beijing's attempt to cast itself as a responsible power is likely to be taken ever more seriously in Chinese foreign policy considerations.

However, influencing Chinese activity in Africa is becoming less and less straightforward. Chinese trade with Africa has become, in many ways, "normalized," i.e., diverse and involving multiple actors and individuals, rather than being—as previously—arguably state-directed and under the direct control of central organs of the government. Working out production networks, where things are made and/or finished and how such products reach markets is increasingly complicated.[14] This is perhaps why much talk of Sino-African engagement reduces relations between China and Africa to an almost bilateral level. This is heuristically useful but analytically inadequate.

To return to a point made above, the concept of a "China, Inc.," complete with master plan, either at home or abroad, is intrinsically flawed. The multiplicity of Chinese actors now operating in Africa means that talking of Chinese activities as if they are all representative of what Beijing desires, or, even more implausibly, that such activities are emblematic of a grand Chinese strategy for Africa is inaccurate, as is a vision of China as a monolith. This means that American engagement with China vis-à-vis Africa has to recognize the compacted multiplicity of such ties, as well as the fact that Chinese foreign policy is changing and in a state of flux with regard to the African continent. Close academic and policy-level engagement with Beijing is the only feasible step forward if there are any ambitions to sway Chinese behavior (a difficult task even for the central government in Beijing).

Castigating China as uniquely amoral in Africa or the "new colonizer" will only serve to bolster hardliners in Beijing and cheer the hearts of autocrats in Africa. It is surely not such people that American foreign policy should be aimed at.

Notes

1   T. Fundira, *Africa-China Trading Relationship* (Stellenbosch: Trade Law Centre for Southern Africa, 2008).

2   I. Taylor, *China and Africa: Engagement and Compromise* (London: Routledge, 2006).

3   Hong Eunsuk and Sun Laixiang, "Dynamics of Internationalization and Outward Investment: Chinese Corporations' Strategies," *China Quarterly*, vol. 187, 2006.

4   Wang Hongying, "Linking Up with the International Track," "What's in a Slogan?" 2007.

5   Erica Downs, "The Fact and Fiction of Sino-African Energy Relations," *China Security*, vol. 3, no. 3, 2007.

6   T. Fishman, *China, Inc.: How the Rise of the Next Superpower Challenges America and the World* (New York: Scribner, 2006).

7   J. Kurlantzick, *Charm Offensive: How China's Soft Power Is Transforming the World* (New Haven, CT: Yale University Press, 2007).

8   R. Sutter, *Chinese Foreign Relations: Power and Policy Since the Cold War* (Lanham, MD: Rowman & Littlefield, 2008).

9   R. Ong, "Peaceful Evolution," "Regime Change," and "China's Political Security," *Journal of Contemporary China*, vol. 16, no. 53, 2007.

10   D. Burstein and A. De Keijzer, *Big Dragon: Future of China: What It Means for Business, the Economy and the Global Order* (New York: Touchstone, 1999).

11   Inter Press Service, November 15, 2006.

12   Zheng Yongnian, *Discovering Chinese Nationalism in China: Modernization, Identity, and International Relations* (Cambridge: Cambridge University Press, 1999).

13   Wan Ming, "Democracy and Human Rights in Chinese Foreign Policy" in Deng Yong and Wang Fei-ling, eds., *China Rising: Power and Motivation in Chinese Foreign Policy* (Lanham, MD: Rowman & Littlefield, 2005).

14   S. Breslin, "China in the Asian Economy" in B. Buzan and R. Foot, eds., *Does China Matter? A Reassessment* (London: Routledge, 2004).

Red Star Rising in Africa: Strategic Implications of China's Expansion into Africa

Sean McFate

While the U.S. has been preoccupied in the Middle East, the People's Republic of China has been busy in Africa. Some worry that China's growing influence in Africa poses a strategic threat to U.S. interests there, provoking a proxy Cold War over resources and influence. Yet others, including the recent Bush administration, claim that there is no zero-sum competition with China for resources or influence in Africa, and that China's presence is simply a manifestation of its increasing role in world affairs. In truth, China needs Africa more than Africa needs China, which has driven its rapid expansion onto the continent. What does China need so badly? At least two things: economic goods and political goods.

While the U.S. has been preoccupied in the Middle East, the People's Republic of China has been busy in Africa. It is difficult to find an African capital without a gleaming new sports stadium, ministry building, or other magnificent edifice, courtesy of China's largess. Some worry that China's growing influence in Africa poses a strategic threat to U.S. interests there, provoking a proxy Cold War over resources and influence.[1] Yet others, including the recent Bush administration, scoff at such a notion, claiming that there is no zero-sum competition with China for resources or influence in Africa, and that China's presence is simply a manifestation of its increasing role in world affairs.[2] Both are wrong. Precious little of this issue concerns the competition between an existing superpower and an emerging one. In truth, China needs Africa more than Africa needs China, which has driven its rapid expansion onto the continent. True, this has had third and fourth order consequences, such as altering Africa's political landscape and piquing relations with other donor nations, but this should not be mistaken for Chinese policy. What does China need so badly? At least two things: The first is economic goods: access to natural resources and new markets, and the second is political goods: developing diplomatic ties and demonstrating global leadership.

Pay Dirt

China's commercial interests in Africa are driven by China's own economic successes. China requires Africa's rich natural resources to fuel its economy and needs Africa's hungry markets to sell its commercial goods. As a result, China has looked for new economic and commercial opportunities in Africa, witnessing a substantial increase in Sino-African engagement since 2000. Chinese businesses flourish in Cape Verde and Senegal, its investments are funding industrial expansion in Mauritius, and it is rebuilding the war-torn infrastructure of Angola and Liberia. China is buying ferrous metals from Mauritania, South Africa, and Zimbabwe; copper from Zambia and South Africa; cobalt from South Africa and Congo; feed from Burkina Faso, Ethiopia, Nigeria, Sudan, and Tanzania; chemicals from Niger; and oil from anywhere it can find it.[3]

China is now Africa's third largest trading partner after the United States and France but ahead of Great Britain. Bilateral trade skyrocketed from $10 billion in 2000 to $70 billion in 2007. It is expected to top $100 billion in 2008, two years earlier than predicted, according to a report by China's General Administration of Customs.[4] In 2003, China's direct investment in the continent was approximately $491 million. Three years later, it exceeded $2.5 billion, and continues to grow. Africa ran an overall trade surplus with China between 2004 and 2006, evidencing that China has become an important source of export revenue for the continent.

As remarkable as these numbers might seem, it should be noted that the value of China's trade with Africa represents only a fraction of its trade in the Middle East, Latin America, or Asia. Furthermore, China's foreign direct investment (FDI) in Africa is only 3 percent of China's total FDI, according to a 2007 U.N. report.[5] However, what is remarkable about these numbers is the velocity, not the volume, of China's investment in Africa.

Much of this velocity comes from China's insatiable appetite for oil and other natural resources. China's economy has maintained an incredible average of 9 percent growth per annum over the last two decades, nearly tripling the country's GDP. African oil fuels this growth. Until 1993 China was a net exporter of oil; now it is the world's second-largest energy consumer, after the United States, obtaining 30 percent of its oil from African sources, especially Angola, Republic of the Congo, Equatorial Guinea, and Sudan. It has also sought supplies from Chad, Nigeria, Algeria, and Gabon.[6] Angola has now overtaken Saudi Arabia as China's biggest oil supplier.

China's appetite for oil is expected to grow substantially over the coming decades. The International Energy Agency projects China's net oil imports will jump to 13.1 million barrels per day by 2030 from 3.5 million barrels per day in 2006.[7] Much of this will have to come from Africa. At present, Africa holds only a small fraction of the world's proven oil reserves: 9 percent compared to the Middle East's nearly 62 percent. However, some industry analysts believe it could hold significantly more undiscovered reserves. This, combined with the volatility of the Middle East, has led China to seek increased oil imports from Africa. Although it currently consumes only 9 percent of the continent's oil exports in 2006, compared to the United States' purchase of 33 percent, the growing global demand for oil represents a looming strategic concern for the United States. In fact, Chinese officials have publicly stated that they plan to increase oil and gas imports from Africa by up to 40 percent in the next five to ten years.[8]

China is also seeking new export markets for its consumer goods, having saturated markets in North America, Asia, and elsewhere. Small private Chinese investors have invested millions of dollars into opening enterprises in Africa that operate in textiles, light manufacturing, construction, and agriculture. Africa's demand for China's low-cost goods, combined with the fact that more countries are privatizing their industries and opening their economies to foreign investment, has led to a huge upsurge in bilateral trade over recent years. The diversity of Chinese investments in Africa varies. Some cases are high-profile, such as the Industrial and Commercial Bank of China's October 2007 purchase of a 20-percent stake in South Africa's Standard Bank, or a $9 billion loan and investment package for Congo that will be repaid in cobalt and copper from Congolese mines. Other investments are reportedly meant to circumvent U.S. and European quotas on Chinese exports, especially in the textile sector.[9]

Although the advent of low-cost goods has been generally a welcome occurrence, it is not without criticism. In 2008, for example, there were public protests in Zambia and Namibia over alleged poor working conditions and low pay by Chinese firms. Also, China has been accused of flooding the market with excessively cheap, inferior consumer goods that have denuded some local economies of entrepreneurship. This has sparked public outcries in a number of states, particularly those less endowed with mineral resources. In November 2007, for example, local street vendors in Lesotho attacked Chinese-owned businesses, throwing rocks and chanting anti-Chinese slogans, and accusing Chinese investors of colluding with government to force them out of the city center of the country's capital, Maseru.[10] Although China's ascendency in Africa is rapid, it is hardly guaranteed.

Making Friends and Influencing People

The second driver behind China's rapid insertion into Africa is the need to forge strategic alliances and demonstrate global leadership. Currently there are over 700 Chinese state companies conducting business and over 750,000 Chinese nationals working in every corner of the continent.[11] Such expansion is not purely organic economic growth. China is engaged in multilateral efforts to build strategic partnerships in Africa. As China's policy paper on Africa bluntly asserts: "The Chinese Government encourages and supports Chinese enterprises' investment and business in Africa, and will continue to provide preferential loans and buyer credits to this end."[12] To this end, President Jiang Zemin in 1999 petitioned the Organization of African Unity (now the African Union) to create a Forum on China-Africa Cooperation (FOCAC). A year later the first ministerial conference took place at Beijing with forty-four African states participating. In 1995 two-way trade between Africa and China hovered at less than $1 billion. Now it is near $100 billion.

These commercial ventures are buttressed by a series of diplomatic initiatives, aimed initially at isolating Taiwan but also at broader policy objectives. Currently, China has diplomatic relations with forty-eight of Africa's fifty-two states, and offers limited, but not inconsiderable, development assistance in exchange for diplomatic support contra Taiwan. Similarly, China rewards assistance to governments that grant favorable treatment to Chinese companies. Unlike the Western development assistance, Chinese assistance typically comes without conditions, such as commitments to good governance, human rights, poverty reduction, peace-building, and so forth. In this way, China uses foreign development assistance as a diplomatic spur and trade tool, which needles the international community.[13]

Africa's importance to Chinese diplomacy is further accentuated by the fact that African countries constitute the largest single regional grouping of states of any international organization in which they belong. Furthermore, African countries tend to engage in "bloc-voting" in international organizations, such as the United Nations, which is an effective tactic for influencing multilateral processes, such as rules formulation or complex negotiations. China has relied on African support in the past to overcome staunch international criticism. For example, African votes were crucial to block U.N. Commission on Human Rights resolutions that condemned Chinese human rights abuses.[14] As Premier Wen Jiabao describes it: "China is ready to coordinate its positions with African countries in the process of international economic rules formulation and multilateral trade negotiations."[15] Strategic relationships with Africa will give China, at relatively low cost, the means to secure its position in the World Trade Organization and other multilateral venues.

Buying African regimes through the guise of development assistance rankles the international community, development agencies, and human rights organizations. The U.S., for example, admonishes China not to support "resource-rich countries without regard to the misrule at home or misbehavior abroad of those regimes."[16] Beijing has secured many African alliances, public and private, through direct aid and concessionary loans with "no political strings" attached. As Premier Wen told African delegates at the 2003 China-Africa Cooperation summit at Addis Ababa: "We do offer our assistance with the deepest sincerity and without any political conditions."[17]

Perhaps the best-known beneficiary of China's "don't ask, don't tell" policy regarding foreign assistance is Sudan. China is both the largest foreign direct investor in and the largest customer of Sudan's petroleum production, as China owns thirteen of the fifteen largest companies and purchases more than 50 percent of Sudan's crude oil.[18] However, according to Amnesty International reports, China is also violating the U.N. arms embargo by illegally importing weapons—including fighter jets—to the Khartoum regime at the height of the Darfur conflict. By Amnesty International's estimation, China has exported $24 million worth of arms and ammunition, nearly $57 million worth of parts and military equipment, and $2 million worth of helicopters and airplanes.[19] This is supported by 2007 television footage, obtained by Human Rights First, of a Sudanese military parade celebrating the country's Fifty-second Independence Day showing Chinese late-model battle tanks, infantry fighting vehicles, and Chinese military trainers.[20]

If this is true, then the fact that China, a permanent member of the U.N. Security Council, would willingly abet genocide in contravention of the Security Council's own mandatory arms embargo (UNSCR 1591) puts it squarely at odds with the international community. Global pressure, human rights outrage over Darfur, and even African voices comparing China to a colonial power have put the Chinese government on the defensive. President Hu Jintao has repeatedly asserted that China would "not do anything harmful to the interests of Africa and its people."[21] From a Western perspective, this statement is less than compelling. However, from a non-Western and African orientation, China's strategy in Africa is far more persuasive.

China has successfully positioned itself as a new type of global actor: the non-Western superpower. Like African countries, it was colonized and exploited by European powers. As such, China makes the case that it better understands Africa's development needs and is better able to advocate for Africa at international trade negotiations. Its approach implicitly states that the Western model of development is flawed, which seemingly aspires to transform African countries into Westphalian nation-states, whether this political model is appropriate for Africans or not. Moreover, it took Europe hundreds of bloody years to achieve "development" status, yet donors expect African countries to achieve development in only a few decades or less. This is unrealistic.

China offers an alternate model for development, which could be termed the "slow developer" model. It recognizes the inherent flaws in Western development theory and makes allowances by offering African governments greater patience, flexibility, and self-determination in deploying assistance, even if this means tolerating the "bad behavior" of some tyrannical regimes, such as Sudan or Zimbabwe. Moreover, China lavishes personal attention on African leadership, sending mainland Chinese diplomats and leaders to Africa on a frequent basis, as compared to their U.S. or European counterparts, to develop personal ties. This has conveyed a strong message of commitment to African governments. Lastly, China does not carry the stigma of a former colonial power, as many European countries do. In fact, China shares this grievance with Africa, since it too was exploited by Western colonialization. This aggregate of factors induces simpatico between Chinese and African leaders that the West simply cannot emulate.

China bolsters its slow developer model with a sophisticated public diplomacy campaign to win the "hearts and minds" of elites and non-elites alike. Chinese media enthuses about Africa's future, as opposed to Western media's typical gloom and doom outlook. For example, in 2000 the British newsmagazine the *Economist* featured a cover picture of Africa with the title: "The Hopeless Continent."[22] China actively promotes Chinese language and cultural studies across the continent. It provides scholarships for an estimated 120,000 students to attend Chinese universities. It sponsors a number of professional exchange programs, including the military. China is also expanding its capacity for public diplomacy by enlarging its diplomatic core and upgrading its media outlets, such as Xinhua news service.

Xinhua now often gets picked up in international news wires, such as the AP or Reuters, even though Xinhua is not an independent news service. Lastly, the fact that China has emerged as one of Africa's top trading partners has warmed the hearts of the business community.[23] As Abdoulaye Wade, president of Senegal, puts it: "China's approach to our needs is simply better adapted than the slow and sometimes patronizing post colonial approach of European investors, donor organizations and non-governmental organizations."[24]

Conclusion: Strategic Implications

China's push into Africa is noteworthy for its velocity, not its volume. This rapid expansion is not necessarily an effort by Chinese leaders to flex their geopolitical muscles, but rather an urgent scramble for natural resources and commercial opportunities to feed China's voracious economy. To achieve this, China has utilized foreign assistance, often without meaningful conditions, as a trade tool and diplomatic spur, cementing important strategic alliances. However, its propensity to support despotic regimes, such as Sudan or Zimbabwe, with minimal accountability or regard for the tenets of democracy has irked many in the international community.

However, China's success on the continent cannot solely be attributed to what some consider bribing regimes for economic or political favors via foreign aid. China has generated much interest on the continent because it also offers a potent new model for development, the "slow developer" model, which recognizes the inherent flaws of traditional Western development assistance. Taken in isolation, this model tolerates bad behavior of tyrannical regimes, which is reprehensible. But the other component of this model is a broader, soft-power campaign that seeks to establish China as a new type of actor in world affairs: the non-Western superpower. This holds a great deal of promise for African leaders, long exacerbated by their perception of the West's slow and patronizing approach.

China's ascendancy in Africa has raised many eyebrows in the U.S. and Europe. Some observers fret that intensifying Sino-African relations threatens both the stability of the continent and Western strategic interests there. Others view this in a more matter-of-fact manner, claiming it is a normal outcome of an emerging world power. However, both viewpoints are wrong. Shifts in world affairs do not denote threat, but change; and assessing China's expansion with the traditional metrics used by Western powers in the past misses the point. China's rise in Africa signals what many non-Western thinkers have known for a long time: the twenty-first century will witness the waning of Western powers and the waxing of non-Western powers, complete with their new ideas, norms, and models. China's greatest future competitor in Africa will not be the U.S., France, or Great Britain. It will be India.

Notes

1   Donovan C. Chau, "Political Warfare in Sub-Saharan Africa: U.S. Capabilities and Chinese Operations in Ethiopia, Kenya, Nigeria, and South Africa," *Strategic Studies Institute Monograph* (Carlisle, PA: U.S. Army War College, March 26, 2007).

2   "China in Africa: Implications for U.S. Policy," prepared remarks of Thomas J. Christensen, Deputy Assistant Secretary for East Asian and Pacific Affairs, and James Swan, Deputy Assistant Secretary for African Affairs, Statement Before the Subcommittee on African Affairs of the Senate Foreign Relations Committee, Washington, D.C., June 5, 2008.

3   Christopher Alden, Daniel Large, and Ricardo de Oliveira Hurst, eds., *China Returns to Africa: A Superpower and a Continent Embrace* (London: Hurst, 2008).

4   "Sino-African Trade to Hit $100 bln in 2008, China Predicts," *Xinhuanet News*, September 3, 2008, http://news.xinhuanet.com/english/2008-09/03/content_9764690.htm (accessed October 10, 2008).

5   "Asian Foreign Direct Investment in Africa: United Nations Report Points to a New Era of Cooperation Among Developing Countries," *United Nations Press Release*, UNCTAD/PRESS/PR/2007/005, March 27, 2007 (accessed October 10, 2008). http://www.unctad.org/Templates/webflyer.asp?docid=8172&intItemID=4431&lang=1.

6   David H. Shinn, "Africa, China, the United States, and Oil." *CSIS Online Africa Policy Forum,* May 8, 2007, http://forums.csis.org/africa/?p=34 (accessed October 10, 2008); Tony Capaccio, "Securing African Oil a Major Role for New Command (Update1)," *Bloomberg.com*, May 18, 2007.

7   *World Energy Outlook 2007 Fact Sheet: China*, International Energy Agency (IEA), 2007, **http://www.iea.org/textbase/publications/free_new_Desc. asp?PUBS_ID=1987** (accessed October 10, 2008).

8   Kerry Laird, "China Looks to Increase Oil Imports from Africa to 40%," *Rigzone* March 17, 2008, **http://www.rigzone.com/news/article.asp?a_id=58422** (accessed October 10, 2008).

9   Stephanie Hanson, "China, Africa, and Oil." *Washingtonpost.com*, June 9, 2008.

10 Hany Besada, "China and Africa," *International Herald Tribune*, June 19, 2008.

11 Howard W. French and Lydia Polgreen, "Entrepreneurs from China Flourish in Africa," *New York Times*, August 18, 2007.

12 "China's African Policy," *Xinhuanet News*, http://news.xinhuanet.com/ english/2006-01/12/content_4042521_3.htm (accessed October 10, 2008).

13 See remarks of Thomas J. Christensen.

14 Chris Alden, "Emerging Countries As New ODA Players in LDCs: The Case of China and Africa." *Institut du dévelopement durable et des relations internationales*, N° 01/2007.

15 Speech by Chinese Premier Wen Jiabao at opening ceremony of China-Africa Cooperation Forum, Addis Ababa, Ethiopia, December 15, 2003, **http://www. chinaembassycanada.org/eng/xwdt/t56420.htm** (accessed October 10, 2008).

16 *The National Security Strategy United States of America*, March 2006, 42.

17 Speech by Chinese Premier Wen Jiabao, December 15, 2003.

18 Peter Pham, "China Goes on Safari," *World Defense Review*, August 24, 2006.

19 "Sudan: Arms Continuing to Fuel Serious Human Rights Violations in Darfur," *Amnesty International Report*, AI Index: AFR 54/019/2007, May 2007; "China: Sustaining Conflict and Human Rights Abuses: The Flow of Arms Continues," *Amnesty International Report*, AI Index: ASA 17/030/2006, June 2006.

20 "China's Arms Sales to Sudan Fact Sheet," *Human Rights First*, **http://www. humanrightsfirst.info/pdf/080311-cah-arms-sales-fact-sheet.pdf** (accessed October 10, 2008).

21 Craig Timberg, "Hu Defends China's Role in Africa," *Washington Post Foreign Service*, February 8, 2007, A14.

22 "The Hopeless Continent," *The Economist*, May 13–19, 2000.

23   Joshua Kurlantzick and David Shinn, "China's Africa Strategy: A New Approach to Development and Diplomacy?" A public discussion at the Carnegie Endowment for International Peace, Washington, D.C., December 12, 2006.

24   Abdoulaye Wade, "Time for the West to Practice What It Preaches," *New African*, March 2008, 20.

Sino-African Strategic Engagement: Opportunities, Constraints, and U.S. Policy Implications

Michael P. Argosino

This chapter examines the evolution of Sino-Africa engagement to inform U.S. security policies toward the continent. After reviewing the history of China's foreign policy toward and engagement with Africa states, the chapter concludes with recommendations for U.S. policy.

The George W. Bush Administration's *2008 Annual Report to Congress on the Military Power of the People's Republic of China* concluded that China has "not publicly articulated an explicit, overarching 'grand strategy' that outlines national strategic objectives and the means to achieve them." The report cites Deng Xiaoping's "24 Character Strategy" as providing the framework of an engagement strategy designed "to maximize future options through avoiding unnecessary provocations, shunning excessive international burdens, and building up China's power over a long-term." Similar themes run through China's *National Defense in 2006* white paper. In addition to upholding "world peace," China would "promote common development and seek cooperation."[1] China continues to emphasize peaceful cooperation, harmonious relations, and the creation of additional opportunities for engagement abroad.

Beijing has also addressed critics of China's rising economic and military power, maintaining that China will not become a hegemonic power. President Hu Jintao emphasized 'diversity' and 'equality' in international relations along with traditional People's Republic of China (PRC) foreign policy dictums of 'noninterference' and the 'democratization of international relations' in his 2007 "Harmonious World" philosophy[2]. Adhering to the principles of "peaceful rise," China is taking "full advantage of the good opportunity of world peace to develop itself and at the same time safeguard world peace with its development."[3] Beijing has declared a "purely defensive" military strategy that frames its military activities within the Five Principles of Peaceful Coexistence,"[4] which are:

- firmly upholding the principle of sovereign equality;

- respecting and maintaining the diversity of the world's civilizations;

- promoting common development of the world's economies;

- maintaining peace and security through dialogue and cooperation; and

- giving full scope to the important role of the UN and other multilateral mechanisms.[5]

Critics argue that "harmonious relations" rhetoric and pro-cooperation policies are merely part of a grand strategy to become a global super-power and a regional hegemon. Energy security is one of the areas where observers can measure China's stated engagement philosophy against its behavior. For example, China's five-part energy strategy has the following aims: (1) geographical diversification of its energy supplies; (2) increasing energy efficiency; (3) diversifying its reliance on oil toward nuclear power, hydroelectric power, and natural gas, the supply of which is less susceptible to sea-lane interdiction; (4) reducing reliance on international majors, while conversely increasing the share of energy imports flowing through Chinese owned or controlled intermediaries; and (5) developing the military capability to independently protect Chinese energy supplies.[6]

The evidence is that China is pursuing all these strategies simultaneously, with the strongest emphasis on the first four. In light of the above overview of Beijing's foreign policy and energy strategies, this chapter explores elements of China's Africa strategy and assesses the implications for U.S. security policy toward Africa. Africa is the region with the most potential for Chinese military involvement to protect energy supplies and to prevent disruption and destabilization in the global energy market.

Sino-African Engagement: Complexity, Consistency, Opportunities, and Constraints

As global competition for new oil increases, and as stability of energy extraction and transportation becomes more vital, China's military capabilities will become more important. By late 2008, China's dependency on international sea lanes had enhanced Chinese interest in naval deployments to help combat piracy off the Somali coast. China is also "acquiring direct control over overseas oil and gas reserves"[7] and shifting from long-term off-take agreements toward ownership of foreign mines.[8]

Sino-Africa relations are increasingly important to understanding China's larger foreign policy objectives. Some argue that China is building its navy and expanding its maritime activities to safeguard oil and gas transportation networks and to balance against U.S. power in Africa. In addition, China is criticized for providing arms and military equipment to states in exchange for oil and gas exploration and extraction rights, often to countries to which the U.S. will not provide weapons.[9] Because China does not attach conditions to its trade agreements and foreign aid, there are fears that corrupt African leaders and governments will align with China to avoid pressure from the U.S. and Europe to reform government.

To understand the complexities of Sino-African engagement and its consistency with PRC policy and history it is helpful to pursue a more balanced assessment of the evolving strategic opportunities and constraints that China faces.

Sino-African relations evince a consistent decades-long history. In Mao's socialist internationalism, "world revolution was taking the form of 'surrounding the cities from the countryside' on a global scale"—with "North America and Europe as 'world cities,' and Asia, Africa, and Latin America as the 'world countryside.'"[10] During the revolutionary 1950s China engaged the developing world. The new leaders of Communist China first engaged newly independent African nations at the 1955 Bandung Conference. Then, as now, China's approach was what current parlance terms "soft power," an ideological approach that would later be characterized as "non-interference." Prime Minister Zhou En-lai affirmed the tenets of the Chinese approach in a 1963 trip to Africa: "the exclusion of conditional ties for the delivery of its aid, the non-interference in other countries' affairs, the sovereignty doctrine, and the primacy of the state."[11]

As a soft power exemplar, Sino-Ethiopian relations date to cultural exchanges in 1960 and have seen such endeavors as: "provision of free assistance" from 1996-2001; six-figure donations to the African Union peace fund; donation of demining equipment; the "Ethio-China Friendship Avenue" road project; and a 2004 agreement on "cooperation in water resources development."[12] Comparatively, "Whereas the West began by exploiting Africa, China initiated its relations with Africa with 'people-to-people' medical and technical assistance missions in the sixties and seventies, the most famous of which was the now-fabled construction of the Tanzania-Zambia (Tanzam) Railway."[13]

Today's Sino-African trade, development, and humanitarian agendas follow the same three tenets outlined in the 1960s but are more ambitious in scope. At the autumn 2006 Forum on China-Africa Cooperation, sweeping continental goals were declared:

- $100 billion in trade by 2010, comparative to $40 billion in 2005;

- 3-5 "trade and economic cooperation zones" by 2009;

- $3 billion in "preferential loans in the next three years and the cancellation of more debt";

- establishment of 10 "special agricultural technology demonstration centers"; and

- construction of 30 hospitals and 100 rural schools.[14]

What does this mean for United States security policy toward Africa? The U.S. should realistically view the history of the Chinese soft power approach and the increased level of engagement as a rational capitalization on strategic opportunities by China in accordance with its declared strategic objectives. In addition, China is deepening Sino-African historical ties to maximize China's political and economic ascent as a great power and leader of developing nations. This creates opportunities for Sino-African-U.S. cooperation on the continent, especially if China partners with Western nations on security and stabilization missions. Finally, it is important to consider the nature of the "soft power" competition being waged by China, India, Russia, and other European powers in Africa. The most important strategic consideration is the potential for the non-interference principle to undermine multilateral efforts to influence African leaders to reduce corruption, improve governance, and be more accountable to their citizens.

Non-Western Approaches in Sino-African Engagement

Critics contend that "because China does not insist on commitment to democracy, good governance and respect for human rights as a precondition for development assistance, Western pressure to that effect is diluted.... [Non-conditionality also] has the potential to nullify all the progress made in fighting corruption."[15] Yet Western expectations may overlook two historical realities.

1. There was no dearth of 'Somalias' and 'Liberias' in seventeenth- and eighteenth-century Europe; and

2. The major problem with the implementation of human rights in the Third World is the fact that the concept of human rights owes it empirical validity to the existence and successful functioning of the...states of Western Europe and North America.[16]

African leaders hold "deep suspicion of criticism of their regimes on the grounds of 'western-centric' norms of human rights and liberal democracy...China taps into this suspicion."[17] A so-called "Beijing Consensus" has arisen to challenge the "Washington Consensus" development model and has seized Africa's attention: "Fifty years of aid hasn't worked, and the G8 is failing to deliver. China, on the other hand, has experienced nine per cent growth a year for more than two decades and raised 400 million people out of poverty."[18] From the African perspective,

> What compounds the West's worries is the fact that everyone can now clearly see through its inconsistencies, such as the colonial legacy which contradicts claims of democratization…its notable Cold War protection and support of corrupt dictators and, even worse, its stark failure to come up with any real economic success story in Africa…The West and its multilateral institutions are in crisis.[19]

By "tapping into" African resentments of Western criticisms, China is rationally extending the historical opportunities of South-South Cold War solidarity. However, China faces potential image-identity constraints: its advantageous non-Western image-identity may be dispelled if Chinese presence becomes perceived in Africa—accurately or not—as yet another breed of exploitive political economy. At a 2005 Beijing conference, one observer warned: "Africa sells raw materials to China and China sells manufactured products to Africa. This is a dangerous equation that reproduces Africa's old relationship with colonial powers."[20] At the 2007 World Social Forum in Nairobi, another observer assessed: "First, Europe and America took over our big businesses. Now China is driving our small and medium entrepreneurs to bankruptcy."[21] After the 2006 Zambian elections, "Anti-Chinese resentment boiled over…after it became clear that an opposition candidate who had accused Beijing of 'exploitation' had lost."

Sino-African Energy/Extractive Engagement

In terms of energy policy, the stakes are high in Africa with respect to conditions that may reduce ecological and environmental damage, climate change, and the spread of anti-Western ideologies. Encapsulating the trajectory of Sino-African energy ties: in 2004, China imported 45 percent of its crude from the Middle East versus 29 percent from Africa—but from 1995-2004, the Middle Eastern share remained flat, while African imports surged up from 10 percent. [22]

Within China's energy strategy, "overseas oil and gas equity purchased by Chinese oil companies has only been part of the political, diplomatic, and economic game."[23] Vis-à-vis strategic minerals, "Chinese companies will not shy away from countries which might be considered 'too risky' politically, or from where traditional transnational mining companies will not operate due to a poor respect for human rights or lack of governance."[24] Chinese national oil companies (NOCs) and extractive enterprises are parastatal, under the direction of governmental "energy policy, industrial policy, social policy, and foreign policy." However, among NOCs themselves, motivations "relate principally to corporate survival and corporate ambition for expansion."[25]

Some argue that African leaders pursue energy deals with Chinese corporations because they provide funding and assistance to create a more robust, end-to-end energy industry with infrastructure required to support exploration and extraction.[26] In mining opportunities, a representative 2007 Sino-Congolese deal features "$6.5 billion-worth of improvements to the country's infrastructure and $2 billion-worth of construction and refurbishment of mines." Congolese leaders have expressed that this deal "might encourage Western governments to drop their 'patronizing attitude, that we know what's best for you.'"[27] Furthermore, "China went to the countries where the U.S. either had withdrawn, such as Sudan, or had a very weak presence, because it did not want to provoke the U.S."[28]

But Chinese parastatals often find that deals backed by or "sweetened" by the Chinese government can be an obstacle, adding complications. CNOOC's attempted takeover of Unocal in 2005 was blocked based on arguments that CNOOC "was an agent of the government."[29] Similarly, "While Beijing's deep pockets have, for example, helped Sinopec acquire some assets in Angola,... [other] oil-for-infrastructure deals have not won China's NOCs attractive exploration and production assets elsewhere in Africa."[30]

Sino-African Regime and Security/Military Relations

Sino-African security relations and military commerce have a consistent history. After the Soviet collapse, Beijing balanced against American power by increasing ties with certain states, including some pariah or rogue nations. China also reacted against the pro-democracy 'colored revolutions' that spread throughout Europe and the Caucasus, defending other authoritarian governments when they were pressured by the West. In Africa, China threatened to veto UN sanctions on Sudan in 2004 and, in 2005, supported Zimbabwe's President Mugabe with a weeklong state visit to China "at the height of international outrage over the Zimbabwean government's Operation Drive Out Trash."[31]

China's philosophy toward UN intervention, however, has evolved. Whereas "China had long insisted that the massacres in Darfur were an internal matter," in 2006 it made "crucial interventions to secure the Sudanese government's agreement" to the proposed UN-AU peacekeeping force. Energy security risks and constraints may have driven the peacekeeping policy shift on Sudan: "the fighting in Darfur had escalated, spreading across the border into Chad, in whose nascent oil sector Beijing had just promised to invest."[32] China has also supported enhancing "the UN's image as a universal organization, viewing with concern the perception that UN missions have been dominated by some Western powers."[33]

Still, China has not shifted on Zimbabwe and continues its longstanding solidarity with Mugabe, who "uses the Look East Policy to reassert Zimbabwe's role on the international stage to gain greater prestige and legitimacy."[34] In 2008 China vetoed a U.S.-led UN Security Council resolution to sanction the Mugabe regime, in response to the violent protracted electoral crisis. China maintains that the crisis "has not exceeded the context of domestic affairs" and that "sanctions would 'interfere with the negotiation process.'"[35]

Intra-African politics have come to the fore in the Zimbabwe crisis as lead negotiator, South African President Mbeki, "is accused of showing too much loyalty to Mugabe out of respect for the Zimbabwean leader's past as an anti-colonial hero."[36] As Sino-African engagement deepens, China will become inexorably vested in the outcomes of such crises. These will present

China with diplomatic opportunities and constraints alike, which highlight the limitations of noninterference and nonconditionality. Chinese diplomacy will face a revealing test in Darfur as the International Criminal Court is considering arrest warrants for Sudanese President Bashir on genocide charges.

Conclusion

There are number of ways forward for U.S. policy when it comes to China's non-interference approach. Some African states may seek to integrate the benefits of both the Western-styled market economy, which aims to viable markets, institutions, and development activities, with the Beijing approach to trade and economic growth. On the other hand, as China is perceived as pursuing its own interests at the expense of African development, some African leaders may impugn both the U.S. and China as exploitive capitalists, calling for an alternate South-South consensus on development. China, moreover, is likely to continue to pursue opportunities for its own South-South engagement and leadership, seeking to evade any "neocolonialist" images or attachment to the American and European approaches based on conditionality.

Strategically, the U.S. should neither overestimate nor discount Sino-African energy/extractive opportunities as an impetus for PRC military power projection: Africa is of rising, but not (yet) overriding, importance. Commercially, Chinese parastatals must ultimately participate in open markets for African resources—bound by the same competitive constraints as U.S. and other firms. These could induce China to further adopt Western-styled business practices, including privatization, labor standards, transparency, and environmental and social responsibility.

U.S. and international pressures and constraints may push China into further solidarity with pariah regimes. Yet China's demonstrated policy shifts and evolving attitudes hold opportunities for measured Sino-U.S. cooperation in transformational diplomacy. U.S. strategy should incentivize more active and positive Chinese diplomacy by framing the improvement of African governance as a win-win outcome. The U.S. should emphasize that the opportunities springing from good African governance far outshine the long-run risks and constraints from poor governance.

Notes

1   Government White Paper: China's National Defense in 2006. (Translation), pp. 195-201.

2   2008 Annual Report to Congress on the Military Power of the People's Republic of China, p. 8.

3   Abanti Bhattacharya, "Revisiting China's "Peaceful Rise": Implications for India," *East Asia: An International Quarterly*, Winter 2005, Vol. 22, no. 4, p. 61-65.

4   Government White Paper: China's National Defense in 2006. (Translation), pp. 195-201.

5   Wen Jiabao. Speech: "Carrying Forward the Five Principles of Peaceful Coexistence in the Promotion of Peace and Development." June 28, 2004, http://www.fmprc.gov.cn/eng/topics/seminaronfiveprinciples/t140777.htm

6   Kent Calder, "Coping With Energy Insecurity: China's Response In Global Perspective." *East Asia: An International Quarterly*, Fall 2006, Vol. 23, Issue 3,. p. 54.

7   Heinrich Kreft, "China's Quest For Energy." *Policy Review*, Sep/Oct 2006, p. 66.

8   Walter Kansteiner, Presentation at The George Washington University, April 7, 2008.

9   Yi-Chong Xu, "China's Energy Security." *Australian Journal Of International Affairs*, Jun 2006, Vol. 60, no. 2, p.267.

10 Zhimin Chen, "Nationalism, Internationalism and Chinese Foreign Policy." *Journal of Contemporary China*, Feb 2005, Vol. 14, No. 42, pp 41-44.

11 "China in Africa: Why the West is worried." *New African*, March 2008.

12 Donovan Chau, "Political Warfare in Sub-Saharan Africa: US Capabilities and Chinese Operations in Ethiopia, Kenya, Nigeria, and South Africa." Strategic Studies Institute, March 2007, pp. 21-35.

13 Walden Bello, "China Eyes Africa." *Multinational Monitor*, Jan/Feb 2007, Vol. 28, no. 1, p.24.

14 Firoze Manji and Stephen Marks, eds. *African Perspectives on China in Africa*. Fahamu, 2007, p. 2.

15 Ibid., pp. 15-16, 26.

16 Chester Crocker, Fen Hampson, and Pamela Aall, eds. *Managing Global Chaos.* USIP, 1996., pp. 40-43.

17 Ian Taylor, "China's Oil Diplomacy in Africa." *International Affairs,* 2006, Vol. 82, no. 5, p. 939

18 Charlie Furniss, "The Hungry Dragon And The Dark Continent." *Geographical,* December 2006, p. 61.

19 "China in Africa: Why the West is worried." *New African,* March 2008

20 Firoze Manji and Stephen Marks, eds. *African Perspectives on China in Africa.* Fahamu, 2007, p. 5.

21 Walden Bello, "China Eyes Africa." *Multinational Monitor,* Jan/Feb 2007, Vol. 28, no. 1, p.23.

22 Ma Xin and Philip Andrews-Speed. "The Overseas Activities Of China's National Oil Companies: Rationale And Outlook." *Minerals & Energy*, Mar 2006, Vol. 21, no. 1, p. 24.

23 Yi-Chong Xu, "China's Energy Security." *Australian Journal Of International Affairs*, Jun 2006, Vol. 60, no. 2, pp. 276-77.

24 Damian Brett and Magnus Ericsson. "Chinese Expansion to Create New Global Mining Companies." October 2006, **http://www.rmg.se/RMG2005/pages/ attachments/COMMODITIES_NOW_2006_Oct,_Chinese_Expansion_to_ Create_New_Global_Mining_Companies.pdf**, p. 28.

25 Ma Xin and Philip Andrews-Speed. "The Overseas Activities Of China's National Oil Companies: Rationale And Outlook." *Minerals & Energy*, Mar 2006, Vol. 21, no. 1, pp. 18-20.

26 Linda Jakobson and Zha Daojiong. "China And The Worldwide Search For Oil Security." *Asia-Pacific Review*, Nov 2006, Vol. 13, no. 2, p. 67.

27 "A Ravenous Dragon: A Special Report on China's Quest for Resources." *Economist,* March 15, 2008, pp.13-14.

28 Yi-Chong Xu, "China's Energy Security." *Australian Journal Of International Affairs*, Jun 2006, Vol. 60, no. 2, p. 278.

29 Ma Xin and Philip Andrews-Speed. "The Overseas Activities Of China's National Oil Companies: Rationale And Outlook." *Minerals & Energy*, Mar 2006, Vol. 21, no. 1, p. 21.

30 Erica Downs, "The Fact and Fiction of Sino-African Energy Relations." *China Security,* Summer 2007, Vol. 3, no. 3.

31   Stephanie Kleine-Ahlbrandt and Andrew Small. "China's New Dictatorship Diplomacy." *Foreign Affairs*, Jan/Feb 2008 (electronic version, no pagination).

32   Ibid.

33   Zhongying Pang, "China's changing attitude to UN peacekeeping." *International Peacekeeping*, Spring 2005, Vol. 12, no. 1, pp. 89-94.

34   Jeremy Youde, "Why Look East? Zimbabwean Foreign Policy and China." *Africa Today*, Spring 2007, Vol. 53, no. 3, p. 4.

35   "Russia, China Veto Sanctions on Zimbabwe." July 11, 2008, http://www.cbsnews.com/stories/2008/07/11/world/main4255091.shtml

36   "Diplomatic Row Over Zimbabwe Veto." July 12, 2008, http://www.cbsnews.com/stories/2008/07/12/world/main4255604_page2.shtml

China's Military Ties to Africa: Simultaneously Fostering Instability and Stability

Michael Radosh

China's interests in Africa have changed dramatically since the late 1970s. No longer concerned with exporting revolution, China's goals in Africa are to secure access to energy and mineral resources, garner international political support, find trade and investment opportunities, and diplomatically isolate Taiwan. China's military involvement in Africa is at the same time destabilizing and stabilizing. In order to encourage China to become a purely stabilizing force in Africa, the United States should encourage further Chinese peacekeeping efforts, and needs to convince Beijing that creating instability in Africa runs counter to China's own national interests.

From the 1950s to the mid-1970s, China aided African liberation movements in an effort to export Mao Tse-tung's brand of international communism. In addition to providing ideological support and training to these groups, Chinese assistance between 1955 and 1977 also included modest arms sales worth $142 million.[1] Although China has since abandoned its ideological foreign policy, its military ties to Africa have grown exponentially over the past thirty years. Between 1998 and 2005 alone, Chinese arms sales to Africa were valued at $1.1 billion.[2]

China's extensive military involvement in Africa is not limited to arms sales. As of 2007, Beijing had at least fourteen military attaché offices in Africa, while eighteen African nations have defense attaché offices in Beijing.

Between 2001 and 2006, Chinese military leaders traveled to Africa approximately thirty times, visiting nearly every African country that has diplomatic relations with China. Other military-to-military activities include Chinese naval ship visits to Africa, Chinese technical support and financial assistance to African militaries, and professional education exchanges. China also provides troops to several U.N. peacekeeping missions operating in Africa.[3]

China's military engagement with Africa is truly a continent-wide phenomenon. China holds bilateral security consultation meetings with South Africa;[4] signed a military cooperation agreement with Sierra Leone in 2006; and docked a naval vessel in Alexandria, Egypt, as part of China's first around the world naval voyage in 2002.[5] In every sub-region of Africa, China has a growing military presence.

This chapter analyzes the impact of China's military relationships in Africa. First, it examines two cases where Sino-African military ties are particularly strong: Sudan and Zimbabwe. Second, it examines China's role in supporting U.N. peacekeeping operations in Africa. Finally, it discusses implications for U.S. policy. The chapter concludes that Chinese military cooperation, assistance, and arms sales to Africa have contributed to instability and, in some cases, human rights abuses. However, at the same time, China's contributions to U.N. peacekeeping forces foster stability.

Sudan

During the 1990s, China began to take the place of Western oil companies that were pulling out of Sudan amid growing instability and international criticism over Sudan's human rights abuses.[6] In 1996 China's state-owned China National Petroleum Corporation (CNPC) bought into Sudan's Greater Nile Petroleum Operating Company, purchasing a 40 percent stake in the Heglig and Unity oil fields. In the years that followed, CNPC built pipelines connecting these oil fields to the Red Sea,[7] and co-built Sudan's largest refinery with Sudan's Energy Ministry. CNPC and other Chinese state-owned companies, such as the Sinopec Corporation, have also funded various other oil infrastructure projects.[8]

What has essentially developed since the mid-1990s is a relationship where Sudan trades oil for weapons with China. By the beginning of 2007, China was importing roughly two-thirds of Sudan's oil,[9] providing Sudan with most of its estimated annual oil revenue of $500 million. Sudan, in turn, spends as much as 80 percent of its total oil revenue on weapons,[10] many of which are purchased from China. And many of these Chinese weapons were used in Sudan's north-south civil war (which ended in 2005) and remain in use in the current Darfur conflict, where over 200,000 have died and roughly 2.5 million have been displaced.[11]

Sudan has purchased a wide array of weapons from China in the past decade, including tanks, small arms, towed artillery, antitank and antipersonnel mines, ammunition, helicopters, and fighter aircraft.[12] According to a report issued by Human Rights First, China is Sudan's largest small arms supplier. Between 2004 and 2006, Chinese small arms sales to Sudan totaled over $50 million, and equaled 90 percent of the total small arms sales to Sudan.[13] China's aircraft sales to Sudan are also notable. The Sudanese air force purchased Shenyang fighter planes valued at roughly $100 million. Among these aircraft are twelve supersonic F-7 jets.[14] China also assisted Sudan in constructing three weapons factories, including one that assembles T-55 tanks.[15]

Chinese weapons have been directly linked to the Darfur conflict, as a U.N. panel found after analyzing vehicles and shell casings in Darfur.[16] Likewise, in June 2006 Amnesty International issued a report detailing how Sudan has used Chinese weapons to perpetuate conflict in both the civil war and Darfur. In one of several examples, the report cites how a Chinese-made helicopter gunship, owned by the Sudanese government, killed seventeen civilians in 2002.[17]

Zimbabwe

China's close ties to Zimbabwe date back to 1970, when Beijing sided with Robert Mugabe after the Soviet Union declared its support for Mugabe's rival.[18] Chinese President Hu Jintao has referred to Mugabe as a "much respected old friend of the Chinese people,"[19] while Mugabe has deemed China to be Zimbabwe's "number one friend."[20]

China is interested in Zimbabwe's vast supply of mineral and precious metal deposits, including gold, silver, ferrochrome, copper, and the world's second-largest deposits of platinum.[21] China imports significant quantities of these resources and is one of Zimbabwe's top trading partners.[22]

In 1989, China sold its first J-7 fighters and radar to Zimbabwe. Since then, Beijing's arms sales to Harare have increased dramatically. One of the more notable arms transactions is the 2004 sale of twelve FC-1 fighter jets, armored personnel carriers and other military vehicles, and assault rifles, together valued at approximately $240 million.[23] A year later, Zimbabwe's air force purchased six K-8 jets to train fighter pilots and for use in "low intensity" military operations.[24] And, in May 2006, China donated construction equipment and machines to Zimbabwe's military worth $1.5 million.[25] Most recently, in April 2008, China tried to deliver to Zimbabwe seventy-seven tons of rifles, small arms, mortar shells, and rocket-propelled grenades valued at $1.25 million. The ship was turned away after dock workers from neighboring South Africa refused to unload the cargo.[26]

In addition to weapons sales, China has assisted Mugabe's repressive policies in other ways. Beijing has provided Harare with jamming devices used to block anti-Mugabe broadcasts originating from both inside and outside Zimbabwe. In addition, China has given Zimbabwe's security forces electronic surveillance devices used to monitor Mugabe's political opponents.[27]

Mugabe's crackdowns have caused a massive refugee problem that undermines the stability of Zimbabwe and its neighbors. By March 2007, over three million Zimbabweans, a quarter of Zimbabwe's population, had fled to neighboring South Africa, Botswana, Zambia, and Mozambique. Zimbabwe's neighbors have had a hard time coping with the large influx of refugees.[28] For example, the large number of Zimbabwean refugees in South Africa has created resentment, as some South Africans accuse the refugees of taking away local jobs and committing violent crime. As of January 2008, approximately 4,000 Zimbabweans were crossing into South Africa daily.[29] Thus China, which has provided Mugabe with much of the coercive tools that enables him to commit human rights abuses, has only helped to create instability in Zimbabwe's neighborhood.

Peacekeeping

The cases of Sudan and Zimbabwe indicate that Beijing's growing military involvement in Africa fosters instability. However, in recent years, China has dramatically increased its personnel contributions to U.N. peacekeeping missions in Africa. This reflects China's desire to be seen as a responsible stakeholder in the international community. Thus, peacekeeping efforts reveal there is a portion of China's military involvement in Africa that actually helps maintain stability.

China's foray into peacekeeping operations (PKO) is a recent phenomenon, as Beijing typically has apprehensions about becoming involved in the internal affairs of other countries. However, China is now taking active parts in several PKO, although Beijing has vowed only to do so with the explicit permission of a host country.[30] Beijing committed its first PKO observers and police abroad in 2000, and deployed its first PKO soldiers abroad in 2003. By 2007, China had over 1,500 PKO troops deployed overseas,[31] contributing a substantial number of soldiers to two of the six African PKO missions: the U.N. Mission in the Sudan (UNMIS) and the U.N. Mission in Liberia (UNMIL).

By March 2007 China provided 446 out of 8,766 PKO soldiers to UNMIS.[32] On January 1, 2008, UNMIS officially took over PKO from exhausted African Union forces. Once this switch took place, 140 additional Chinese PKO troops and engineers were some of the first reinforcements to arrive in Sudan. With them came new Chinese bulldozers, armed personnel carriers, and additional equipment to be used in PKO. In the coming months, 175 additional troops are expected.

China's emergence as a leader in UNMIS is not by coincidence. UNMIS, which aims to eventually have 26,000 PKO troops in Sudan, has had problems increasing the PKO troop presence in Darfur in part because of Khartoum's general unwillingness to allow non-African PKO troops in Sudan. The main exception to this rule is China. Beijing's friendly relations with Sudan have facilitated the relative ease with which Chinese PKO forces have entered Darfur.[33] Although UNMIS is still short on critical supplies and personnel, UNMIS forces are creating some sense of stability, patrolling refugee camps and protecting displaced people.[34]

As of March 2008, China also contributed 558 of the 13,841 UNMIL peacekeepers. The Chinese peacekeepers contribute to Liberia's stability by providing logistical support for other UNMIL deployments, constructing and maintaining roads and supply routes, transporting fuel and water, and repairing airfields, helipads, and bridges. In March 2008, 137 Chinese PKO soldiers in Liberia were awarded U.N. medals for their work by the U.N.'s Special Representative of the Secretary-General.[35]

Although much of China's peacekeeping efforts have focused on Sudan and Liberia, Beijing has also provided peacekeeping personnel support in a number of other African countries as well. By March 2007 this included:

- 218 soldiers and twelve military observers to the U.N. Mission in the Democratic Republic of the Congo,

- seven military observers to the U.N. Mission in Cote d'Ivoire,

- seven military observers to the U.N. Mission in Ethiopia and Eritrea, and

- thirteen military observers to the U.N. Mission for the Referendum in Western Sahara.[36]

Understanding China's Military Ties to Africa

The preceding discussion reveals two seemingly contradictory facets of China's military involvement in Africa. On one hand, China's military ties to Sudan and Zimbabwe have helped sustain or exacerbate conflict and instability. In contrast, China's growing peacekeeping efforts have helped to increase stability in some of Africa's most troubled countries. The contradictions of Beijing's security policies in Africa become particularly apparent in the case of Sudan. In Darfur, Chinese peacekeepers are protecting civilians who are threatened by fighting between rebel groups on one side, and Sudanese forces and Janjaweed militia armed with Chinese weapons on the other!

It is certainly in the U.S. national interest to promote the stabilizing elements of China's Africa policies. However, before any potential U.S. polices can be examined, it is important to understand why China has pursued the policies it has. China's military-to-military relationships with Sudan and Zimbabwe must be seen in the context of Beijing's larger goals in Africa: gaining access to oil and other natural resources, securing diplomatic allies, isolating Taiwan, and pursuing trade and investment opportunities.[37] China's military engagement with Sudan, Zimbabwe, and other African nations is motivated by Beijing's desire to pursue these national goals. Furthermore, China's general policy of noninterference in the internal affairs of other countries has enabled it to look past the destabilizing consequences of its military relationships.

However, one of Beijing's other broad goals is to ultimately gain the international respect, prestige, and dignity befitting of a rising power. China wants to assure the world of its "peaceful rise" and that there is no emerging China threat. Beijing's growing role in peacekeeping seems to be motivated by its desire to be seen abroad as a responsible leader in the international community of nations.

Implications for U.S. Policy

The United States can and should encourage China's military engagements in Africa, shaping them into more constructive efforts. First, America should engage China and publicly commend it for its growing contributions to U.N. peacekeeping operations in Africa. If China sees that its contributions to peacekeeping are noticed and well received by the United States, it stands to reason that China will continue to support peacekeeping efforts. After all, China and the United States are major trading partners, and it is very much in China's interest to be on good terms with America.

Perhaps more difficult is convincing China to curtail its destabilizing military relationships in Africa. Publicly condemning China for accommodating some of the world's worst human rights violators is not the way to do this. Excessive public criticism of Beijing may simply lead to an increased nationalistic backlash in China. Indeed, this is exactly what has happened in response to sustained Western criticism over China's actions in Tibet.

Instead, the United States must convince China that its destabilizing military relationships in Africa actually harm Beijing's fundamental economic interests and energy security in the long run. Indeed, close Chinese military ties to some African governments have already brought rebel group attacks on Chinese investments in Africa, and accusations that China is simply a new imperialist power that must be defeated. For instance, on April 24, 2007, approximately two hundred gunmen from the rebel group Ogaden National Liberation Front killed nine Chinese workers and kidnapped seven others during an attack on a Chinese energy exploration facility in Ethiopia.[38]And in Sudan, the rebel group Justice and Equality Movement (JEM) has increasingly threatened the growing Chinese presence in the country. JEM perceives that Beijing's arms sales to Khartoum are fueling the Sudanese government crackdown, and the rebel group thus sees Chinese facilities as being legitimate targets.[39] In short, the United States needs to make China realize that its military assistance and arms sales draw Beijing into internal conflicts that in turn threaten Chinese commercial interests.

Thus, China has a choice to make. If it continues to fuel conflict in Africa through irresponsible weapons sales and military cooperation with aggressive regimes, it will invite both criticism from the West and increasing security risks to Chinese infrastructure in Africa. In contrast, if China steps up its peacekeeping efforts it will win accolades from the West and will promote a stable environment where Sino-African commercial ties can thrive. The United States should make it clear to Beijing that behaving responsibly in its military relationships with Africa is the right road to take.

Notes

1   Esther Pan, "China, Africa, and Oil," *Council on Foreign Relations*, January 26, 2007, http://www.cfr.org/publication/9557 (accessed April 20, 2008).

2   Richard F. Grimmett, "Conventional Arms Transfers to Developing Nations, 1998–2005," *CRS Report for Congress*, October 23, 2006, http://www.fas.org/sgp/crs/weapons/RL33696.pdf (accessed April 20, 2008).

3   Susan Puska, "Military Backs China's Africa Adventure," *Asia Times* Online, June 8, 2007, http://www.atimes.com/atimes/china/ifo8ado2.html (accessed April 20, 2008).

4   Puska.

5   David Shinn, "Africa and China's Global Activism," National Defense University Pacific Symposium, Fort Lesley J. McNair, June 20, 2006.

6   Ali Askouri, "China's Investment in Sudan: Displacing Villages and Destroying Communities," *African Perspectives on China in Africa* (Oxford: Fahamu, 2007), 71–86.

7   Robert Sutter, *Chinese Foreign Relations* (Lanham: Rowman & Littlefield, Inc., 2008), 376.

8   Peter S. Goodman, "China Invests Heavily in Sudan's Oil Industry," *The Washington Post*, December 23, 2004, http://www.washingtonpost.com/wp-dyn/articles/A21143-2004Dec22.html (accessed April 20, 2008).

9   Pan.

10 Peter Brookes, "Into Africa: China's Grab for Influence and Oil," *The Heritage Foundation*, March 26, 2007.

11 Lydia Polgreen, "China, in New Role, Presses Sudan on Darfur," *International Herald Tribune*, February 23, 2008, http://www.iht.com/bin/printfriendly.php?id=10322602 (accessed April 21, 2008).

12 Sutter.

13 "China Denies Report That It Increased Small Arms Sales to Sudan as Darfur Violence Escalated," *International Herald Tribune*, March 14, 2008, http://www.iht.com/bin/printfriendly.php?id=11105979 (accessed April 20, 2008).

14 Ian Taylor, "China's Oil Diplomacy in Africa," *International Affairs*, 82, 2006, 937–959.

15 Joshua Eisenman, Eric Heginbotham, and Derek Mitchell, eds., *China and the Developing World* (Armonk, NY: M.E. Sharpe, Inc., 2007), 33.

16 Polgreen.

17 "People's Republic of China: Sustaining Conflict and Human Rights Abuses— The Flow of Arms Accelerates," *Amnesty International* (New York: Amnesty International, 2006).

18 Joshua Eisenman, "Zimbabwe: China's African Ally," *China Brief* 5.15 (The Jamestown Foundation, 2005), 9–11.

19 Sutter.

20 Joshua Eisenman and Joshua Kurlantzick, "China's Africa Strategy," *Current History*, May 2006, 219–224.

21 Joshua Eisenman, "Zimbabwe: China's African Ally."

22 David Shinn, "Africa and China's Global Activism."

23 Ibid.

24 Joshua Eisenman, "Zimbabwe: China's African Ally."

25 "China, Zimbabwe to Strengthen Military Ties," *People's Daily* Online, August 1, 2006, http://english.peopledaily.com.cn/200608/01/eng20060801_288665.html (accessed April 20, 2008).

26 Celia W. Dugger and David Barboza, "Arms for Zimbabwe May Turn Back," *New York Times*, April 23, 2008, http://www.nytimes.com/2008/04/23/world/africa/23zimbabwe.html (accessed April 23, 2008); Celia W. Dugger, David Barboza, and Alan Cowell, "Zimbabwe-Bound Ship Heads Back to China," *New York Times*, April 25, 2008, http://www.nytimes.com/2008/04/25/world/Africa/25zimbabwe.html (accessed April 25, 2008); "Zimbabwe Weapons Ship Headed for Angola," CNN.com (accessed April 19, 2008), http://www.cnn.com/2008/WORLD/africa/04/19/safrica.china (accessed April 19, 2008).

27 Peter Brookes, "Into Africa: China's Grab for Influence and Oil."

28 Brett D. Schaefer, "The Crisis in Zimbabwe: How the U.S. Should Respond," *The Heritage Foundation*, March 23, 2007, http://www.heritage.org/Research/africa/wm1407.cfm#_ftn40 (accessed April 21, 2008).

29 "S. Africa Police Raid Zimbabwean Refugee Sanctuary," *Reuters*, January 31, http://www.reuters.com/articlePrint?articleId=USL31429959 (accessed April 25, 2008).

30 Ian Taylor, "The Future of China's Overseas Peacekeeping Operations," *China Brief* 8.6 (The Jamestown Foundation, 2008), 7–8.

31 "China: Peacekeeping and the Responsible Stakeholder," *Stratfor Strategic Forecasting, Inc.*, August 28, 2007, http://www.stratfor.com/china_peacekeeping_and_responsible_stakeholder (accessed April 29, 2008).

32 Puska.

33 Alfred de Montesquiou, "Sudan Welcomes Chinese Peacekeepers," Associated Press Writer, February 1, 2008 www.boston.com/news/world/africa/articles/2008/02/01/sudan_welcomes_chinese_peacekeepers/ (accessed April 29, 2008).

34   Lydia Polgreen, "Darfur Peacekeeping Force at Risk of Failing, Already," *International Herald Tribune*, March 23, 2008, http://www.iht.com/bin/printfriendly.php?id=11347925 (accessed April 29, 2008).

35   "UN Envoy Describes UNMIL Chinese Peacekeeping Role Crucial in Liberia's Recovery," UNMIL, March 28, 2008, http://unmil.org/article.asp?id=2706 (accessed April 29, 2008).

36   Puska.

37   Joshua Eisenman, Eric Heginbotham, and Derek Mitchell, eds., *China and the Developing World* (Armonk, NY: M.E. Sharpe, Inc., 2007), 33.

38   "China, Ethiopia: Facing the Price of Engaging Africa," *Stratfor Strategic Forecasting, Inc.*, April 24, 2007 http://www.stratfor.com/china_ethiopia_facing_price_engaging_africa (accessed April 30. 2008).

39   "Sudan: What Can Militants Do, and What Can China Tolerate?" *Stratfor Strategic Forecasting, Inc.*, December 13, 2007, www.stratfor.com/analysis/sudan_what_can_militants_do_and_what_can_china_tolerate (accessed April 30, 2008).

The Ambivalent Nexus:
The Rise of China, National Oil Companies, and Energy Security in Africa

Peng Claire Bai

Increasing demand for oil and natural gas has focused attention on Africa's untapped energy resources. This chapter examines energy exploration activities of three major Chinese oil companies in Angola, Sudan, and Nigeria as well as Beijing's long-standing political interests in Africa. The chapter also explores implications for U.S. energy security and concludes with policy recommendations for strengthening Sino-American cooperation in both government and corporate domains.

China's engagement in Africa is rooted in more than fifty years of friendly, respectful, and supportive relations. Since the founding of the PRC, China has sought to align with nations with shared interests in order to culti-vate support for issues important to its foreign policy objectives. China's multifaceted African development agenda includes constructing a new in-ternational economic and political order for the third world, facilitating South-South economic cooperation, and promoting the interests of de-veloping countries. China also sees Africa as being ripe for an economic takeoff when conflicts and instability that began in the 1990s finally end.[1] China became Africa's third most important trading partner in 2004 and seeks to increase its economic influence on the continent.[2]

Since the 1990s China's burgeoning economy and double-digit growth rate have driven the country to embark on a sustained quest for energy resources. China's increased engagement in Africa has been dubbed the dragon's turn toward "oil diplomacy."

American reactions to China's engagement with African states have become polarized. One camp acknowledges that China's political and economic interests in Africa will create tensions with the U.S. but consider any U.S.-China competition over resources as an inevitable outcome of China's growing economic power and integration into global affairs. Others argue that China's behavior and intentions are a cause for alarm, viewing China's presence in Africa as inherently threatening to U.S. interests and part of a wider plan to counter American power. For the alarmists, China is essentially reducing the influence of the "Washington consensus" of economic liberalism and democracy, and instead promoting a "Beijing consensus" of state-led development and authoritarian rule in African states.[3]

A fundamental problem with the alarmists, however, is their tendency to characterize Washington-Beijing competition over African resources and markets as wholly political or dominated by state actors. To explore the more complex nature of Chinese engagement in Africa, this paper examines the energy exploration activities of three major Chinese oil companies: China National Petroleum Corporation (CNPC), China Petroleum & Chemical Corporation (Sinopec), and China National Offshore Oil Corporation (CNOOC). While some see China's national oil companies (NOCs) as the tool with which the Chinese government realizes its strategic objectives in Africa, these companies in fact make independent economic decisions that are not necessarily coordinated, or even approved, in Beijing.

Introduction to Chinese Interests in Africa

In the 1960s China actively sought to engage the sub-Saharan states as diplomatic partners and Chinese Foreign Minister Zhou Enlai made a celebrated "Safari to Africa." China saw Africa as a significant source of support in the United Nations and other international organizations. Indeed, African votes were crucial to Beijing securing representation at the U.N.

China's Africa policy subsequently shifted to include gaining access to resources essential for sustaining China's economic growth and to the long-term goal of opening new markets for Chinese goods. Indeed, sub-Saharan

Africa's 800 million people represent a sizable potential market for Chinese products. Sino-African trade grew by 700 percent during the 1990s, reaching $55 billion in 2006, and is expected to hit $100 billion by 2010.

In the 1990s China became a critical provider of African assistance. China's various aid programs have brought about economic growth and promoted development on the continent. The Forum on China-Africa Cooperation (FOCAC), launched in 2000, is a new vehicle through which China manages its relationship with Africa. China promised to facilitate the entry of African products into the Chinese market, increase investment and assistance, reduce African debt, continue supporting African defense building and peacekeeping operations, and encourage Chinese enterprises to build infrastructure in Africa.

China's official assistance and aid programs include the following activities:

- In 2004, China provided the Angolan government a $3 billion package of loans and credit line to rebuild infrastructure ruined by its civil war.[4]

- By 2006, China's Exim Bank ran a total of 259 projects in thirty-six African countries, amounting to $20 billion, 79 percent of which are committed to infrastructure development in countries like Sudan and Nigeria.[5]

- China currently deploys over 1,500 security assistance and international peacekeeping personnel in Liberia, Congo, and Sudan, and has sold Sudan's Khartoum government weapons and $100 million's worth of Shenyang fighter planes.

- In 2008 Sinosure, China's export credit guarantee agency, offered $50 billion worth of export guarantee facilities to help fund projects and encourage investment in Nigeria over the next three years.[6]

China has also invested in Africa with investment and loans. In 2004 Chinese foreign direct investment (FDI) in Africa reached $900 million. Chinese loans to African countries are three times the total development aid provided by Organization for Economic Cooperation and Development

(OECD) members. In 2006 China lent nearly three times as much to African countries as the World Bank.

Domestically, China's economic bureaucratic agencies encourage Chinese NOCs and other state-owned enterprises to increase their investment and trade with Africa. This is part of China's efforts to shape new markets, continue to expand China's international role and presence in political and economic sectors, and gain access to natural resources. The promise of economic growth, access to Chinese investment funds, and the opening of new sources of political, economic, and even military support all encourage African leaders' support for increased Chinese engagement.

Western observers often attribute the behavior and actions of Chinese companies operating in Africa as being controlled by the Chinese government. In reality, there is far less coordination between Chinese NOCs' activities and the government. China's multiple bureaucracies with responsibilities over energy production at home and abroad possess limited capacity for control and coordination, and there is often confusion among the different organizations about priorities and objectives. In certain cases, bureaucratic actors are actually politically weaker than the NOCs.

Beijing's ability to rely on its corporate agents to dependably advance its strategic, economic, and diplomatic interests in Africa is also in question.[7] These companies implement China's aid projects, extract natural resources, and then either export back to China or sell in the international marketplace for profit. Independent corporate decision making, such as that of CNPC's involvement in Sudan, has already presented challenges to China's global influence and the "soft-power" goals in its national security strategy.

The Chinese energy sector experienced decentralization and liberalization during decades of sustained economic transition. Power and resources shifted from the central government toward state-owned oil companies. In 1988 China abolished its ministries of coal and oil to form a ministry of energy, subsequently abolished in 1992. Since then, no ministerial-level agency has performed the basic function of compiling and presenting authoritative data on the country's energy industry, including overseas investment activities.[8] China's Foreign Ministry does not exercise direct supervision over Chinese

NOCs' operations in Africa; nor does it have the necessary channel to communicate or enforce China's foreign policy goals in corporate policy making vis-à-vis target countries.

China's lending and investment practices have been criticized in the West. Western governments traditionally attach conditions to foreign aid and loans. Conditions include building democracy; promoting transparent, accountable governments; reducing human rights' violations; and financial sector reform. Laws and agreements prevent Western companies from engaging in business deals involving bribes, secondary payments, or guarantees of income. China does not attach the same conditions on its investments and Chinese companies are not required to adhere to anticorruption practices or other agreements. But it is also not clear that Beijing has insights into or control over the structure of the NOCs' agreements with African governments and businesses, especially those that are done under the table.

In cases where the state has provided low-interest loans and investments as part of a deal, China defends its practices and argues against linking trade and investment decisions to political or economic reforms. China views such investments as critical to building infrastructure required to support long-term development; they argue for a long-term perspective that focuses on building regional capacity needed for sustained political and economic stability.

Chinese Oil Companies in Africa

As the world's biggest consumer of many commodities with a rapidly growing need for oil, China seeks a steady flow of raw materials. This requires opening new sources of energy, developing the transportation infrastructure to bring raw materials to China, creating new markets for its goods, and promoting stability.

With respect to energy resources in Africa, Chinese NOCs have adopted a proactive approach since China became a net importer of oil in 1993. They quickly engaged producers such as OPEC member country Nigeria, also the largest oil producer in Africa; Angola, the continent's second-largest oil producer with major offshore sources of gas; and Sudan, producer of light, sweet crude—the most easily refined and most desirable oil.[9] A summary of their recent involvements in select countries tells much of the story:

- Since its initial engagement in Sudan in 1996, CNPC has acquired a 40 percent stake in Sudan's Greater Nile Petroleum Operating Company, pumping over 300,000 bbl/day of oil.[10]

- In 2005 CNPC signed an $800 million crude oil sale deal with the Nigerian National Petroleum Corporation to supply 30,000 bbl/day of crude oil to China.[11]

- In 2006 Sinopec offered a record price of $2.4 billion for the right to explore for oil in three of Angola's offshore blocks.[12]

- In 2006 CNOOC announced a $2.37 billion deal to buy a 45 percent stake in a substantial offshore oil field in Nigeria.[13]

The NOCs' activities have stirred fears that Chinese oil companies, in collaboration with their shareholders in government, are blocking Western access to emerging resources. In reality, however, Chinese oil companies usually invest overseas in partnership with Western firms or other NOCs. Moreover, they tend to be passive shareholders, exercising little day-to-day control over the investment, and mostly sell their share of the oil produced on the open market, rather than shipping it back to China.[14]

Driven by higher prices in the global market, China's NOCs often sell large quantities of their foreign equity oil on the international market rather than to Chinese consumers. This is an example of the NOCs' ability to make decisions independent of China's domestic political or economic agenda. The State Council's 2004 policy of capping retail prices for oil, insulated consumers from the rising global cost of oil and enabled China to keep its petroleum goods lower than other global producers. Large NOCs such as CNPC suffered as a result. Their profits were squeezed as costs went up but prices in China remained flat.[15] Under such pressure, the response from NOCs was an act of defiance against authorities: the amount of oil sold in China was drastically reduced and several large refineries were put on "scheduled maintenance."[16]

The Chinese government does subsidize NOCs, which some view as contributing to unfair trade practices. Beijing, however, views subsidies as necessary to offset the NOCs' history of being handicapped in the global competition for oil reserves as latecomers to the international oil business.[17] Additionally, China has argued that Western companies are not sharing or providing access to advanced exploration and extraction technologies. While some decry subsidies as an unfair trade policy, others contend that Chinese oil subsidies exert a long-run stabilizing effect by increasing exploration and extraction, opening new sources to satisfy rising demand, and moderating prices by offsetting risk incurred from investment in conflict-prone regions.[18] At the global level, China's NOCs are essentially expanding rather than contracting the amount of oil available to other consumers through their overseas operations, especially by developing fields others are unable or unwilling to invest in.

China has focused on engagement with Angola, Sudan, and Nigeria. All three nations recognize the legitimacy of the Beijing government as well as support the One China principle. Although these three countries reap high oil revenues, an overwhelming majority of the population still lives in abject poverty. Additionally, political situations in these countries are constantly interrupted by internal upheavals and unrest. Much of Sudan's regions with huge potential for energy reserves are inaccessible due to conflicts.

The rationale for China's outreach to countries like Sudan and Angola is partly a response to strategies that Western and international oil companies traditionally pursued vis-à-vis Africa. Since its discovery of oil, Nigeria has been a major oil supplier to both Western Europe and the United States. Chinese NOCs are latecomers to the Nigerian businesses, and thus face fierce competition with their Western peers. Over the past three decades, major international oil companies, such as Chevron-Texaco, Exxon-Mobil, Shell, and Total, dominated exploration and production in Nigeria. Since it was fairly difficult to enter the Nigerian market, Chinese companies pursued opportunities in Sudan and Angola.

China's NOCs have a particularly interesting history of engagement in Sudan. China came into Sudan when Western companies were scaling back operations for security reasons and when the Sudanese government was eager to develop its own oil industry with external support. Chinese NOCs' capital and technology assisted Sudan in its development of a domestic oil industry. Sudan's rich reserves enabled Chinese oil companies to expand their business operations. China is the largest foreign investor in Sudan's oil sector and receives 64 percent of Sudan's oil exports.[19] Although the amount imported from Sudan accounts for only a fraction of China's total, China's Sudan activities remain one of its largest, most comprehensive, and most integrated (both upstream and downstream) overseas oil projects.[20]

Darfur Crisis: Corporate vs. National Strategy

In the case of Sudan, due to CNPC's operations in the country's oil fields for over a decade, Beijing has been able to forge a particularly close relationship with the government in Khartoum. Observers thus deem that China's extensive economic involvement in Sudan gives it enormous leverage over Khartoum. On the issue of Darfur, the Chinese government has endorsed the U.N.'s three-phase program for deployment of a peacekeeping force, and has shown interest in helping to convince the Sudanese government to accept it. In March 2007 China's National Development and Reform Commission took Sudan off the list of resource-rich countries that could receive soft loans from China's Exim Bank. China's special envoy to Africa also expressed China's commitment to working hard to persuade the Sudanese authorities to cooperate with a hybrid U.N-African peacekeeping force that is being deployed in Darfur.[21] In addition, China has dispatched 136 personnel in 2005 for peacekeeping operations in Sudan—the largest number of peacekeepers sent by the five permanent members in the U.N. Security Council.

In spite of the criticism prompted by China's close economic ties with Sudan that China has weakened international efforts to halt the violence in Darfur, CNPC has at times sold more of the oil from Sudan to Japan than it has at home.[22] Western observers see FDI made by China's NOCs as part of a highly-coordinated quest for oil and natural gas, in which the companies are merely puppets of the state, executing the directives of their political masters. This perception stems from a combination of the authoritarian nature of the Chinese government, the state ownership of China's oil companies, and the country's growing demand for oil.[23] Admittedly, the Chinese government has encouraged China's NOCs to expand internationally and provided them with diplomatic and financial support. However, in terms of investment decisions and choosing the final destination, the NOCs almost always have the final say. Sudan's recent omission from the Chinese Exim Bank's catalog of soft-loan receivers has not prevented CNPC from continuing to invest in the country's oil fields.

Meanwhile, Chinese analysts have criticized the poor coordination both between China's NOCs and the central government, and among the companies themselves. Some Chinese scholars argue that Chinese NOCs have become powerful interest groups, and in certain cases like the Darfur Crisis, even hijacked China's foreign policy.[24] The power of the NOCs vis-à-vis the central government has grown substantially at the turn of the century, due to their surging profits, their listing of subsidiaries on foreign stock exchanges, their globalizing senior management, and their reliance on international banks and consultancies for investment advice. China's government agencies face enormous difficulties coordinating the formulation and implementation of energy decisions among themselves, let alone with the NOCs.[25] In this light, large state companies now operate under purely economic motivations, and it is imperative that further regulations be created and enforced by the government to constrain the NOCs' behavior overseas, so as not to harm China's broader strategic interests.

Implications for U.S. Security Policy

The United States and China share similar concerns in their security policies, as both are highly dependent on foreign sources of energy, and both have a keen interest in keeping global energy supplies open, secure, and at an affordable price level. Africa is a key region through which both countries secure their supply of energy resources. China's NOCs face the same problems that Western oil companies do in conflict zones such as the Niger Delta. The

Movement for the Emancipation of the Niger Delta has threatened operations of Chinese NOCs as well as Chinese nationals working in the area.

The United States must continue engaging China and seek to develop new concepts of bilateral cooperation to advance common security interests. The two sides should cooperate through joint or parallel actions to promote economic and political developments in Africa, as well as further engage regional countries into global affairs.

The United States should pursue a two-track approach with China in order to ensure energy security in Africa. At the governmental level, the U.S. administration needs to make a concerted endeavor at moderating China's negative influences in key areas such as governance, and needs to continue to urge China to become a responsible international stakeholder. At the corporate level, U.S. oil companies should engage their Chinese counterparts in exploration and production activities, and bridge their shared interests.

Good governance is a prerequisite for secured flows of trade and investments in Africa and ensures that investor interests are safeguarded. It is crucial that Chinese and American activities help promote or at least not undermine good governance on the continent.[26] The United States and China must reach a mutual understanding of what good governance and transparency entail. Mindful of its previous "no questions asked" investment approach that contributed to current volatility in the Middle East, the U.S. views Africa as a chance to "get it right."[27]

Meanwhile, constrained by its commitment to the principle of noninterference, China abstains from initiatives that would help bring equity and transparency to Africa. The United States must keep in mind China's status as a developing country and its political considerations in order to set realistic expectations.[28]

Cooperation instead of competition is the key to U.S.-China relations in Africa. The United States' security interests lie not in curtailing China's involvement, but in promoting cooperation that would support international norms in the long run. It is imperative that American policy makers and corporate executives understand the dynamic between the Chinese NOCs' decision making and the Chinese government's broader strategies.

Notes

1   Alex Vines, "China in Africa: A Mixed Blessing?" *Current History*, 106:700, May 2007, 218.

2   Esther Pan, "China, Africa, and Oil," *Backgrounder*, CFR, January 26, 2007, http://www.cfr.org/publication/9557.

3   James Swan, Deputy Assistant Secretary for African Affairs, "Africa-China Relations: The View from Washington," an address at SIPA, Columbia University, February 9, 2007, http://www.state.gov/p/af/rls/rm/80453.htm.

4   Greg Mills and Chris Thompson, "Partners or Predators? China in Africa," *China Brief*, vol. 8, no. 2, January 17, 2008, http://www.jamestown.org/china_brief/article.php?articleid=2373910; Pan, "China, Africa, and Oil."

5   Linden J. Ellis, "China Exim Bank in Africa: Opportunities for Strengthening Environmental Standards for Hydropower in Sudan," lecture given at the China Environment Forum, Woodrow Wilson International Center for Scholars, March 22, 2007, http://www.wilsoncenter.org/index.cfm?topic_id=1421&fuseaction=topics.event_summary&event_id=224956.

6   Matthew Green and Richard McGregor, "China in $50bn Move to Woo Nigeria," *Financial Times*, April 2, 2008, 4.

7   Bates Gill and James Reilly, "The Tenuous Hold of China Inc. in Africa," *The Washington Quarterly*, 30:3, Summer 2007, 39.

8   Zha Daojiong and Hu Weixing, "Promoting Energy Partnership in Beijing and Washington," *The Washington Quarterly*, 30:4, Autumn 2007, 109.

9   Angola and Sudan are China's top energy suppliers, while Africa's top three receivers of Chinese FDI are respectively Angola, Nigeria, and Sudan.

10 Chietigj Bajpaee, "The Eagle, the Dragon and African Oil," *Asia Times* Online, October 12, 2005, http://www.atimes.com/atimes/China_Business/GJ12Cb01.html.

11 Ian Taylor, "China's Oil Diplomacy in Africa," *International Affairs*, 82:5, October 2006, 945.

12 "China's Sinopec Wins Bid for Stakes in Angola Oil Blocks," *Forbes* Online, June 13, 2006, http://www.forbes.com/business/feeds/afx/2006/06/12/afx2810979.html.

13   Peter S. Goodman, "CNOOC Buys Oil Interest in Nigeria," *Washington Post*, January 10, 2006, D1.

14   Downs, "Sino-African Energy Relations," 47.

15   Fred Bergsten, Bates Gill, Nicholas Lardy, and Derek Mitchell, *China: The Balance Sheet*, New York Public Affairs, 35.

16   Geoff Dyer and Richard McGregor, "China's Champions," *Financial Times*, March 17, 2008, 7.

17   Erica S. Downs, "The Fact and Fiction of Sino-African Energy Relations," *China Security*, vol. 3, no. 3, Summer 2007, 52.

18   "A Ravenous Dragon," *The Economist*, March 15, 2008, 4.

19   Ibid.

20   Wu Qiang, "Sudan weiji tiaozhan zhongguo haiwai shiyou liyi [Sudan Crisis Challenges China's Overseas Oil Interests]," *Nanfengchuang*, September 16, 2004, 24.

21   James Blitz, "Sudan Arms Sale Claims Exaggerated, Says China," *Financial Times*, February 23, 2008, 4.

22   Geoff Dyer and Richard McGregor, "China's Champions," *Financial Times*, March 17, 2008, 7.

23   Downs, "Sino-African Energy Relations."

24   Richard McGregor, "Chinese Diplomacy Hijacked by Companies," *Financial Times*, March 17, 2008, 2.

25   Downs, "Sino-African Energy Relations."

26   Mills and Thompson, "Partners or Predators?"

27   Daniel Morris, "The Chance to Go Deep: U.S. Energy Interests in West Africa," *American Foreign Policy Interests*, 28, 2006, 226.

28   J. Anyu Ndumbe, "West African Oil, U.S. Energy Policy, and Africa's Development Strategies," *Mediterranean Quarterly*, Winter 2004, 23.

SECTION III:

Security and Development Challenges

U.S. and Chinese Development Assistance in Africa

Angela Sapp Mancini

Africa has historically stood below the rest of the world in terms of living standards, economic development, and access to food and health care. But in recent years, booming commodity prices and increased trade capacity have boosted average growth rates to over 5 percent per year, and increasing resource competition among major powers has led to sharply rising interest in Africa's rich energy and mineral resources. Both the U.S. and China have rapidly increased foreign assistance flows to Africa in recent years, albeit with different goals and strategies for the aid. This chapter will discuss U.S. and Chinese foreign aid flows to Africa in terms of size, mechanisms, and trends; explore the motives behind that aid; and offer ideas for the new administration to consider regarding the approach to foreign aid to Africa in light of increasing assistance flows from China.

With over 15 percent of the world's population, Africa has historically stood below the rest of the world in terms of living standards, economic development, and access to food and health care. But in recent years, booming commodity prices and increased trade capacity have boosted average growth rates to over 5 percent per year, and increasing resource competition among major powers has led to sharply rising interest in Africa's rich energy and mineral resources. At the same time, both the U.S. and China have rapidly increased foreign assistance to Africa, particularly to support trade, infrastructure, and resource-related development. The U.S., whose assistance to Africa focuses most heavily on HIV/AIDS prevention and health and education issues, has grown increasingly apprehensive about the motives and impact of China's rising aid flows, which include loans and state-sponsored investments tied to industrial contracts.

The U.S. is also wary of the "China model" of assistance that is built on noninterference in domestic African affairs. This model stands in sharp contrast to the U.S. approach that links aid to institutional reform and improved standards in areas such as governance and the environment. This chapter compares the objectives and relative size of U.S. and Chinese development assistance flows to Africa, explores the differences between the U.S. approach and the China model, and outlines recommendations on ways the new administration might approach foreign aid to Africa in light of increasing assistance flowing from China.

Recent Trends: Rising Funding for Africa

U.S. aid to Africa has historically ebbed and flowed; it reached a peak of over $2.5 billion in 1985, as the U.S. was both competing with the Soviet Union during the Cold War for influence in Africa and responding to famine on the continent, and rose again in the late 1990s as the U.S. pursued both humanitarian relief and economic development. Today, U.S. Official Development Assistance (ODA)[1] aid to Africa—primarily economic development and welfare—has risen from $2 billion in 2000 to $5.3 billion in 2006, though it still averages less than $9 per African per year.[2] Immediately prior to the 2005 G-8 summit in Gleneagles, Scotland, President Bush pledged to double ODA to Africa between 2004 and 2010 (i.e., from $4.5B to $8.9B).[3] While this pledge has not yet been met, ODA to Africa is now over 20 percent of the total U.S. assistance budget of approximately $23 billion and, assuming the same growth trajectory, the U.S. will likely reach this goal by 2010.

The U.S. government clearly states its objectives of foreign assistance to Africa. Aid is provided based on "humanitarian need, the foreign policy interests of the United States, and the commitment of a country and its leadership to reform."[4] A specific goal for "stable" African countries includes supporting economic growth, which is accomplished primarily through the African Global Competitiveness Initiative, a $200 million, five-year Presidential Initiative that works with African states to improve private sector development and expand trade. Other goals include health, democracy, governance, and improving agriculture. Aid to "fragile" African states focuses on conflict prevention and democratic reforms.

U.S. assistance is provided primarily through the U.S. Agency for International Development (USAID);[5] USAID has twenty-three bilateral missions and three trade hubs in sub-Saharan Africa. The U.S. also provides assistance through multilateral agencies such as the World Bank, though the Bush administration has focused on bilateral, rather than multilateral, approaches during its tenure.[6] The U.S. has also used debt relief to promote development in African countries. Significant recent programs include Nigeria ($597 million in 2006) and the Democratic Republic of the Congo ($689 million in 2006).[7]

In addition to providing support through traditional USAID programs, the U.S. launched two major initiatives in 2004 that have provided significant assistance to Africa. The President's Emergency Plan for AIDS Relief (PEPFAR) is an initiative to increase funding to fight HIV/AIDS and other diseases by $10 million over five years. Although some have criticized the growing imbalance of assistance focused on HIV/AIDS (25 percent of all U.S. bilateral assistance to Africa in 2006 focused on HIV/AIDS),[8] PEPFAR is considered one of the most significant foreign policy successes of the Bush administration. The Millennium Challenge Account (MCA) is another significant initiative, which has been praised for its innovative approach in providing aid to countries that qualify for eligibility based on quality of governance and other specific criteria. Increasingly, the U.S. is also providing assistance through the Department of Defense's United States Africa Command (AFRICOM), which in addition to its military mandate is focusing also on development, health, education, democracy, and economic growth objectives.[9]

While China's assistance to Africa includes technical assistance, debt relief, and other forms of aid similar to what the U.S. provides, China's support also includes preferential trade and investment agreements, many of which are related to extractive resources that can support China's explosive growth. China's growth rates have routinely been in the double digits, and China's energy demands have been increasing at 4 to 5 percent per year, compared to 1 percent for industrialized countries. China's primary domestic focus is stability and economic growth, and the government's key goals include securing energy resources and export markets that will sustain that growth. These objectives increasingly appear to drive China's investment, trade, security—and foreign aid—agreements with other countries.[10]

China has taken an increasing interest in Africa's significant energy resources and ability to serve as a potential export market. China/Africa bilateral trade expanded sevenfold between 2000 and 2007, making China a key trading partner with Africa. China's direct investment in Africa increased from $491 million in 2003 to $2.5 billion in 2006.

China is not a newcomer to providing assistance to Africa—it has been doing so since 1956. As China's commercial interests in Africa have grown, so have its foreign aid flows to the continent. Unlike the U.S., China has not published its budgets for African assistance flows, nor its specific development objectives for Africa. As such, precise information on China's bilateral assistance flows to Africa is difficult to obtain, but experts estimate it is between $1 to 2 billion per year.[11] This amount is small compared to the $5 billion provided by the U.S., the $18 billion (including debt relief) provided by EU member countries, and the $9 billion from multilateral institutions.[12] However, China provides assistance to Africa through additional mechanisms, including the Export-Import Bank of China, the Ministry of Commerce, and the China Development Bank in forms such as "concessional loans, trade deals, and state-sponsored investments…that may far surpass U.S. ODA."[13]

Regardless of the precise figures, it is clear that Chinese aid to Africa is increasing. In 2006, China and Africa held the first summit of the Forum on China-African Cooperation (FOCAC), at which China pledged to double its aid to Africa by 2009. If met, this could result in aid to Africa of up to $1 billion per year.[14]

U.S. vs. Chinese Assistance Models

National security objectives play an important role in formulating U.S. development strategy. During two decades following the Camp David Accords, for example, Egypt and Israel were the largest recipients of foreign aid. Today, Iraq and Afghanistan top the list. Following 9/11, the Bush administration included development in a new three-pronged foreign policy strategy (i.e., the 3 D's—diplomacy, defense, and development—with a strong emphasis on the military element). The U.S. has highlighted the link between security and development, and increased the focus on combating terrorism as a foreign aid objective. Programs that promote democracy, civil society, and economic growth are aimed not only at meeting traditional development objectives that improve quality of lives, but also at reducing the effectiveness of terrorist recruitment efforts.

The economic development model promoted by the U.S in recent decades has been the so-called "Washington Consensus," which advocates reducing state involvement in markets and promoting open trade and financial flows, privatization, and deregulation. These ideas led to shock therapy for Asia and Russia during the financial crises of the 1990s. This model faced criticism when these countries underwent painful market corrections but still faced significant economic growth challenges. Today, in the wake of the massive bailouts of the Western financial systems following the global financial crisis, donor recipient countries are extremely wary of adopting these ideas without considerable tailoring for local conditions. U.S. foreign aid approaches have also been questioned as they relate to promoting democracy and human rights following 9/11; some claim that America's zeal in pursuing these goals has created a backlash among some recipient countries and has crowded out other important objectives, such as economic development.

China's model for development assistance differs from the U.S. model in three key respects: the goals of the assistance, the strategy of development, and the terms of aid.[15] The China model puts short-term economic gain and infrastructure development ahead of longer-term institutional reforms, and it supports the strengthening of states that will pursue incremental reforms, rather than advocating potentially destabilizing ideas like democratization, deregulation, and quick transitions to free and open markets.[16] China also holds firm in its view of noninterference with internal matters of recipient countries, and it does not link aid to any policy changes, such as governance or environmental standards. China believes its win-win model is better, and will be more readily accepted than the U.S. model by countries who want to emulate China's growth, see quick, tangible results in infrastructure, and are disillusioned with the strings of governance and democracy that U.S. places on its aid.

Indeed, some African leaders have noted that China's emphasis on quick delivery, without any ideological strings, allows for more rapid benefits. Senegal's President Wade noted, "I have found that a contract that would take five years to discuss, negotiate, and sign with the World Bank takes three months when we have dealt with Chinese authorities. I am a firm believer in good governance and the rule of law. But when bureaucracy and red tape impede our ability to act…African leaders have an obligation to opt for swifter solutions."[17]

But actually the China model does often come with strings, albeit not to ideological policy changes. Instead, there is a strong link between the development assistance and its promotion of Chinese trade, investment, and access to natural resources. Certainly there are many positive impacts of China's increasing aid flows to Africa. Infrastructure is improving, African exports to China are increasing, Africa is receiving new sources of finance, and China's activities have led to a renewed interest in Africa by the U.S. and others.[18] China has undertaken student and professional exchanges with Africa, and is sending an increasing number of technical experts to advise on agricultural and other issues.

However, many development experts worry that this model of Chinese aid of exchanging support for resource concessions, irrespective of human rights and environmental, governance, or accountability standards, may be detrimental to Africa in the long-term. This approach can strengthen rogue African regimes and encourage the sale of national resources without any framework to invest the gains back into local development. Others question

Chinese arms sales to governments accused of violating human rights, such as Zimbabwe and Sudan, the increase in African indebtedness, and the long-term environmental damage resulting from certain Chinese-funded projects. An additional concern is that the prevalence of Chinese assistance may ultimately reduce the impact of U.S. assistance and slow down reforms that can improve health, livelihoods, and economies across Africa.

Whether China will continue to pursue this model without any adaptation is unclear. There has been increasing international backlash against China's support of certain regimes, such as Sudan. They have also faced embarrassment from non-Western countries, such as when South African dockworkers in Durban recently refused to unload a Chinese arms shipment bound for Zimbabwe, and the ship was forced to leave the port. Ultimately it is the decision of individual countries in Africa as to how they choose to move forward with accepting foreign assistance. This will depend largely on how effective the two models—or some hybrid—prove to be in the longer term.

Challenges Ahead: Global Recession

In recent years, there has been a debate over the strategy and terms of U.S. and Chinese assistance to Africa. But one of the most significant factors that may influence the trajectory of this assistance may be a new issue: the global financial crisis. Prior to the crisis, Africa had been one of the brightest spots in the emerging market world. Increased trade flows and high commodity prices increased Africa's earnings, which meant that foreign assistance, while critical to many on the continent, was playing less of a vital role in providing foreign exchange to the continent. African financial systems were not heavily integrated with Western markets and as such have been more immune from the crisis than other markets. But due to the global financial turmoil, the IMF is predicting slower GDP growth, tighter credit markets, and weakening of banking systems throughout Africa.[19] As the global economy weakens, both demand for African exports and worker remittances sent back to Africa will drop. Africa has been one of the most attractive destinations for foreign investors, but the reduction in investor resources will surely reduce investment flows to Africa.

The real issue is whether the U.S. and China will continue to be able to afford providing foreign assistance flows to Africa, especially at the current rising pace. U.S. President-elect Obama ran on a platform of doubling foreign aid, but since then American financial commitments have soared with multiple government bailouts, and the U.S. faces a prolonged recession. Even in the earlier days of the crisis, Vice President-elect Biden admitted that one campaign promise that may have to be curtailed was the increase in foreign aid. China faces similar constraints on its resources. And both countries may also face impatient citizens who prefer their governments fund internal development and/or infrastructure before sending assistance abroad.

However, the fact remains that Africa needs assistance, perhaps now more than ever. Even if Africa's economies slump less than others, growth will drop and the continent faces significant humanitarian and development needs. And given the fact that Africa will continue to be of strategic interest due to its role in providing energy, trade, and influence (i.e., voting rights) in international institutions, many hope that both the U.S. and China will continue to prioritize the continent and retain at least an even flow of foreign assistance.

Looking Forward

Looking ahead, there may be three scenarios that unfold. The first is that the recession produces a similar impact on both U.S. and Chinese foreign assistance flows to Africa wherein both countries keep flows level or drop them equally. The U.S could approach this "muddling through" scenario by continuing to engage China within the international aid architecture in order to promote transparency regarding the terms and impact of aid, and perhaps develop common minimum performance standards. Even though the countries employ different assistance strategies, they have many overlapping interests in Africa, including preventing failed states, combating disease, and ensuring supplies of natural resources. As President Bush noted, the U.S. doesn't view the two countries' interests in Africa as a zero-sum competition, nor do experts expect that China's activities in Africa aim to reduce U.S. influence.[20] Vice President–elect Biden agreed that "there is a view in Washington that the United States and China are fated to confrontation...but I believe this view is mistaken. The place to start is sustained, high level engagement...across every issue area."[21]

China has already recently begun increasing its engagement with the international aid architecture. It has donated to the World Bank's International Development Association and joined the Financial Action Task Force. China's Export-Import Bank is also now collaborating with the World Bank to jointly finance transportation and energy infrastructure projects in Ghana, Uganda, and Mozambique.[22] World Bank President Robert Zoellick noted that China is open to discussing the issue of African indebtedness with other stakeholders as well, as "they want to get paid back, too."[23]

The second scenario is that the U.S. economy is impacted more severely than China's and the gap between the two countries' assistance flows widens. In this case, the U.S. would see a drop in its own ability to promote governance and other American foreign aid objectives in Africa. Clearly the U.S. should do whatever it can to avoid this worst-case scenario.

A third scenario, which could be called "seize the opportunity," could see both countries keep relatively even assistance flows, but work in closer concert as a result of a restructuring in multilateral systems. The financial crisis is generating much discussion around changing structures and/or voting rights of international institutions, while at the same time the Obama administration seems poised to increase the U.S. focus on multilateral mechanisms. As the U.S., China, and other countries work more closely together in international forums, there may also be opportunities to create joint frameworks for African foreign assistance. For example, the U.S. could lead efforts to reform rule of law while China leads infrastructure development, through a framework that promotes transparency in aid flows and impact.

The third scenario suggests the possibility of engaging constructively with China on common points of integration. Crises provide unique opportunities for change, and the current financial crisis and subsequent reworking of certain international mechanisms could offer an opportunity for the U.S. and China to work together more closely on this issue. But no matter which scenario occurs, the U.S. should strive as much as possible to retain or increase foreign assistance to Africa, while improving aid effectiveness to stretch funding further and maximize impact. Doing so will not only provide Africa with critically needed support and engage with China in constructive way, but also provide an opportunity for the Obama administration to bolster America's image in the developing world while making an early statement about America's commitment to a leadership role within the international aid architecture.

Notes

1   This article uses the definition of Official Development Assistance (ODA) as outlined by the Development Assistance Committee (DAC) of the OECD. According to the Center for Global Development, DAC defines ODA as grants and subsidized loans whose main objective is to support economic development and welfare. Unless otherwise stated, all ODA figures quoted in this article will exclude debt relief.

2   Steve Radelet and Sami Bazzi, "U.S. Development Assistance to Africa and the World: What Do the Latest Numbers Say?" Center for Global Development, February 15, 2008. Note figures are in constant 2005 dollars.

3   Ibid.

4   USAID Strategic Framework for Africa, February 24, 2006.

5   Note that through the so-called "F process," a series of reforms initiated by Secretary of State Condoleezza Rice in 2006, USAID and the State Department are coordinating assistance efforts through a new "Foreign Assistance Strategic Framework."

6   Sheila Herrling and Steve Radelet, "Modernizing U.S. Foreign Assistance for the Twenty-First Century, The White House and the World: A Global Development Agenda for the Next U.S. President," ed. Nancy Birdsall, Center for Global Development, 2008.

7   Radelet and Bazzi, "U.S. Development Assistance to Africa and the World."

8   Ibid.

9   White House press release, February 6, 2007, http://www.whitehouse.gov/news/releases/2007/02/20070206-3.html.

10   Chris Blanchard, et al, "Comparing Global Influence: China's and U.S. Diplomacy, Foreign Aid, Trade and Investment in the Developing World," Congressional Research Report RL34620, August 15, 2008.

11   Thomas J. Christensen and James Swan, "China in Africa: Implications for U.S. Policy," Statement Before the Subcommittee on African Affairs of the Senate Foreign Relations Committee, June 5, 2008.

12   Ibid.

13   Blanchard, et al.

14   Ibid.

15   Harry Harding, "Blazing a New Trail," *China Security*, vol. 4, no. 2, Spring 2008.

16   Ibid.

17   "China's Foreign Policy and 'Soft Power' in South America, Asia and Africa," a study prepared by the Congressional Research Service for the Committee on Foreign Relations of the U.S. Senate, April 2008.

18   Blanchard, et al.

19   Zephania Ubwani, "Africa to Be Hit Hard by Credit Crisis, Says IMF," *Daily Nation*, November 7, 2008.

20   Christensen and Swan, "China in Africa: Implications for U.S. Policy."

21   Senator Joe Biden, press conference on May 15, 2008, http://biden.senate.gov/press/press_releases/release/?id=143f5fd3_1cae-46ac-8675.

22   "World Bank Reiterates Intention to Collaborate with China in Africa," Bank Information Center, January 18, 2008, http://www.bicusa.org/en/Article.3650.aspx.

23   Ibid.

Risky Business:
Modifying Risk in Africa

Blair Sondker

The U.S. and China are undertaking an exceptional amount of activities throughout Africa. From China's investment in the oil fields of Sudan to the United States' establishment of the Combined Joint Task Force—Horn of Africa (CJTF-HOA) base in Djibouti, these two superpowers are operating in an environment that holds many risks. This chapter will present a general overview of risk throughout Africa that affects nation-state actors and will examine potential avenues of reward that can be achieved by properly mitigating the risk associated with these endeavors.

The nature of operational activities in business, general everyday activity, or in diplomatic maneuvering is predicated upon the amount of risk and reward associated with a given activity, the balancing of which is called risk perception. The perception of risk by nation-states, investors, or other non-state entities, will affect how each undertakes operations within its respective environment. If an actor is too risk averse within a given environment he may so limit his exposure that he can no longer achieve any tangible rewards. On the other hand, countries that tolerate high levels of risk are likely to suffer from the negative consequences that are inherent in their operating environment. With this in mind, Africa is an appropriate case study to examine operational risk on a continent-wide basis, as it is a source of tremendous risk for varying types of actors operating throughout the region. As such, it is important for actors to understand the nature of these risks so they may also understand the nature of the potential rewards present throughout the continent.

Actors, in this case the United States and China, are undertaking an exceptional amount of activities throughout Africa. From China's investment in the oil fields of Sudan[1] to the United States' establishment of the CJTF-HOA base in Djibouti,[2] these two superpowers are operating in an environment that holds many risks. However, due to the nature of these actors, traditional risks can at times be transformed into a reward of their own. This chapter will present a general overview of risk throughout Africa that affects nation-state actors and will examine potential avenues of reward that can be achieved by properly mitigating the risk associated with these endeavors.

Operational Risk and the Superpower

Under the conventional understanding of risk management, all actors who undertake enterprise functions or organizational strategy inevitably face "a risk of loss resulting from inadequate or failed processes, people and systems, or from external events."[3] It is the responsibility of an actor's risk manager to properly transfer or mitigate the known risks associated with their organization's behavior. Within the traditional confines of risk management, this is handled by four processes: risk avoidance, risk reduction, risk transfer, and risk retention.[4] These four processes are readily available to normal actors through common risk management activities. However, for actors that must maintain an operational presence in inherently risky environments—the U.S. and China, or a commodities-based company like Anglo Platinum operating in Zimbabwe[5]—risk modification is a fundamental, if often unrecognized, tool used to transform unmitigatable risks into potential strategic rewards.

While operating in Africa, the U.S. and China face a wide variety of risks that threaten their physical security, economic wellbeing, and political goals. The process of risk modification, similar to hedging risk in investment, allows nation-states to absorb a certain amount of loss by leveraging their unmitigatable risk through political and economic investments. In other words, the risk of loss can be offset, or modified, by altering the goals of investment from traditional end states by directly combating the risk through a nation-state's elements of national power. This survey will examine briefly the three macro variables of physical, political, and economic risk throughout Africa, their effects on U.S. and Chinese interests, and how these actors attempt to modify these risks.

Physical Risk

The risk of economic loss stemming from physical insecurity is a common occurrence for all actors, including nation-states like the U.S. and China. Physical insecurity traditionally emanates from three sources: organized force-on-force conflict, terrorism, and rampant criminality. These sources of physical insecurity represent a significant risk to the United States' and China's physical assets and personnel located in Africa. Additionally, these issues contribute to the overall instability in regions of Africa and can eventually weaken economic growth and productivity and destabilize a region.

The Horn of Africa, and the surrounding interior regions, are host to a number of ongoing low-grade insurgencies and failed states. These areas, most notably, Somalia, Sudan, the Democratic Republic of the Congo (DRC), as well as the recent violence in Kenya demonstrate the varied nature of physical insecurity throughout the region. It is important to note that the violence perpetrated within these regions often stems from neighboring countries.

One example of this transnational movement of violence is Uganda's Lord's Resistance Army (LRA).[6] The LRA's main goal is to destabilize and remove the Ugandan government, yet it conducts its attacks from rear bases in southern Sudan and the DRC, thus also destabilizing the countries surrounding Uganda.[7] This regional instability complicates the diplomatic and economic activities of both the U.S. and the Chinese.

The Darfur region of Sudan is another regional conflict that represents a significant physical risk to both American and Chinese goals throughout Africa. China's active involvement with Sudan, predominately motivated by its energy needs, has motivated groups to target Chinese nationals for kidnapping.[8] So far the attacks have been fairly restricted to Chinese nationals working on oil contracts; whereas American nationals have been targeted by the Janjaweed while delivering aid to refugee and internally displaced persons.[9]

Rampant criminality, as demonstrated by the absence of government functions, such as law enforcement in failed states like Somalia, Zimbabwe, Nigeria, Chad, the DRC, and the Central African Republic, are another source of physical insecurity for both Chinese and U.S. interests.[10] Cocaine smugglers from South America have begun taking advantage of the absence of capable law enforcement authorities in western Africa. Guinea-Bissau, in particular, has proven susceptible to the lure of drug smuggling. Its military and security services appear to be complicit in the trafficking industry that undermine U.S. interests in the region, and Europe, the final destination of the trafficked narcotics.[11] Additionally, organizations such as the Movement for the Emancipation of the Niger Delta (MEND), have repeatedly kidnapped American foreign nationals operating in Nigeria.[12]

The absence of governmental functions, notably the lack of an effective security apparatus, has also led to the evolution of transnational terrorist organizations throughout the unstable regions of the continent. The 1998 attacks against the U.S. embassies in Kenya and Tanzania, coupled with the many attacks by Al Qaeda in the Islamic Magreb (AQIM), have demonstrated Al Qaeda's development of an operational presence on the continent. These elements clearly represent a physical security risk for both Chinese and U.S. goals in the region due to their capability to attack the assets of both countries. The presence of transnational terrorist organizations in the region indicates a strategic loss due to the existence of safe havens. However, despite their presence, a strategic diplomatic advantage can be gained by directly confronting these threats with African actors. The Department of State's Anti-Terrorism Assistance (ATA) program is an example of strategically investing political capital in order to build local capabilities to fight terrorism and regional instability.[13] Specifically, the ATA's Trans-Sahara Counterterrorism Initiative "aims to strengthen regional counterterrorism capabilities and cooperation in the Sahel and Maghreb states of Algeria,

Morocco, Tunisia, Mauritania, Mali, Niger, Chad, Senegal, and Nigeria."[14]

The many ongoing conflicts, failed states, terrorist organizations, and the rampant lawlessness throughout the many different regions of Africa pose a significant risk to both U.S. and Chinese objectives. These risks, however, if approached creatively, could become a valuable asset for both nations. Transnational terrorism and crime present the U.S. and China with an opportunity to strategically engage governments and local populations craving assistance in efforts to reform their security institutions. The U.S. currently participates in a number of programs that help build local capacity throughout the continent. The Department of Justice Office of Overseas Prosecutorial Development, Assistance and Training (OPDAT) have helped Kenya's prosecutorial service to develop its ability to pursue and investigate complex criminal activities and terrorism cases.[15] Another Justice Department program, known as the International Criminal Investigative Training Assistance Program (ICITAP), develops a host country's police and security services throughout Africa, helping host nations combat narcotics, sex crimes, and human trafficking.[16] These programs seek to combat the pervasive physical risk that endangers the U.S. and China, while at the same time developing a politically sensitive relationship among the power brokers of the host country. Actively engaging the problem has allowed the United States to modify the existing physical risk by balancing new gains made on the strategic level.

Economic Risk

The risk of loss stemming from adverse economic conditions within Africa is not a new problem. The continent has faced economic instability for a considerable period of time, the causes of which range from the negative effects of colonial subjugation, to food insecurity, to its current massive debt. These problems affect Chinese and American interests due to their reliance on specific commodities located on the continent. Instability caused by economic conditions can endanger the political and economic courses of action of the superpowers just as easily as physical risk factors can, this can be seen by the dramatic consequences of the recent food riots, and the endemic problem of low economic performance.

Today's food crisis has hit Africa particularly hard. This is due in part to Africa's low per capita income that has forced many families to devote a greater amount of their income toward food expenditures. Violent riots and massive protests have broken out in over ten countries in the past year as the price of basic food stuffs such as rice, wheat, corn, barley, and cooking oil have risen dramatically.[17] The United Nation's Food and Agriculture Organization has estimated that Africa's average price of cereals and other imported staples has increased by 74 percent in the past year.[18] The ramifications of the food riots are particularly visible in that they can endanger U.S. and Chinese investments in both personnel and assets located in the affected countries.

The African continent as a whole is host to a number of systemic economic conditions that endanger stability for the region as well as pose a threat to U.S. and Chinese interests. Despite the World Bank's claims of record growth for the continent in the *2007 African Development Indicators Report*, Africa remains the poorest region in the world.[19] The United Nation's Millennium Development Goals have so far failed to reduce poverty within the region to their desired levels, and continued political unrest has hindered private investment. Economic conditions, in tandem with the global rise in food prices, have created a situation in which economic instability could potentially result in punctuated violence and unrest and damage the U.S. and Chinese by increasing instability throughout the region.

So long as extraordinary poverty, endemic health concerns, low growth, and food insecurity affect the continent, Chinese and American goals in Africa remain at risk to economic factors. As such, both nations are undertaking vigorous efforts to help build the basic aspects of industry throughout the continent so they may be able to function and grow economically. China's Foreign Ministry has made it explicit policy to increase Chinese/African interaction by encouraging "cooperation in transportation, communication, water conservancy, electricity and other infrastructures. It will vigorously encourage Chinese enterprises to participate in the building of infrastructure in African countries."[20] One project China has undertaken, through the China Harbor and Engineering Company, will build a six-lane road around the city of Port Harcourt in Nigeria. According to the African Finance Corporation, the road will be the largest municipal highway project in Africa, and is expected to generate significant economic development for the region.[21]

The United States is pursuing a similar strategy of investment in general infrastructure throughout the continent through the Millennium Challenge Corporation (MCC). The MCC has ten grants with African countries totaling over 4 billion dollars. The recipients include: Benin, Burkina Faso, Cape Verde, Ghana, Lesotho, Madagascar, Mali, Morocco, Mozambique, and Tanzania.[22] In Cape Verde, the MCC has provided $78 million for the development of infrastructure, such as bridges and small roads, in order to "ensure improved transportation links to social services, employment opportunities, local markets, ports and airports."[23] At the same time, the MCC program in Mozambique aims to "improve access to markets, resources, and services and to reduce transport costs for the private sector to facilitate investment and commercial traffic" by repairing nearly 500 kilometers of the country's central highway.[24]

The Chinese and U.S. governments have both undertaken diplomatic aid programs that directly address the systemic economic challenges of the African continent. Traditional actors utilizing risk management principals would have avoided the majority of African countries due to their low rates of growth, their lack of basic infrastructure, and growing food insecurity. Despite these issues, both governments have directly attempted to modify the risk of fundamental economic weakness by helping foster and develop indigenous capability. These aid programs effectively hedge the risk of potential economic unrest through investment into economic and infrastructure programs. These projects not only help to alleviate the negative economic conditions within a country, albeit on a long-term scale, but they also serve as a public diplomacy reward for the donor countries as they appear to the recipient host nation to be magnanimous and generous benefactors. Additionally, these programs can curry favor with the ruling government, facilitating future negotiations.

Political Risk

Political realities in any environment change on a near constant basis, but when that political change could negatively affect an actor's investment of time, assets, or personnel it is known as a political risk. Any change on the political scene could result in an increase or decrease of political risk depending on the nature of an actor's operational activities. Hence, it's important to pay attention to changes in overall political stability on a macro scale. Accordingly, Africa with its endemic state weakness, poor national economies, and colonially drawn borders is a frequent source of political instability for U.S. and Chinese interests.

Early 2008 witnessed two significant political crises in Africa that contributed to regional instability. The first crisis began when claims of massive voter fraud delegitimized the results of Kenya's presidential elections in late December 2007. The Kenyan political crisis eventually resulted in the death of over 1,000 people, the assassination of several prominent political leaders, and the displacement of over 500,000 people.[25] During this time, the state ceased functioning as a government, eliminating interstate transportation, empowering criminals, and shattering one of the continent's strongest economies. Additionally, the Kenyan crisis impacted U.S. goals in the region by eliminating the Port of Mombassa as a viable point of entry for development aid destined for areas such as Southern Sudan, Uganda, and Rwanda.

The second crisis occurred in June 2008 in Zimbabwe and centered upon the country's presidential election. President Mugabe and forces aligned with his congressional ZANU-PF political party forced the resignation of opposition candidate Morgan Tsvangirai through mass violence.[26] The crisis resulted in the displacement of thousands of families, massive arrests of the political opposition, and the further disruption of the economy—already one of the worst economic disasters in Africa. During the crisis, China's quiet support of the Mugabe regime became public when the Chinese transport ship, the *An Yue Jiang*, was held at the docks of Durban, South Africa.[27] Its cargo, a massive arms shipment intended for Zimbabwe's military, contained millions of rounds of ammunition and explosives. The

Zimbabwean political crisis helped further damage China's reputation in the region, as evidenced by the numerous anti-Chinese protests in South Africa, Namibia, and Zambia. Additionally, U.S. assets in Zimbabwe were damaged during the crisis and their diplomats were physically threatened by elements of ZANU-PF.

These two instances of political unrest demonstrate the unique nature of political risk for nation-state actors. Unlike physical or economic risks, these events are uniquely political in nature and cannot be addressed in the same way as discussed in the previous sections. Instead, the U.S. and Chinese, while not willing to directly abandon a politically risky situation, need to engage diplomatically in a unilateral, bilateral, or multilateral capacity in order to influence and thus reduce the risk of political instability. The U.S. response to the Zimbabwean political crisis has been to apply and enhance a sanctions regime intended to punish the political powers of the country. For its part, China has rejected the effort and has vetoed the measure in the United Nations Security Council saying, "It will interfere with the negotiating process and lead to the further deterioration of the situation."[28] These two options demonstrate that there is no clear way to modify or transfer political risk due to the complex nature of a political crisis due to the meager rewards and frequently significant risk. However, these situations do require direct diplomatic action, which, if handled skillfully, can help stabilize and thus mitigate the existing political risk.

Conclusion

As demonstrated by the three-macro variables described above, the process of risk modification can play a significant part in hedging political risk. China and the U.S., due to the nature of their foreign policy goals, can't avoid certain risks. They can, however, invest in alternate strategies that produce rewards that both mitigate the initial threat on a long-term scale, as the U.S. is pursuing through its security sector reform in Kenya. Risk modification, like hedging an investment, can also produce competing rewards that offset the various unmitigatable risks threatening actors. These rewards are often diplomatic victories gained from operations like ICITAP's work in West African nations attempting to reform the internal security service's investigative techniques to combat human trafficking, or the State Department's ATA program in the Sahara region. These aid missions have the potential to mitigate the risk by directly harnessing the economic, military, and political power that only a nation-state, particularly a superpower, can bring to bear. Properly managing the risk modification process will be critical to successfully fulfilling either the U.S. or Chinese ambitions within Africa. The state that properly balances their operational risk will be better suited to identify and take advantage of the rewards available throughout the continent.

Notes

1   Scott Baldauf, "Hu's Trip to Sudan Tests China-Africa Ties," *Christian Science Monitor*, February 2, 2007 http://www.csmonitor.com/2007/0202/p06s01-woaf.html.

2   Nick Childs, "US Plans Anti-Terror HQ in Horn," BBC News, November 3, 2002, http://news.bbc.co.uk/2/low/africa/2392831.stm.

3   Loannis Akkizidis and Vivianne Bouchereau, *Guide to Optimal Operational Risk* (New York: Taylor & Francis Group, 2006), 9.

4   Atlantic Global, "Introduction to Risk Management," Programme and Project Portfolio Management Blog, August 11, 2007, http://www.project-portfolio-management-blog.com/2007/08/11/introduction-to-risk-management.

5   Percy Zvomuya, "Will Foreign Companies Stay the Course in Zimbabwe," *Mail* and *Guardian* Online, July 16, 2008, http://www.mg.co.za/article/2008-07-16-will-foreign-companies-stay-the-course-in-zimbabwe.

6   Joe Powell, "Children in Conflict: the Lord's Resistance Army, Uganda," *Guardian*, http://www.guardian.co.uk/journalismcompetition/resistance.army.

7   Joe Bavier, "LRA rebel threat haunts Central African Republic," *Mail* and *Guardian* Online, July 8, 2008, http://www.mg.co.za/article/2008-07-08-lra-rebel-threat-haunts-central-african-republic.

8   "Abducted Chinese Escapes to Safe Place in Sudan," *Xinhua*, March 20, 2004, http://www.chinadaily.com.cn/english/doc/2004-03/20/content_316632.htm.

9   "Aid Worker Shot and Injured in Darfur," UN Office for the Coordination of Humanitarian Affairs, March 23, 2005, **http://www.irinnews.org/report. aspx?reportid=53552.**

10   "Failed States Index 2008," *Foreign Policy*, August/September 2008, http://www. foreignpolicy.com/story/cms.php?story_id=4350&page=1.

11   "How Cocaine Pours through Africa," *The Economist*, June 7, 2007, **http://www. economist.com/world/africa/displaystory.cfm?story_id=9304402.**

12   Rebecca Roberts and Ofeibea Quist-Arcton, "Nigerian Rebels Kidnap American Workers," National Pubic Radio, May 10, 2007, **http://www.npr.org/templates/ story/story.php?storyId=10108236.**

13   "Antiterrorism Assistance Program," U.S. Department of State, **http://www. state.gov/m/ds/terrorism/c8583.htm.**

14   "The Antiterrorism Assistance Program—Report to Congress for Fiscal Year 2005," U.S. Department of State, 2005, **http://ww.state.gov/documents/ organization/75780.pdf.**

15   "DOJ/OPDAT Counterterrorism Programs," Department of Justice, **http:// www.usdoj.gov/criminal/opdat/ctu/ctu.html.**

16   "Africa and the Middle East," Department of Justice, **http://www.usdoj.gov/ criminal/icitap/programs/africa-mideast/.**

17   Ban Ki-Moon, "Food Costs Soaring, So Poor Hurt," *Milwaukee Journal Sentinel*, March 22, 2008, **http://www.jsonline.com/story/index.aspx?id=730868.**

18   Finfacts team, "United Nations' FAO says cereal import bill of world's poorest countries to rise 56% in 2007/2008; Food riots reported in 10 countries; world cereal production in 2008 to increase by 2% ," Finfacts, April 15, 2008 **http:// www.finfacts.ie/irishfinancenews/article_1013178.shtml.**

19   "UN Chief: Africa Anti-poverty Efforts Lag," Associated Press, April 21, 2008, **http://www.usatoday.com/news/world/2008-04-21-un-africa_N.htm.**

20   "China's Africa Policy," Ministry of Foreign Affairs of the Peoples Republic of China, January 12, 2006 **http://www.fmprc.gov.cn/eng/zxxx/t230615.htm.**

21   Nick Tattersall, "Chinese Firm to Build $1 bln Road in Nigeria Oil Hub," *Reuters*, July 13, 2008, **http://www.alertnet.org/thenews/newsdesk/L13281960. htm.**

22   "MCC in Africa: A Partnership for Success," Millennium Challenge Corporation, **http://www.mca.gov/programs/africa/index.php.**

23   "Cape Verde," Millennium Challenge Corporation, http://www.mca.gov/
     countries/capeverde/index.php.

24   "Mozambique," Millennium Challenge Corporation, http://www.mca.gov/
     countries/mozambique/index.php.

25   "Resettling Kenya's Internally Displaced Persons," United States Institute of
     Peace, http://www.usip.org/events/2008/0617_kenya_idp.html.

26   "MDC Confirms Zimbabwe Vote Pullout," Al Jazerra, June 25, 2008, http://
     english.aljazeera.net/news/africa/2008/06/20086240129359181.html.

27   "Zimbabwe Arms Ship Quits S. Africa," BBC News, April 19, 2008, http://news.
     bbc.co.uk/2/hi/africa/7354428.stm.

28   "Russia, China Veto U.S.-drafted Resolution on Zimbabwe," Xinhua, July 12,
     2008, http://english.sina.com/world/p/1/2008/0712/171118.html.

Thwarting Transnational Islamic Extremism

Joshua Aaron Vogel

Achieving stable and peaceful relations among African states while fighting terrorism and securing commerce is critical to America's security in the twenty-first century. With a sizable Muslim population and large swaths of ungoverned territory, some argue Africa is destined to become a haven for Islamic militants. Regardless of whether jihadists develop new safe havens on the continent, the U.S. should avoid conflating regional and local Islamic insurgent groups with global pan-Islamic militants like al-Qaeda. It is essential for the United States and its allies to interdict pan-Islamic jihadists and work with more peaceful Islamic grassroots organizations. This chapter examines measures to increase the capacity of African nations to fight regional terrorists and to build economic potential of the continent, an area where the United States must engage diplomatically.

There are many reasons to believe Africa is headed into a century of economic development and greater stability. American, European, and Asian nations share common interests in African stability and development; they also share aversions to terrorism, civil wars, and the disruption of economic activities. Renewed global interest in African natural resources and economic development has created conditions ripe for new regional cooperation initiatives. But there is a darker side to development.

Some fear that a more vicious pattern of development and instability is likely to emerge. Additional factionalism and violence stemming from recent economic, political, and social disparities may lead to alienation among the lower and middle classes, especially as the price of oil decreases and elites manipulate government policies and economic institutions, reduce government spending, and pursue efforts to preserve their own wealth. Similarly, some fear that the continual absence of civil society and good governance across African nations undermines attempts to build accountable, responsible governments that can sustain viable regional development strategies. When governments fail to accommodate or appease the growing demands of citizens to share in the spoils of resource extraction and development there is greater potential for mobilization along ethic, class, religious, and tribal affiliation. It is widely believed that militant Islamism feeds on repression and class divisions, especially when governments flaunt corruption and deny basic services. The conditions that open opportunities for regional cooperation and stability, therefore, may also be setting the conditions for terrorists, insurgents, and political violence, especially in the sprawling African slums.

Evaluating U.S. engagement strategies in Africa to understand the long-term impact on decreasing Islamic radicalism requires assessing several issues. First, it is critical to understand the true potential for Africa to become the next major staging ground for al-Qaeda. Second, apart from the loose affiliation of groups considered part of the al-Qaeda terrorist network, what engagement options exist for moderate pan-Islamic groups that reject terrorism and violence? And finally, how does the U.S. leverage its power (military and diplomatic) to ensure the continued development of African nations and American national security needs are met?

To answer these questions, the U.S. must develop a counterterrorism strategy that thwarts terrorist inroads, bolsters good governance, and denies Islamic extremists safe-haven. To meet this challenge, the U.S. must alter its current strategy for counterterrorism operations.

Islam and the Threat of Pan-Islamic Terrorism in Africa

As a consequence of colonial rule, national borders in Africa were set arbitrarily, creating several nations that lack a unifying language, religion, or ethnic heritage. This has led to the formation of insurgent groups that seek their own ethnic enclave, a larger share of power, and/or wealth. Today, many of these insurgent groups recognize Islam as a unifying factor. Many of these groups are at risk of being co-opted by pan-Islamic groups like al-Qaeda.

The effect of pan-Islamic movements in Africa cannot be understood without first addressing the role of Islam in African society. Islam is not new to Africa. In some respects, Africans have adapted Islam to local spiritual and religious traditions. Slightly more than half of all Africans practiced Islam in 2006; there remains a wide range of adaptation in African Muslim practices.[1] Indeed, the majority of Muslims in Africa practice *Sufism*, which traditionally avoids explicit involvement in government and politics.[2] African Muslims have integrated traditional African religious practices into their Islamic faith and the extremist, fundamental theology of Islamic jihadists has had marginal success.

Still, fundamentalist mosques and *madrasas* (religious schools) have grown in number in Africa since the 1990s. This has led to a growing influence from more radical *Salafist* groups funded by "charity organizations" based in Saudi Arabia and the Persian Gulf.[3] These "charity" organizations provide the people with basic social services that poor African governments cannot afford. At the same time they espouse a fundamentalist interpretation of Islam and inculcate these values to young children at madrasas.

Salafism can be grouped into two broad currents: the *Salafiyya Ilmiyya* and *Salafiyya Jihadiyya*. The *Salafiyya Ilmiyya* (scholarly *Salafists*) is a conservative sect that urges obedience to the state, but abstains from political involvement.[4] *Salafiyya Ilmiyya's* belief system could be exploited and encouraged as a bulwark against the movement for a global jihad that subverts secular states. The *Salafiyya Jihadiyya* (fighting *Salafists*) reject the standing political order and permit the use of violence to defend Islam against those groups or regimes they see as "apostates." *Salafiyya Jihadiyya's* numbers grew significantly in Africa as a result of the Soviet Union's invasion of Afghanistan in the 1980s.[5] Many Africans traveled to the region to fight the Soviets and were exposed to this type of *Salafism*. This is a troubling trend, but the vast majority of Muslims in Africa are not radical in their beliefs. It should be noted that these radical elements, while growing, are still a minority opinion with minimal support for the general population in most nations.

U.S. Counterterrorism Policy in Africa

Since 9/11, the U.S. has predicated its counterterrorism strategy in Africa on the belief that localized insurgencies by Islamist groups are part of a monolithic movement toward Islamic terrorism in Africa. This is based on flawed generalizations about Islam in Africa (there are 540 million Muslims who have varying views on Islamic practice) and the belief that extreme poverty, social cleavages based on ethnicity and religious, rampant corruption, weak governance, and porous borders create a fertile breeding ground for transnational Islamist terror.[6]

In linking local and regional terrorist groups to al-Qaeda the U.S. risks pushing groups with valid grievances and moderate localized objectives toward the global pan-Islamic jihadist movement. Al-Qaeda's inroads with several groups were accelerated by U.S. efforts to link regional insurgent groups to the greater pan-Islamist terrorist movement.

The 2006 National Security Strategy of the United States argues, "The War on Terror is a battle of ideas, it is not a battle of religions. The transnational terrorists confronting us today exploit the proud religion of Islam to serve a violent political vision."[7] Both statements are valid. The U.S. must differentiate between conservative interpretations of Islam and the militant Islamism advocated by leaders of the global pan-Islamic insurgency. Since 9/11 the United States has worked with its allies to shut down several Islamic charities that wittingly or unwittingly aided Islamic militant groups in Africa.

In forming a counterterrorism policy for Africa, it is critical that the U.S. differentiate between organizations and Imams espousing militant pan-Islamism and similar actors preaching strict adherence to Islam. This may be a difficult endeavor but there is a difference between missionaries preaching religious renewal and Islamic militants that seek to use violence to create one expansive Islamic nation. To effect change it may be necessary to work at the grassroots level to assure good governance by African governments.

It is not the intention of the author to suggest that the U.S. allow terrorist organizations in Africa to grow. Groups that support al-Qaeda and similarly minded organizations must be identified and their membership destroyed. It is critical to make the distinction that all African Muslims not be seen as sympathetic to the struggle of pan-Islamic terrorists. Instead of being considered synonymous with terrorism, Islam could be leveraged as an anchor for stability in the region and a unifying force in many African nations.

Evaluating Regional Insurgency vs. Global Pan-Islamist Movement

The willingness of policy elites to associate local and regional African insurgent groups into a monolithic enemy is unwise, overly simplistic, and inherently flawed. There is the need for a paradigm shift in how the United States engages Africa's Muslim population. A new policy must include a nuanced understanding of the objectives of local insurgent groups versus the objectives of pan-Islamic extremists.

The worldwide jihadist campaign is "a diverse confederation of movements that uses terrorism as its principal, but not its sole tactic."[8] Jihad is waged by Islamist groups in separate theaters around the world, connected through religious, cultural, ideological, financial, and historical links. Al-Qaeda operates at the highest level in this global jihadist movement. It provides ideological guidance and propaganda for a pan-Islamic movement that seeks to create one monolithic Islamic state that stretches from the Atlas Mountains in Morocco to the Hindu-Kush Mountains in Asia. In Africa, al-Qaeda communicates at the local level with insurgent groups through regional intermediaries. These affiliates often co-opt, exploit, and redefine local grievances in pan-Islamic, jihadist terms.

In Africa, many local Islamic insurgent groups form by uniting the population around a common heritage. Many of these Islamic groups have no desire to spread Islam beyond their own borders. These groups resort to terrorism as a tactic to further their struggle against a current regime. Many of these groups have formed in areas of prolonged disorder, especially in states with weak or repressive political structures. They offer morality and stability to their constituencies, two prized assets in nations characterized by oppression and anarchy. The success of global-level jihadists has been their ability to fuse dozens of dissimilar, localized groups into the greater pan-Islamist movement.

By lumping local African Islamic groups with al-Qaeda and its pan-Islamic movement, the U.S. risks a self-fulfilling prophesy. By relying on hard power options, the U.S. risks alienating more moderate elements within these local groups. This causes radical factions to gain control/influence, which leads to the U.S. helping al-Qaeda recruit and diversify its pool of terrorists. In uniting these groups to fight a new common enemy (the U.S.), the U.S. only strengthens the global Islamic insurgency.

As part of a global counterinsurgency strategy, the U.S. should instead focus on denying sanctuary to foreign operatives that seek to co-opt local insurgent groups. To buffer these advances it may also be necessary to increase the capacity of African nations. This could include humanitarian assistance (building political/economic capacity) as well as counterterrorism assistance (e.g., law enforcement, intelligence, military training).

U.S. Efforts in North Africa

In 2002 the Pan-Sahel Initiative (PSI) was created by the State Department to enhance regional cooperation with the Sahel nations and to combat terrorism, track the movements of people through the Sahel and Sahara, and protect the region's borders.[9] In 2005 this program was renamed, the Trans-Sahara Counter Terrorism Initiative (TSCTI), and was expanded to include more North African nations. Operation Enduring Freedom—Trans Sahara (OEF-TS) is the military component of the TSCTI. It conducts "military-to-military engagements and exercises designed to strengthen the ability of regional governments to police the large expanses of remote terrain in the trans-Sahara."[10]

New counterterrorism capabilities were tested by the Salafist Group for Preaching and Combat (GSPC), a domestic Islamic group that came into existence during the Algerian Civil War. In 2003 the group changed its tactics, abandoning attacks against the Algerian government. Instead they focused on kidnapping Western tourists. In the post–9/11 mindset, the

GSPC's attacks on Western tourists and exploitation of sparsely patrolled areas seemed to reinforce the raison d'être for OEF-TS: Stop a terrorist group from using lawless areas to attack Western interests, and build domestic capacity for counterterrorism operations.

The linkage of the GSPC with the global pan-Islamic insurgency played directly into al-Qaeda's hands. Despite initial GSPC reluctance to associate with al-Qaeda, Osama bin Laden and Ayman al-Zawahiri used propaganda videos to portray counterterrorism operations against GSPC as part of the worldwide conflict between Islam and the "crusaders."[11] Operations by the OEF-TS denied the group the freedom of movement, crippled its leadership, and froze finances.

Short on funds, racked with infighting among its leadership, and increasingly unpopular in the region, joining the global jihadist movement was the only way the organization could survive. By 2007 the group officially renamed itself the al-Qaeda Organization in the Islamic Maghreb (AQIM). For the first time, its membership included foreign jihadists. AQIM increased direct financial links and began to carry out al-Qaeda–style attacks, including coordinated suicide bombings.

While this group's ability to engage in terrorist attacks was significantly diminished, a tactical and operational victory for TSCTI, AQIM is still capable of limited attacks in North Africa. AQIM's continued existence is a victory for al-Qaeda and its war to unite and radicalize Islamists at the local level in Africa. AQIM is now part of the greater pan-Islamic insurgency and is more radicalized than at any time in its history.

U.S. Efforts in the Horn of Africa

The Combined Joint Task Force—Horn of Africa (CJTF-HOA) was established in 2002 with the objective to "prevent conflict, promote regional cooperation, and protect U.S. coalition interests, to prevail against extremism."[12] The group's areas of operations include the Horn of Africa as part of the Arabian Peninsula. CJTF-HOA is based in Djibouti and has conducted "short-term assistance…providing clean water, functional schools, improved roadways and improved medical facilities."[13] The objective is to better the lives of those in the region. Missions also include a support component, especially interdicting pirates along Somalia's maritime borders and engaging militants in Africa as well as nations in the Arabian Peninsula such as Yemen.[14]

CJTF-HOA was put to the test following the rise of the Islamic Courts Union (ICU), an unabashedly Islamist group, that seized control in Somalia in 2006. The ICU won favor, not because of a radicalized population, but because they promised to bring law and order to one of the most chaotic nations in the world. The ICU's head, Sheik Hassan Dahir Aweys was noted to have links to al-Qaeda (including links to operatives that conducted a 2003 attack in Mombassa, Kenya). The message of the organization's leadership was not pan-Islamic militancy but a localized message of law and order.[15] Somalia's internationally acknowledged government, the Transitional Federal Government (TFG), lacked the legitimacy and broad-based support to contest the ICU's rise. The TFG did, however, have the support of Ethiopia and the U.S. The TFG positions itself as a secular, "anti-terrorist" movement and sought to cast the ICU as being a direct link to al-Qaeda.

Shortly after the invasion of Somalia by Ethiopia troops, Ayman al-Zawahiri issued an audio message entitled "Set Out and Support Your Brothers in Somalia." In it, he calls the Horn of Africa "a new battlefield of the Crusaders' war."[16] The U.S.-backed Ethiopian invasion brought the TFG back to power. In the process several high ranking foreign jihadists, who came to the region in the wake of the Second Persian Gulf War, were killed. Despite these tactical successes, the ICU (now backed by international jihadists), continues to fight an insurgency against the TFG, and Somalia remains lawless.

Evaluation of Regional Counterterrorism Efforts

Counterterrorism operations in North and East Africa have yielded tactical successes but the U.S. risks bringing regional and local insurgent groups into contact with al-Qaeda, thereby creating a greater likelihood of these local and regional groups becoming radicalized. It is critical that the U.S. assist African militaries by sharing intelligence and personnel to eliminate foreign Islamic terrorists when possible. This has been done by assisting African nations to build their indigenous capacity to secure their borders (land and maritime) and perform counterterrorism operations.

The U.S. must distinguish its fight against al-Qaeda from local and regional Islamic insurgent groups, lest future operations inspire resentment toward the U.S. This is especially true given Africa's sizeable Muslim population. In the long run, hard power options will harm, not further, American interests in Africa. It is important to push Islamist groups apart, not allow them to build similar objectives and foster continued communication and coordination in the future. The newest combatant command, Africa Command (AFRICOM), will play a critical role in building African stability in the coming years.

A New Organization for a New Security Environment: AFRICOM

Previously, U.S. foreign policy toward Africa was administered by both the Department of State and the Department of Defense. With the foundation of Africa Command, operations for Africa will be united under one combatant command.[17] AFRICOM brings together experts in intelligence, diplomacy, economics, health, and other applicable disciplines. Assisting African nations to effectively use their resources will go a long way to create institutions and build transparent institutions, therefore alleviating the need for insurgent groups.

AFRICOM can be leveraged to enhance security cooperation, extend humanitarian assistance, build military capacity, and perform limited military interdiction. This does not necessarily mean the U.S. must have a large military footprint in Africa. The U.S. should expand its naval presence off Africa's coastline to assure continued safe maritime commerce. Maritime security is critical to the expansion of commerce in the region, especially in the Horn of Africa, which has experienced a surge of piracy. Security cooperation and assistance, especially with the African Union and its peacekeeping force, will allow for African nations to solve their own problems and avoid large commitments of U.S. forces.

AFRICOM may be particularly susceptible to criticism if sporadic "hard power" operations overshadow its "softer" initiatives. African leaders may become skeptical of American preference for shorter-term, strictly military solutions and America's desire to capitalize on resource abundance. To prevent skepticism, AFRICOM must show that it is willing to provide civil-military as well as economic assistance. AFRICOM can provide necessary training for African governments in aspects of contingency operations related to health, natural disaster response, and humanitarian aid.

AFRICOM will be critical to capacity-building operations and civic actions, whereby military units undertake projects that result in infrastructure that is useful to the local population (e.g., road construction, well building, etc.). CJTF-HOA has seen positive results from these types of initiatives. These soft power initiatives support struggling African nations, allowing them to provide services to the people and are fairly easy to expand. By helping African governments to meet the needs of the people, the populace may no longer need to depend on to Islamic charities for basic human services.

Sustained and systematic application of all the elements of national power to root out transnational Islamic extremists is vital to successfully combating terrorism. This will require the U.S to assist African states to build law enforcement, intelligence, and other military capabilities. The critical element for supporting African governments is to help build institutions that will allow African states to maintain a monopoly of violence within their own borders. Meeting new complex objectives requires a transformational combatant command that breaks out of the Cold War mindset. AFRICOM is the instrument best equipped to meet these new and complex objectives and counter pan-Islamic terrorist groups in Africa.

A New American Policy for Security in Africa

The U.S. has a national strategic interest in Africa's continued economic development and stability. Maintaining stable and peaceful relations among African states and securing commerce is critical to America's security in the twenty-first century. With a sizable Muslim population and large swaths of ungoverned territory, some argue that Africa will be the next front in a global battle against Islamic militants. To avoid this, U.S. policy should distinguish between Islamic groups that have local and regional objectives and those who openly support the global jihad espoused by al-Qaeda. Seeking a monolithic enemy could create a self-fulfilling prophesy.

It is critical for the United States and its allies to interdict pan-Islamic jihadists and work with more peaceful Islamic groups, seeking out moderates where possible. By acting too forcefully, the U.S. risks alienating more moderate voices in Africa. A reliance on hard power solutions and tactical victories ensures failure in denying the global jihadist insurgency a foothold in Africa. In partnering with African nations in matters of intelligence sharing, law enforcement, military cooperation, and countering the conditions that breed disaffection, the U.S. will strengthen African governments.

The United States, through AFRICOM, can play a productive role in bringing about this vision of a more peaceful, prosperous Africa. It is critical that the U.S. engage in transformational diplomacy in order to bolster the capacity of African nations. Building the foundations for stability and addressing the root causes of conflict will be vital roles for AFRICOM as part of a comprehensive African security policy. The U.S. must form effective relationships with governments, NGOs, religious leaders, and regional and international organizations to resolve existing and emergent conflicts. This course of action will foster positive growth and ensure the stability in an area critical to American national security in the twenty-first century.

Notes

1   "African Muslim Population." http://www.islamicpopulation.com/africa_islam. html (numbers based on figures in 2006 in CIA World Factbook).

2   International Crisis Group. "Islamist Terrorism in the Sahel: Fact or Fiction?" Africa Report. Number 92, March 2005, 4, http://www.crisisgroup.org/library/ documents/africa/west_africa/092_islamist_terrorism_in_the_ sahel_fact_ or_fiction.pdf

3   International Crisis Group. "Islamist Terrorism in the Sahel: Fact or Fiction?" 4.

4   Baz Lecocq and Paul Schrijver, "The War on Terror in a Haze of Dust: Potholes and Pitfalls on the Saharan Front," *Journal of Contemporary African Studies*, vol. 25, no. 2, January 2007, 14, http://www.kidal.info/docs/War-on-Terror-JCAS.pdf.

5   International Crisis Group, "Islamism in North Africa I: The Legacies of History," Middle East and North Africa Briefing, Number 12. April 2004, 3, http://www.crisisgroup.org/home/index.cfm?id=2618&CFID=40874116 &CFTOKEN=65337346.

6   Princeton N. Lyman and J. Stephen Morrison, "The Terrorist Threat in Africa," Foreign Affairs, vol. 83, no. 1, January/February 2004.

7   George W. Bush, "National Security Strategy of the United States of America," March 2006, 9, http://www.whitehouse.gov/nsc/nss/2006/nss2006.pdf.

8   David Kilcullen, "Countering Global Insurgency," Small Wars Journal, November 2004, http://www. smallwarsjournal.com/documents/kilcullen.pdf.

9   "Pan Sahel Initiative," U.S. Department of State, Office of the Coordinator for Counterterrorism, November 7, 2002, www.state.gov/s/ct/rls/other/14987.htm.

10   "Operation Enduring Freedom—Trans Sahara, http://www.globalsecurity.org/ military/ops/oef-ts.htm.

11   Evan F. Kohlman, "Two Decades of Jihad in Algeria: the GIA, the GSPC, and Al-Qaida," The NEFA Foundation, May 2007, http://nefafoundation.org/ miscellaneous/nefagspc0507.pdf.

12   "Combined Joint Task Force—Horn Of Africa Fact Sheet," Web site of U.S. Central Command, http://www.hoa.centcom.mil/factsheet.asp.

13   Combined Joint Task Force—Horn of Africa Fact Sheet.

14   Lyman and Morrison, "Terrorist Threat in Africa."

15   Eliza Griswold, "Occupational Hazard: The Other Failed Invasion," The New Republic, August 6, 2007, http://www.netnomad.com/2007/08/other-failed-invasion.html.

16   Dr. Ayman al-Zawahiri, audio message issued by as-Sahab addressed to Muslims: "Set Out and Support Your Brothers in Somalia," January 2007, http:// counterterrorismblog. org/site-resources /images/SITE%20Institute%20-%20 1-4-07%20 %20Zawahiri%20Audio%20Support% 20Somali%20Brothers.pdf.

17   "About U.S. Africa Command," http://www.africom.mil/AboutAFRICOM .asp.

Africa's Offshore Future

Richard Mehring and Daniel Trapp

Africa's importance to U.S. strategic interests derives from many sources, but particularly in the continent's energy supplies. Some commentators have speculated that ensuring the security of oil supplies sits high atop the agenda of AFRICOM, the United States' new combatant command for the continent. West Africa has geostrategic value, with oil reserves that lie substantially closer to the United States and Europe than those of the Persian Gulf states, yet in countries such as Nigeria and Angola, conflict threatens energy extraction.[1] As African energy has started to play an increasingly important role on the world stage and failed states or troubled governments become an important part of decisions made around the globe, U.S. policy makers need to understand the basic issues at play and the main geopolitical and market issues that will shape the debate for decades to come. This chapter will examine future opportunities in western Africa from two angles: the developments and trends in relations to western African offshore reserves, and the security environment in which energy companies are forced to operate when lifting oil in Africa's two largest producers.

The future of African energy lies off its shores in new fields far from most of the marauding bandits that threaten energy production. Nigeria and Angola form the centers of gravity in current and future West African energy. The two countries have a respective 36.2 and 9 billion bbl of proven oil reserves. According to the *Oil & Gas Journal* in 2008, "Offshore West Africa is poised to become an important source of oil and gas supplies for global consumption, with 6.5 billion bbl of oil discovered in the last 2 years alone."[2] Deepwater[3] African discoveries are particularly important. In 2005, the *Oil and Gas Journal* made the dramatic prediction that deepwater production would climb from "just 1% of total production across West Africa" in 2000 to as much as 50 percent by 2010, potentially approaching 3.5 mbpd of liquids production.[4] In short, the future of West African oil lies off its shores.

This chapter will examine future opportunities in western Africa from two angles. First, it will consider recent developments and trends in relation to western African offshore reserves. Second, it will consider the security environment in which energy companies are forced to operate when lifting oil in Africa's two largest producers.

Overview of Offshore Resources in West Africa

Exploration and production in West Africa is centered around the Gulf of Guinea, with the majority of economically viable energy reserves lying on and around Nigerian and Angolan territory. These nations have traditionally represented challenging operating environments, having never developed institutions to maintain either transparency or an equitable distribution of wealth.[5]

In the past decade, offshore operations have enjoyed increased viability thanks in part to high oil prices. Geographic distance from the shore has fostered a better security environment for offshore production, making for more palatable conditions for international oil companies (IOCs). There are several other reasons for the upward trend of deepwater production in Africa. Recent high prices made deepwater production viable as the expensive technological investment required to recover oil was offset by high or projected revenues. In certain areas, instability and unrest have made offshore development an attractive alternative to more vulnerable onshore production. The offshore environment has also provided a certain haven for IOCs operating in West Africa, and not only in terms of physical security; the offshore environment has at times provided more technologically endowed IOCs a degree of liberty from the official regulatory constraints that, onshore, might be more stifling.[6] Offshore wells also provide a measure of convenience, as oil pumped from them can be loaded directly onto tankers. In short, rising global demand for oil, and its correspondingly rising price, along with less hospitable onshore conditions, has made these areas newly viable.

Despite corrupt governments and instability, IOCs continue to see value in developing fields in the region. Foreign companies operate in Nigeria under joint ventures with the National Nigeria Petroleum Corporation (NNPC) and include Shell, ExxonMobil, Chevron, ConocoPhillips, Total, Agip, and Addax Petroleum. Angolan development is led by its NOC, Sociedade Nacional de Combustiveis de Angola (Sonangol), which has both joint ventures and production sharing agreements (PSAs) with several Western firms. Recently, Chinese oil company Sinopec has become involved in Angola. Nigerian and Angolan offshore production represents a sizeable component of IOC portfolios. Shell, for instance, counts 20 percent of its global oil reserves from Nigerian fields. Although these countries may present a challenging environment, the prospect of pulling out of these markets, and incurring a large write-down in oil reserves, is a step that none of these companies appears ready to take.

Nigeria

Nigeria began deepwater oil production in 2003 with the small Abo field. In 2005 the larger Bonga field, with estimated recoverable reserves of 600 million barrels, operated by Royal Dutch Shell, began production of up to 225,000 barrels per day.[7] Exxon-Mobil, whose production in Nigeria accounts for about 750,000 bpd, looks to increase its production in the country to 1.2 mbpd by 2011.[8]

Joint ventures between major IOCs and the NNPC accounted for over 95 percent of Nigeria's production.[9] The Nigerian government has lately undertaken efforts to reform the country's oil sector. Nigerian President Umaru Yar'Adua, elected in May 2007, is, according to one source, "conducting a root and branch reform of the NNPC." In 2007 he announced the disbanding of the NNPC and the forming of a new organization, the

National Petroleum Company of Nigeria (NAPCON) that would reconstitute several of its predecessor's responsibilities, less "its present regulatory and policy-making functions." Partial privatization of the NNPC is also reportedly under consideration. While these reforms have not yet been put fully into practice, Yar'Adua's actions continue a trend among recent leaders to develop more responsible government. President Yar'Adua referred to the NNPC in 2007, however, as "one of the most difficult agencies of government to tackle" due to "the vested interest of very powerful people in the country."[10] Also, the NNPC of recent months has required loans from operators to fulfill its joint venture commitments.

According to the Energy Information Administration, "deepwater projects may represent the future of Nigerian oil production by allowing multinational operators to avoid security risks inherent to the unstable Niger Delta region."[11] Recent developments, however, have not been encouraging. Recent attacks on oil infrastructure in Nigeria have had a substantial effect, forcing repeated shut-ins that are seriously affecting operations in the country.[12] The resulting drop in exports has left the country in second place to fellow OPEC member[13] Angola as Africa's largest oil producer.[14] As of June 2008, of forty-four Nigerian blocks on offer for development, only four have been developed, while of Angola's menu of only twenty-two, the figure was nineteen.[15] The disruptions in Nigeria this summer, coming as they did as Saudi Arabia agreed to increase production by 200,000 bpd, served to demonstrate the influence of Nigerian production on the international energy market.[16] In a global energy market short on spare capacity, even the shortfalls of an individual nation like Nigeria can have broad effects.[17]

At a reported 1.5 mbpd, Nigeria is currently producing well below its potential. Attacks, such as the one in June 2008 on Shell's Bonga field seventy-five miles offshore, have also demonstrated that offshore facilities are not as immune to violence as conventional wisdom previously may have held. Shell has had to declare[18] *force majeure* on a substantial share of its production commitments.[19] It continues to suffer from the effects of corrupt governance and endemic violence.[20]

(Lack of) Nigerian Security Affects the Global Markets

Nigerian oil has been shut in by significant violence and unrest in the Delta. Citizens in the region have complained for decades that although tremendous wealth lies beneath their land, they have had little access to the revenues generated by its extraction. The resulting frustrations have led to near constant violence since the discovery of oil in 1958, including the separatist Biafran War (1967–70) and frequent attacks in the last twenty years from the Movement for the Emancipation of the Niger Delta (MEND), which seeks greater autonomy for the communities of the Delta.

Nigeria faces a combination of other problems, such as corruption, inequality, ineffective development programs, and poor security strategies. Although each problem feeds the other, corruption sits at the heart of why the country is having such a hard time developing.[21] The effects of corruption are not limited to large-scale contracts. The day-to-day activities of average citizens are also affected, creating a systemic challenge that touches on the political, economic, and social lives of the majority of Nigerians who are powerless to confront corrupt officials and merchants.

In 2004 Transparency International wrote that Nigeria has consistently ranked either the most corrupt or second most corrupt nation in the organization's Corruption Perception Index (CPI). Transparency International argues that a number of contributing factors have allowed corruption to take such firm root in the country. Military dictatorships thrived on a culture of corruption. The ruling classes paid no attention to even hiding corruption, thereby established an endemic culture of bribery. There is little political will to curb such activities. Transparency International further commented on Nigeria's youth:

> Serious efforts must be made to salvage the youth, who have developed resistance to every principle of integrity, due primarily to the fact that they have not experienced any other alternative. Integrity doctrines and anti-corruption principles must be incorporated immediately into the school curricula, in order to give young Nigerians a fighting chance.[22]

President Yar'Adua's government has made a priority of such efforts, but has not firmly established solid anticorruption programs during its first two years in office.

MEND funds its activities by stealing oil from pipelines and oil tankers—often with the tacit approval of corrupt Nigerian security officials guarding the facilities[23]—and selling the product in nearby Cameroon. MEND rebels use the revenues to buy arms, pay off corrupt officials, and spread a limited amount to local villages to evoke local support.[24] MEND suspended violence after elections in May 2007, but had decided by October 2007 that the new government was neither willing nor able to address the region's concerns. Since then, MEND has mounted attacks on oil facilities and conducted kidnappings of foreign oil workers and government officials.

The cycle feeds itself. Corrupt government officials have fueled an inequitable system that rewards a powerful few using national resources, while reactionary groups such as MEND will continue to use the pretext of official abuse or neglect to continue their disruptive resistance. Meanwhile, the Delta remains impoverished. Absent a sea change among leaders or outside influences, the cycle will continue.

Angola: Signals of Progress?

Angola, further to the south, shares with Nigeria the African continent's sadly common scourge of violence and unrest. Still, Angola has remained intact and has taken advantage of its oil resources. The majority of the country's 9 million barrels of proven reserves lie offshore, with some important oil reserves both on and offshore of the noncontiguous Cabinda Province to the north. The country's recent distinction as Africa's top oil producer was underlined at the Offshore Technology Conference in Houston, Texas, in May 2008, where Angolan development received attention in the opening session.[25]

Angola has witnessed substantial success in recent years. "Production for 2007 averaged almost 1.7 mbpd and capacity is expected to reach more than 2 mbpd in 2008," with projections that put peak capacity at about 2.5 million.[26] The major IOCs operating in Angola, including Exxon, Chevron, Total, and BP, operate via PSAs and joint ventures with the Angolan

NOC, Sonangol. Angola has a common interest zone with neighboring oil producer Congo-Brazzaville that encompasses blocks that belong to both countries and that are operated by IOCs. The two countries split the profits fifty-fifty.[27]

Though the country is well acquainted with armed conflict, Angola's political leadership has enjoyed significant longevity. The Popular Movement for the Liberation of Angola (MPLA) has ruled the country for the past thirty-three years, and the general election on September 5, 2008 appeared to have legitimized the party's leadership, "with more than 80% of the vote" in elections that appeared to represent some democratic progress.[28]

Sonangol, the Angolan NOC, has a tradition of competence and efficiency. The company emerged from the MPLA's efforts to solidify the nation's oil sector in 1975 and its dominance in the Angolan economy brought a favorable report by the World Bank in the late 1980s.[29] Despite its distinctions at home, however, the company has remained an opaque institution with a tainted history, that included involvement in "the wartime acquisition of arms paid for by future oil production."[30] Yet Sonangol is one of a few resource generators in a country plagued by a poor economic record.

Placing African Offshore Production in a Global Context

The costs and potential benefits of bringing to market an increased supply of African offshore crude warrants examination in comparison with the world's other emerging alternatives for offshore development, such as the Outer Continental Shelf and the deep waters off Brazil. Offshore oil exploration and extraction will likely feature prominently in the industry's future. An author writing in the *Oil & Gas Journal* expressed optimism of offshore oil's prospects in furnishing future supply, noting its historically consistent growth and its importance to production growth, given that "onshore [production] has essentially remained at plateau for more than two decades."[31] Africa's two largest oil producers, Nigeria and Angola, have also witnessed the increased importance of offshore production. As Paul F. Hueper writes in a chapter of the book *Energy and Security*,

The degree to which key producers such as Nigeria and Angola remain among the world's top oil suppliers will depend not only on the favorableness of their ultra-deepwater geology but also on foreign investment for exploration and development. West African oil-producing countries also must implement political agendas and economic policies conducive to ensuring the maintenance of attractive investment environments. This is especially important as the region competes with other newly developing frontier oil and gas provinces around the world.[32]

Conclusion

The global oil market is vulnerable to even local actors, such as MEND, who can produce painful effects by their activities. It is possible that the region could serve to exercise a positive influence on the international oil market by reigning in the problems of corruption and political instability that have hampered development, and by expanding production capacity and hastening development of proven resources. Barring that, allowing for a favorable environment for IOCs to invest and operate offshore, freer from security concerns on land, may serve to bring more oil to market.

Offshore oil production will likely form the cornerstone of West Africa's oil production in the coming decade. Major producers will likely continue to face the political challenges inherent in these markets, including separatist violence and corruption, as well as the technological challenges of drilling in deepwater. Both nations and producers have put some effort into developments that would solve some of the underlying problems inherent in operating in these regions, but neither group has brought about true solutions. International energy companies do not have the capacity to solve each nation's problems. Shell has invested in building projects in the Niger Delta, including schools and infrastructure, but local municipalities either have not had the funding or the will to provide teachers or upkeep, thus leading to potentially good investment faltering at the hands of bad bureaucracy.

In the context of a recovery of global oil demand, high prices will allow countries and energy firms to develop even more expensive fields. Deepwater developments will play an increasingly important role in supplying the market, and with robust growth in China and India as well as the needs of the West, strong demand and high oil prices are likely here to stay. While West Africa has much to offer among its offshore reserves, it suffers from the intractable problems of corruption, unrest, and underdevelopment. While offshore oil production may offer a solution to some of these problems, and warrants the attention and investment of international oil companies, solutions need to be sought if the region is to make good on its potential to be an important, reliable source of supply to the global oil market.

Notes

1   This essay includes Angola in its discussion of West Africa.

2   Uchenna Izundu, "OWA: W. Africa Is Strategic for Global Crude Oil Supplies," *Oil & Gas Journal*, vol. 106:5, February 2008, 31.

3   Defined by Wood Mackenzie Ltd. as 400 meters or more. See Wood Mackenzie's energy glossary, **http://www.woodmacresearch.com/cgi-bin/ wmprod/portal/energy/overview.jsp?overview_title=glossary**

4   James McLennan and Stewart Williams, "Deepwater Africa Reaches Turning Point," *Oil & Gas Journal*, vol. 103:6, February 2005, 18.

5   For more information on transparency in Africa, see Transparency International's "Global Corruption Barometer," **http://www.transparency.org/ policy_research/surveys_indices/gcb**.

6   Shree Vikas, "Part 1: Oil Companies Adjust As Government Roles Expand," *Oil & Gas Journal*, vol. 105, no.12, March 2007.

7   Energy Information Administration, "Country Analysis Briefs: Nigeria," April 2007, **http://www.eia.doe.gov/emeu/cabs/Nigeria/pdf.pdf**.

8   Ibid.

9   Toyin, Falola and Ann Genova, *The Politics of the Global Oil Industry: an Introduction* (Westport: Praeger, 2005), 200.

10   Constance Ikoku, and Juliana Taiwo, "Nigeria: Yar'Adua Restates Resolve to Cleanse Nnpc," *allAfrica.com*, December 15, 2007, http://allafrica.com/ stories/200712150069.html.

11   Energy Information Administration, "Country Analysis Briefs: Nigeria."

12   The U.S. Energy Information Administration reports that current Nigerian
      production is 2.45 million bbl/d, but estimates that the country could
      produce a full 3 million bbl/d if shut-in was reduced (See Energy Information
      Administration, "Country Analysis Briefs: Nigeria"). The June 2008 attacks
      on Shell's offshore Bonga platform temporarily shut-in roughly 200,000 bpd,
      http://m.cnn.com/cnn/archive/archive/detail/128492;jsessionid=5BAAC6BB
      1F4F1092CE752474D86D1C88. The attack on Chevron's pipeline a week later
      shut-in an additional 120,000 bpd, http://www.marketwatch.com/news/story/
      chevron-says-nigerian-oil-pipeline/story.aspx?guid=%7BACF470CE-54D7-
      43A9-B4DB-234FFAEBD108%7D&dist=msr_1.

13   Angola became the twelfth member of OPEC in January 2007, http://www.eia.
      doe.gov/emeu/cabs/Angola/Background.html.

14   "Saudi Arabian Oil Production Hike Negated by Falling Nigerian Output,"
      Energy Business Review Online, June 24, 2008, http://www.energy-business-
      review.com/article_news.asp?guid=50678D1E-7882-4C5E-9F6C-E0753CB3813C.

15   Hector Igbikiowubo, "Oil & Gas Development, Nigeria's Loss, Angola's
      Gain," Vanguard, June 16, 2008, http://www.vanguardngr.com/index.
      php?option=com_content&task=view&id=10308&Itemid=0.

16   "Nigerian Crisis May Spoil Saudi Promise of More Oil," Irish
      Times, June 23, 2008, http://www.irishtimes.com/newspaper/
      finance/2008/0623/1214047001134.html.

17   Daniel Yergin, "Energy Security and Markets" in Energy and Security: Toward
      a New Foreign Policy Strategy, Jan H. Kalicki and David L Goldwyn, eds.,
      (Washington, D.C.: Woodrow Wilson Center Press, 2005) 55; "The Slippery
      Business of Oil," The Economist, June 28, 2008, 55.

18   "Saudi Arabian Oil Production Hike Negated," Energy Business Review Online;
      "Crisis Meeting over Nigeria Oil Attacks," AFP, June 23, 2008, http://afp.google.
      com/article/ALeqM5jlcURE1aBD8_jxzMVIGjVhJ9vMLg.

19   "Crisis meeting," AFP and "Shell extends Force Majeure at Nigerian Terminal,"
      AFP http://afp.google.com/article/ALeqM5hXZPvvrma9iV9S8Kvf1dz7rFHI8A.

20   Cobus De Swardt, "Strategy & Management: Transparency International—
      Counting Corporate Corruption," Ethical Corporation, February 13, 2008,
      http://www.ethicalcorp.com/content.asp?ContentID=5705

21   "Please Hurry Up: People Are Worried about Umaru Yar'Adua's Slow Pace of
      Government," The Economist, October 23, 2008.

22 "Transparency International Country Study Report: Nigeria 2004," *Transparency International*, http://www.google.com/url?sa=U&start=1&q=http://www.transparency.org/content/download/1685/8494/file/nigeria.pdf&usg=AFQjCNF35ssXNc6-XTWQBt502zap7wHKLg, 6–7

23 Braide, Kombo Mason, "The Political Economy of Illegal Bunkering in Nigeria," July 2003, http://www.nigerdeltacongress.com/particles/political_economy_of_illegal_bun.htm.

24 Bestman Wellington, "Weapons of War in the Niger Delta," *Terrorism Monitor*, vol. 5:10, May 24, 2007, http://www.jamestown.org/terrorism/news/article.php?articleid=2373428.

25 Igbikiowubo, "Nigeria's Loss, Angola's Gain," *Vanguard* 2008 Offshore Technology Conference, "Waves of Change," http://www.otcnet.org/2008/release.html.

26 Energy Information Administration, "Country Analysis Briefs: Angola."

27 Ibid.

28 "The People Have Their Say," *The Economist*, September 13, 2008, 56.

29 Ricardo Soares De Oliveira, "Business Success, Angola-style: Postcolonial Politics and the Rise and Rise of Sonangol," *Journal of Modern African Studies*, vol. 45:4 (2007), 602.

30 Ibid., 606–608.

31 Ivan Sandrea, "Exploration Trends Show Continued Promise in World's Offshore Basins," *Oil & Gas Journal*, vol. 105, no. 9, March 2007.

32 *Energy and Security*, 247.

SECTION IV:

AFRICOM and U.S. Military Strategy

U.S. Defense Strategy and African Security

Robert R. Tomes

This chapter provides a strategic perspective on U.S. defense strategy and African security affairs. By placing U.S. defense strategy in context, the intent is to frame issues addressed later in this section and to provide a transition discussions of AFRICOM. The chapter addresses U.S. national security planning and the implications of new security and stability missions. A conclusion suggests areas requiring attention by defense planners.

New requirements to train and equip forces for stabilization, security, transition, and reconstruction missions have cracked the canon of post-Cold War defense strategy and planning. During the 1990s, defense strategy and planning documents struggled for coherence, vision, and relevance. Attempts to provide strategic vision and new planning frameworks failed to link the ends or objectives proscribed in national security strategies to the means or capabilities actually provided by military services, combatant commands, and defense support agencies.

By the mid-2000s, the contours of a new strategic framework for defense strategy and planning gelled among government, think tank, and academic defense strategists. Defense strategists and planners in the Pentagon and warfighting labs were jolted by the experience of Afghanistan and Iraq. Recognizing the mismatch between 1990s force planning and the realities of twenty-first century conflicts, strategists are focused on hybrid conflicts that blur the lines between irregular and conventional missions. While planners in the 1990s believed brigade combat teams and other combat units could be easily adapted to deal with small wars and irregular missions as "lesser included" contingencies, planners in the 2000s have recommended that civil affairs, engineering, and other "support" units be retrained and adapted to be the main effort. Support units have the requisite core skills; maneuver forces are now the supporting units.

The chapters in this section address defense planning challenges in Africa and the creation of the U.S. Africa Command (AFRICOM), a hybrid combatant command reflecting the Defense Department's increasing focus on "Phase Zero" activities. This chapter frames the issues and arguments explored by others to provide additional perspective on key aspects of defense strategy and planning.

Quo Vadis U.S. Defense Strategy?

Defense strategy is in flux. From the 1991-1992 Gulf War through the 2003 Invasion of Iraq, U.S. defense strategy was inundated with the language and arguments about American armed forces exhibiting a significant, discontinuous increase in military effectiveness, loosely defined as the mechanism through which nations turn their resources into military or combat power. Defense strategy in the 1990s was largely a continuation of an "offset strategy" implemented in the late 1970s to increase U.S. military capabilities vis-à-vis the Soviet Union, to bolster the North Atlantic Treaty Organization's (NATO) conventional deterrence posture to reduce reliance on nuclear weapons, and to leverage the power of the dawning information age. The offset strategy worked surprising well.

Vowing "no more Vietnams," the U.S. Department of Defense (DoD) focused on European security issues and the defense of NATO throughout the 1970s and 1980s. By the end of the Cold War, the U.S. had fielded revolutionary intelligence, precision strike, stealth, and other capabilities optimized for high-intensity warfare in Central European. America became proficient in and dominated high-intensity, combined arms conventional warfare. In retrospect, however, dominating the middle—or force-on-force—part of the conflict spectrum encouraged adversaries and competitors to design around U.S. advantages, seeking asymmetric advantages at opposing ends of the spectrum: weapons of mass destruction on the one end and terrorism, insurgency, and other indirect means on the other.

From the 1970s through the early 2000s, meanwhile, military planners assumed the United States would not get involved in protracted counter-insurgency operations, would avoid urban combat, and would not commit significant forces to foreign internal defense or pacification. Any "small war" or intervention mission could be managed by existing forces, which would be deployed only with overwhelming numerical superiority, clear objectives for victory, and a withdrawal plan. Moreover, defense strategists largely focused on keeping American military forces out of third world entanglements and prolonged peace keeping missions.

Defense strategists should take note of an important trend. Whenever transnational, regional, or state-specific security problems are defined as affecting *American* security policies or objectives, they become characterized as threatening American interests and, eventually, are re-defined in military terms. Because the U.S. Defense Department is perceived a) to have abundant resources, b) to have the best planners and easy access to current information, and c) to be an action-oriented culture, it is easier for bureaucrats and policymakers to build momentum for military solutions to what are essentially complex *social* and *political* problems. If history is a guide, the military dimensions of African problems and their solutions will increasingly be amplified within policy debates as military problems or as having a military dimension.

Unfortunately, it is quite difficult to reconcile the capabilities planners and policymakers identify on paper vis-à-vis those that can be operationalized and delivered. It is even harder to sustain operations unless the White House commits political capital to mobilize support when casualties or setbacks occur. Long-term missions become an especially hard sell when the boots on the ground are treading on African soil without clear military objectives and reasonable measurements for success.

The international community, however, has begun adopting a "responsibility to protect" approach that calls upon nations to intervene to protect people from crimes against humanity, natural disasters, and pandemics.

Meanwhile, China, India, Brazil, Russia, the EU, Japan, and others are committing additional resources to Africa, primarily to lay claims to natural resources and to expand trade with African states. Increased engagement is sparking renewed focus on security and stability as a prerequisite for investment, anti-corruption programs, and government capacity building.

When thinking about future conflicts in Africa, Asia, and Latin America, defense planners must recognize and overcome the effects of decades of strategic tunnel vision. Indeed, defense planners have a long history of underestimating the challenges of security and stabilization missions. There is no easy button for security operations.

Resetting expectations for African security missions will be a tough task given that a particular paradox formed at the core of U.S. strategic thought in the 1990s. The paradox stemmed from the incongruity between arguments against expanding capabilities for "small wars" and constabulary missions and others favoring intervention. The paradox was temporarily resolved when planners simply assumed that the ongoing American "revolution in military affairs" would yield forces possessing capacity for any mission. Additionally, when defense budgets decreased in the 1990s, the U.S. Armed Services focused planning activities on saving prized programs designed for Cold War battles.

A number of factors, therefore, coalesced into a defense strategy and planning blind spot in 1990s:

- overconfidence in advanced surveillance and reconnaissance systems and the adaptability of U.S. military forces;

- misplaced dependence on international organizations and regional partners;

- a deep-seated, post-Vietnam cultural antipathy to small wars and interventions;

- an indulgent acceptance of "new world order" theorizing.

This blind spot was exposed by the wars in Afghanistan and Iraq, which suggested even deeper problems with defense strategy and planning processes across the interagency national security complex.

The Quadrennial Defense Review (QDR)

How is defense planning adapting to address the security missions required to deal with hybrid threats? The *Quadrennial Defense Review* is among the most important DoD strategic planning documents, intended to provide a strategic framework and key mission areas to inform defense programming and budgeting processes. The 2006 QDR provided a small set of near-term military threats to shape capabilities-based planning efforts:

- a global Islamic insurgency that thrived on instability, took advantage of failed governments, and required physical and ideological safe havens to survive;

- a rising China with expanding interests and increased military capabilities; and

- the proliferation of weapons of mass destruction and disruption that might threaten the homeland or U.S. forces overseas.

Regrettably, the QDR failed to provide a coherent strategic vision for how the U.S. defense planning bureaucracy might prioritize across these threats or manage risks created by re-allocating funds at the expense of legacy programs. Moreover, the QDR emphasized the requirement to sustain ongoing war efforts and prepare for the advent of budget cuts. The document did not prepare planners to in the Services and Commands "to do more" (sustain the war, modernize, prepare for additional missions) "with less" (shrinking budgets, readiness issues, fewer high-technology platforms).

The 2010 QDR should strive to recast planning and programming assumptions and establish the critical, strategic importance of security missions. From a grand strategy perspective, U.S. vital interests include energy security, managing infectious diseases, and continuing the expansion of the Western, liberal political and economic model that is the core of international political and economic life. Future missions will likely find the Army and Marine Corps on the ground in Africa (including in dangerous, sprawling urban slums), the Navy patrolling African coasts (assuming interdiction and enforcement missions), and the Air Force providing support, over-watch, and mobility for multi-lateral stabilization missions.

The 2010 QDR process can bring additional clarity to future strategic programming and budgeting cycles by developing more realistic scenarios, games, and mission area assessments for security missions. Africa is a region where U.S. national interests are present but ill-defined in terms of threats and opportunities. By working through African security and stability issues with new scenarios and war games, planners can drive security and stabilization capabilities deeper into the capabilities based planning cycle.

The Obama administration will likely seek to establish American leadership by supporting new African peace missions, increase maritime security and patrolling along dangerous African coasts, and prevent future African crises from becoming catastrophes. A number of other issues may receive attention, including slavery and trafficking in humans and drugs.

The 2010 QDR will be the first in which stability and security operations are considered a primary mission, not "lesser included contingencies." No longer do planners adhere to the argument that forces trained for high-intensity conventional operations can manage security missions.

Shifting U.S. defense and military resources to address new missions is difficult under normal circumstances. Doing so is near-impossible today given the U.S. economic crisis, budget deficit, and devastating long-term effects of Afghanistan and Iraq on equipment readiness and recapitalization. It is likely that U.S. defense planners are going to be asked to do more with less. The Obama economic stimulus plan, coming on the heels of economic bailouts, will likely accelerate arguments for budget contraction and reduced commitments. The Obama team will seek to curtail spending, protect party seats in the mid-term elections, and meet 2008 campaign promises to support a 2012 re-election victory.

The Obama administration intends to restore America's image abroad, rebuild confidence in U.S. leadership, and commit American power and influence to what have traditionally been peripheral security issues: human security, the environment and global warming, renewable energy resources, and partnering with international organizations. All of this suggests that his defense leadership will strive to revise the QDR process, find the means to support interventions and security missions, and draft a new defense strategy that incorporates the multilateral, pro-cooperation tone of the 2007 maritime strategy. The next QDR should be validated and assessed by outside experts with an eye to pushing for fundamental changes in U.S. defense strategy and planning processes.

Addressing African Security Missions

Africa is for the first time a contested sphere of U.S. great power influence, leadership, and performance. It is also an emerging continent-sized zone of competition over the future of the liberal, Western, largely American economic, social, and political global political system. Since the late nineteenth century, the American model of economic and political liberalization has been the most important U.S. export. Keeping foreign markets and societies open to U.S. trade and American political ideals has been the route to stability and security at home. Africa is no exception.

Nearly a decade ago, national security strategy documents tended to place Africa last among other regions. 1990s defense strategy and planning documents often described U.S. interests in Africa as limited or did not mention Africa at all. In 2002 the State Department declared West African oil to be a vital U.S. national interest, making energy security the first of many African security issues that were defined as being a "U.S. national interest."

A number of factors prevent African issues and security concerns from influencing planning processes, scenario-based capabilities assessments, and mission area risk analyses—some of the activities that inform QDR and other planning documents.

There are no sizable military forces in Africa. Because there are no serious challenges to U.S. military forces, Africa is a poor replacement for a rising China or other "near-term" peer competitor in planning processes designed to help planners make acquisition trades across billion-dollar weapons systems.

For decades, policies, doctrine, and strategic planning guidance have created the expectation that the United States will not become entangled in counterinsurgencies, small wars, or prolonged peace operations. This excluded serious security mission assessments during planning processes altogether. AFRICOM, which does not have any assigned combat forces, is really a hybrid command intended to focus and support U.S. interagency efforts in Africa. Yet the principle of interagency engagement is not adequately represented in the QDR process and there are no serious external reviews of the logic underscoring the force structure and policy prescriptions embedded in the document itself.

A staggering number of security challenges, driven by environmental, geographical, historical, cultural, and geological factors make African security issues the most challenging and most interesting areas for foreign policy practitioners. Challenges include energy security, water and food security, the promotion of democracy and governance, curbing endemic corruption, grappling with open borders and immigration problems, combating the AIDS/HIV pandemic and controlling other infectious diseases, building regional organizations and security forces, and impeding the emergence and growth of criminal networks, including those engaged in the trafficking of narcotics, humans, small arms, and stolen diamonds, oil, and other resources. Prospects do not look good for containing such a broad range of local crises imbedded with regional and global security implications.

African democracies are developing and maturing and thus featuring dramatically more *peaceful* changes in leadership compared to the postcolonial years. Despite notable exceptions, however, most African democracies are not developing government services and power sharing systems conducive to long-term stability. Corruption remains endemic and the middle class has often accepted corruption and poor governance out of fear that its position will be undermined if the government falls.

African nations may be spared from the worst of the 2008 global economic crisis because they are not as integrated into the global financial system. Modest economic growth projections, nevertheless, will likely not meet the expectations of the exploding youth population. Moreover, forced migration and voluntary immigration have resulted in new waves of African nationalism and xenophobia, with violent protests threatening stability and increasing the attractiveness of gangs, participation in criminal activities, and membership in militias formed to preserve ethnic, kinship, political, religious, or other identities. Military capabilities and intervention cannot directly solve these challenges. Nonetheless, intervention is critical to creating the conditions and opportunities to do so—a topic addressed elsewhere in this volume.

The objective of future deployments will not be regime change, occupation, or counterinsurgency. The United States, with allies and partners, will increasingly deploy military and policy forces to provide the security and stability required for development and government capacity-building efforts. Africa, not Afghanistan and Iraq, will likely be the source of innovation in security, stabilization, peace-enforcement missions.

Recommendations for Defense Strategy

A number of areas hold promise for defense strategists and planners to infuse realism into defense strategy and policy processes regarding the capabilities needed to succeed in hybrid conflicts.

A) Understand what 'Being at War' Means: The most important factor for defense planners is continuing to challenge conventional wisdom regarding the role of the military in twenty-first century conflicts. A starting point is resetting expectations about how defense department resources address vital and significant U.S. interests across all potential mission areas.

Instead of viewing the 1991 Gulf War as the first war of the post-Cold War period, it is more appropriately viewed as the last major war of the twentieth century. The first wars of the twenty-first century—the true post-Cold War conflicts—began in the 1990s. A war has been waging in "cyberspace" for at least a decade, with state and non-state (criminal) belligerents. The long war against Islamic jihadists has been ongoing within Muslim societies for decades but only became a war for the United States when the jihadists changed their strategic focus to the "far enemy"—the U.S. government and American society itself. A global war against criminal networks and cartels also emerged in the 1990s, with a more sophisticated set of global gangs, criminal enterprises, and families collaborating against international policy organizations. Security and stability missions are part of a larger war to preserve and expand the current, Western, largely American vision for international political and economic life. Africa is a key theater in this larger war.

B) Leverage European Partners: Our European partners have vastly more experience in Africa than we do. Some colonial powers retain excellent information and intelligence capabilities, a unique perspective on local conditions that America does not possess, and better training and education institutions (including language training). One of AFRICOM's strategic investments should be building a collaborative network of European information and intelligence services and building the network of experts required to deal with local, unique African security challenges. Africa is an incredibly diverse and dynamic continent that is too often reduced to a homogenous one. Each security challenge is unique, and other nations have far more experience. Listening and learning to European friends and allies will prove to be a strategic enabling factor for defense planners and strategists.

C) Tailor Intelligence and Information Support: AFRICOM will take years, perhaps a decade, to build its information and intelligence capabilities. It is unwise to think that the addition of several hundred people to staff AFRICOM's intelligence analysis billets will provide a net addition to U.S. intelligence capabilities. First, the U.S. intelligence community does not possess a significant number of Africa specialists. AFRICOM is securing its experts from a closed system, drawing its staff from other commands or a small community of think tank academic, and government analysts.

Second, many of the analysts hired to fill AFRICOM positions will be new to their accounts, perhaps even to African security affairs, and thus not truly the "experts" this critical new command requires. They are likely to ask more questions of the intelligence community than they answer. Finally, Africa has never ranked at the top of the list of intelligence priorities. Indeed, one senior intelligence community leader recently commented that, while it is very difficult to say "no" to senior policymakers asking for intelligence support, they still say "no" when it comes to shifting collection and analysis resources to Africa.

AFRICOM is a hybrid command that requires a new intelligence and information support infrastructure. Much of the information required to support AFRICOM operations can be provided by tailored open source collection and analysis. Yet this requires more than merely making huge volumes of open source data available. Analysis and reporting capabilities should be expanded: new, targeted collection and reporting resources should be allocated to AFRICOM and others. AFRICOM should partner with the U.S. State Department in creating a new African Information Support Agency.

D) Build the Africa Map: A critical part of this open source collection and analysis effort must be building the "Africa Map." What is needed is a geospatial intelligence and data layer framework that includes dozens and subsequently hundreds of data layers to provide analysts and policymakers with greater insight into all aspects of African society, history, culture, politics, and environmental conditions. Additionally, airborne sensors can be used to collect and refresh the data layers and provide the basis for new monitoring and reporting capabilities. A priority should be documenting all of the cadastral data we can unearth. The Human Terrain System should be revamped and rendered more operationally relevant.

E) Continue to Make Security Operations the Core of Training: Military planners should consider the early twenty-first century a repetition of the early twentieth in terms of an upswing in American interventionism and military "open door" deployments. The expectation is for America to actually lead, to act, and to join multilateral stabilization efforts as the Obama administration attempts to recast and rebuild America's image as a "humble and restrained" power. Returning officials from the Clinton administration have a history of supporting interventionism, including promoting international efforts to intervene in Darfur. Some criticized President Clinton for amplifying the missionary tradition and militarizing U.S. foreign policy as part of flawed strategy to pursue political and economic derivatives of globalization. Removing barriers and promoting integration to further globalization remains a chief component of U.S. security strategy.

The military services and the Army in particular have pushed significant changes in doctrine, training, and force planning to address security and stabilization operations that were largely ignored in the 1990s. These operations will require shifting some of the shrinking defense budget from high-cost weapons systems that are already being considered too expensive given the economic crisis. But shifting additional funds from weapons systems designed to fight wars to capabilities designed for security and stabilization missions will likely incur Congressional backlash. Security and stabilization missions do not require expensive weapons systems, which means jobs in key districts may be at risk.

F) Adapt the Capabilities Based Planning (CBP) Process: Defense strategy and planning processes should be opened to external participants, input, and perhaps even critical review as outside experts ponder how "capabilities" are derived from planning scenarios, mission analysis, and assessments that are often biased to protect existing Service programs. Done right, the requirement to increase the rigor and objectively of capabilities based planning will strain an already over-burdened and sometimes contrived process, forcing the DoD and the Joint Staff to revamp their processes and include additional representatives.

G) Prepare for Support Roles: The Obama administration seems likely to advocate multilateral missions to address human security challenges, including food security, genocide, and regional crises. In the past, the U.S. has been reluctant to place U.S. forces under foreign leadership or control. It seems unlikely that this preference can continue. At the very least it seems plausible that U.S. support will be provided as an adjunct to maneuver forces provided by others, perhaps playing an advisory role or providing forms intelligence support that does require troops to be on the ground conducting missions under a UN or other commander. At home, defense planners should become more willing and able to lend their talents, resources, and experience to interagency missions that will be led by other departments and agencies.

AFRICOM: An Attempt to Fill Regional Security Voids

Matthew A. Shabat

AFRICOM came to life in the context of three simultaneous trends—the crystallization of U.S. strategic interests in Africa, the emergence of a bias favoring security solutions at regional levels, and the recognition that U.S. interagency coordination is often ineffective, especially at the regional level. While AFRICOM's attributes are necessary to address these matters, the combatant command is not a sufficient solution, due to critical drawbacks. Additional interagency reforms studies should continue, and those related to African regional coordination should maintain AFRICOM in their solution sets.

The context for U.S.-Africa policies and engagement has been changed by four factors. First, there is general recognition that regional engagement strategies have become more important components of national security strategy. Successful regional engagement requires both strong bilateral engagements with key states as well as support to regional and sub-regional organizations. Second, U.S. interagency decision making, policy implementation, and execution capacities are widely criticized as insufficient and unable to manage complex issues. Critics call for an integrated, sustained strategic planning, coordination, and management capability. Better interagency coordination is desperately needed at the national, regional and country levels of engagement.[1]

Third, the imperative to muster and apply all the elements of national power—military, economic, diplomatic, and others—has focused attention on the operational requirements to truly engage in Africa. Finally, on a number of increasingly important issues Africa is emerging as a key regional crossroads for political, economic, and ideological competition or cooperation.

The U.S. Africa Command (AFRICOM) materialized in the context of these four trends after a history of debate on the utility of adding a regional combatant command to pursue American interests on the continent. AFRICOM carries advantages and drawbacks, discussed below. To prevent drawbacks from becoming liabilities, the Obama administration should consider additional interagency reforms to further integrate U.S. instruments of national power. This chapter outlines a way ahead.

U.S. National Security and Africa

AFRICOM's creation followed a "realization that the current state of affairs in sub-Saharan Africa poses a serious threat to American interests."[2] U.S. strategic interests in Africa vary depending on the country or region as well as the specific issue.

U.S. interests in West Africa and the Gulf of Guinea primarily focus on hydrocarbons, manufacturing industries, and potential markets for U.S. goods. Southern Africa is also rich with natural resources, including hydrocarbons and various metals. Some countries in East Africa possess hydrocarbon resources. The primary U.S. interest in the east is the Horn of Africa's counterterrorism efforts, managed by Combined Joint Task Force—Horn of Africa (CJTF-HOA). With respect to Central Africa, natural resources are of interest to the United States, but a central concern is preventing the region's instability and frequent violence from spilling across regions. Forced migration, displaced persons, refugee camps, ethic violence, warlordism, and infectious diseases are among the principle challenges in Central Africa.

In North Africa, U.S. concerns also focus on counterterrorism and energy development, primarily with respect to terrorists from Africa entering Europe and the development of oil and natural gas fields for European markets. Radicalization, a process that feeds on poverty and unmet aspiration, is a key concern. A 2007 estimate concluded that some one quarter of foreign fighters in Iraq are of North African origin.[3] Radicalism and violence within North Africa, meanwhile, threaten the stability of strategic energy projects. The development of natural gas deposits in North Africa will offer Europe an alternative to Russian and Caspian Sea sources, which currently account for over 50 percent of Europe's energy imports.[4]

Additional interests in Africa include overcoming poverty; controlling infectious diseases; promoting social justice and good governance; reversing continued environmental degradation; enhancing agricultural production; building infrastructure; safeguarding water, sea, and land transportation corridors; and moderating ethnic and other conflicts.

Defense Department efforts include the CJTF-HOA, the Trans-Sahara Counter-Terrorism Partnership, the African Contingency Operations Training and Assistance (ACOTA) Program, initiatives with the International Military Education and Training (IMET) initiatives, and a range of other security assistance programs such as the U.S. Naval Forces Europe's African Partnership Station.

The State Department actively oversees and supports ACOTA and other peacekeeper training programs through its Global Peace Operations Initiative while engaging diplomatically with states and multilateral organizations within and outside of Africa. The U.S. Agency for International Development (USAID) oversees numerous development, humanitarian assistance, and governance programs. The Treasury Department participates in World Bank and International Monetary Fund programs targeting development on the continent. The Departments of Agriculture and Commerce assist in knowledge transfers.

Many of these programs also attempt to expose African government, business, and military leaders to U.S. concepts of governance, social justice, and business practices. With such a vast array of programs underway in Africa and focused on unique regions, states, and problem sets, the need for effective coordination is readily apparent.

In pursuit of its interests, the United States is slowly bringing its enormous military, diplomatic, economic, agricultural, technological, and cultural resources to bear. The new Command's headquarters is designed to facilitate interagency coordination, partner with other nations on African security, political, and development efforts, and build bilateral and multilateral relationships.

Importance of Regional Solutions: Africa's Security Complexes

U.S. government activities within any foreign nation are supposed to be coordinated through the Chief of Mission at the U.S. embassy through country teams designed "to grant the Ambassador the means to coordinate all U.S. Government activities to maximize the effectiveness of U.S. foreign policy in the country to which he or she is assigned."[5] Military operations, however, are sometimes coordinated first at the regional combatant command level of organization using a different interagency process that may or may not overlap with the country teams themselves. Initiatives conceived through defense partnerships often lack the U.S. interagency representation required for strategic planning and the regional diplomatic coordination needed to engage in complex operations.

It is helpful to consider security issues facing AFRICOM as bundled into regional "security complexes." The concept is straightforward: "Since most threats travel more easily over short distances than over long ones, security interdependence is normally patterned into regionally based clusters: security complexes."[6] While this observation may seem obvious, it leads to the logical supposition that "[p]rocesses of securitization and thus the degree of security interdependence are more intense between the actors inside such complexes than they are between actors inside the complex and those outside it."[7]

Africa is probably best divided into five regional security complexes.

These include the Maghreb, West Africa, Southern Africa, Central Africa, and the Horn of Africa. Some geographical formations provide physical boundaries for the regions, but they are generally situated around a local state power, such as Nigeria in western Africa, which "sits at the cent[er] of a set of security interactions connecting it to its immediate neighbors, but with limits of power meaning that these individual patterns have not as a rule linked significantly into wider patterns of security interdependence."[8]

A security complex approach focuses attention to regional actors and issues but allows for the inclusion of continent-wide and transnational issues as well. Because the security complex framework places issues and their resolution in the context of local challenges and regional actors, it provides a useful starting point to rethink security policies. Indeed, the U.S. has often sought to impose solutions to social and political problems from the outside rather than patient and sustained engagement within the nations and regions of Africa. African conflicts generally evolve locally and then assume a regional dimension. Regional responses and solutions are necessary earlier on.

This is recognized in the development of regional conflict mechanisms, such as the Economic Community of West African States and the Southern African Development Community (SADC). The emergence of security mechanisms within Africa's regions must be viewed in conjunction with the creation of the African Union (AU) in 2002. Although the nascent AU faces internal coordination and authority issues, especially relating to security, it clearly reflects the desire of African leaders to provide their own solutions to Africa's problems. Collectively, the AU and regional organizations offer international actors, such as the United States, the U.N., the European Union and nongovernmental organizations, legitimate African mechanisms through which to address security concerns.

The U.S. Interagency

Political, economic and social interactions occur more regularly within regions than between them, and more readily within the African continent than between it and its neighbors. Given increasing interest among international actors competing on the continent, AFRICOM will have to work more closely with multiple country teams, interagency representatives, and foreign partners to develop and negotiate multinational, regionally-based strategies. Throughout, the U.S. must keep in mind that it is not always the most influential or most desired "partner."

Interagency coordination problems exist at the national, regional, and country levels. Nationally, the National Security Council (NSC) system, interagency bodies such as the National Counterterrorism Center and the Office of the Director of National Intelligence, and so-called "designated lead agencies" all compete with entrenched, powerful Executive Branch departments and agencies. The NSC staff and others attempt to coordinate and integrate activities but often lack necessary authority. In the absence of centralized control, department and agency personnel tend to operate within their own stovepipes.

Coordination problems do not always improve when the president designates a lead agency, such as the State Department and its Office of the Coordinator for Stabilization and Reconstruction. Lead agency approaches work only when combined with sustained interest and leadership by the president and his most senior staff.

A number of problems plague the lead agency process. A lead agency cannot control the resources of other agencies. Without such control, it lacks necessary influence. Lead agency personnel are not provided clear lines of authority over personnel from other agencies assigned to work the issue. In general, the personnel systems of different agencies are not unified. As a result, lead agencies are not involved in the employee evaluations of personnel from other agencies, which limits the incentives of personnel to follow instructions from the lead agency, especially when those instructions run counter to instructions from their own superiors.

Similar problems present themselves at the country level. At the Country Team, the chief of mission has decision authority over which interagency personnel may work within the Country Team, but he holds no authority over U.S. resources outside of the State Department. As already indicated, he enjoys no authority over Country Teams for which he is not chief of mission. Another country-level mechanism, the Provincial Reconstruction Teams (PRTs) of Afghanistan and Iraq, suffer similar authority, resource, and personnel problems. A PRT leader cannot effectively control the availability of personnel from other departments such as the Departments of Agriculture or Justice.

Interagency coordination is challenging at the national and country levels, where mechanisms and processes have existed long enough for best practices and cross-organizational relationships to evolve. The U.S. government has yet to build coordination processes and organizations optimized for the regional issues, organizations, and complex issues that define many African security problems.

Most departments and agencies have some form of regional integration process, such as regional bureaus at the State Department and USAID or geographic offices at the Central Intelligence Agency. They tend to focus on policy integration to de-conflict and align efforts across the organization, improving coordination and cooperation. Often they focus on improving information sharing. They are often unable to implement or directly execute operations or to integrate operations involving more than one agency. The U.S. government generally creates regional coordination mechanisms for specific issues such as counter-narcotic interdiction in Latin America, the mission of Joint Interagency Task Force—South. Other than these organizations, which are often temporary and focused on specific missions, only the Defense Security Cooperation Agency and regional combatant commands function in both coordination and implementation roles.

The Benefits of AFRICOM

AFRICOM has the potential to improve U.S. policy coordination and implementation in five important areas. First, it consolidates responsibility for African matters within one command and under one combatant commander. The U.S. Unified Command Plan (UCP) assigns an area of responsibility (AOR) to each of the military's unified combatant commands. Revisions to the UCP in 1983 shifted regional combatant command assignments such that four commands—U.S. European Command (EUCOM), U.S. Central

Command (CENTCOM), U.S. Atlantic Command (USACOM)[9] and U.S. Pacific Command (PACOM)—shared responsibility for Africa. Sharing AORs divided responsibility and made it "difficult for the U.S. to prioritize its regional security interests and pursue them consistently."[10]

Such difficulties resulted from two underlying problems. The absence of a command dedicated to Africa "led to institutional disinterest in the region, leaving the military bereft of African expertise," while generally preventing African problems from being "elevated within the Pentagon to a level commensurate with their importance."[11] Unity of command within the military will improve U.S. military coordination on the continent.

Second, AFRICOM's creation promotes the development of an overarching Africa strategy. The African security policy landscape requires a responsive and coherent U.S. strategy, which was difficult even within the Defense Department when Africa was split between combatant commands. The resulting "lack of…overarching strategy and integrated programming hamper[ed] the effectiveness of virtually all security-related U.S. programs in sub-Saharan Africa."[12]

Third, the command increases U.S. military resources available for use on the continent and provides a stronger voice for African affairs and partnerships in Joint Staff decision processes where resources are allocated across all commands. Under Department of Defense Directive No. 5100.1, combatant commanders enjoy direct access to the Secretary of Defense and the Chairman of the Joint Chiefs of Staff. This "puts the new command in a much stronger position to compete with other commands for resources, manpower, and influence over policy making."[13] It also "allow[s] the administration to go to the U.S. Congress and argue that the establishment of AFRICOM demonstrates the importance of Africa for U.S. national security and the administration's commitment to give the continent the attention that it deserves."[14]

AFRICOM's fourth potential benefit involves the commitment the creation of the command signaled to African partners and other nations competing with the U.S for access to and influence within African nations. General William E. "Kip" Ward, AFRICOM's combatant commander, noted that "the elimination of Unified Command Plan boundaries within Africa will position AFRICOM well to establish strong and lasting habitual relationships with…African partners (especially with the African Union), allies, and international organizations" present in Africa.[15] For Liberia's Minister of Defense, "AFRICOM has the potential to 'build partnerships, lead to the convergence of strategic interest, prevent conflict, and conduct operations other than war.'"[16]

Finally, AFRICOM will afford the United States a dedicated command structure to operate various military missions in Africa. These will include current operations, such as train and equip programs, the African Coastal and Border Security Program, CJTF-HOA missions, Joint Task Force Aztec Silence, and naval operations in the Gulf of Guinea. In addition to military activities, AFRICOM will likely provide the infrastructure, logistics, planning, and integration resources required for civilian missions, including infrastructure development, humanitarian assistance, anti-crime efforts, and legal reform.

In recognition of AFRICOM's interagency support role, its headquarters structure differs from those of other combatant commands and is designed "to integrate activities and eliminate 'stovepipes.'"[17] In addition to a three-star Deputy to the Commander for Military Operations (DCMO), there is a civilian Deputy to the Commander for Civil-Military Activities (DCMA). While military flag officers occupy three director positions[18] at the level beneath the DCMO and DCMA, three other director positions are occupied by members of the Senior Executive Service.[19] Embedded beneath them are additional military and civilian personnel. The DCMA is responsible for "direct[ing] the command's plans and programs associated with health, humanitarian assistance, humanitarian mine action, disaster response, and security sector reform."[20]

Challenges for AFRICOM

It will take years for AFRICOM to establish itself. A number of challenges are likely to impede its progress, five of which directly involve the Command's ability to improve regional policy coordination and execution.

First, the command structure may become a *de facto* regional coordinating mechanism. This is the first time that a combatant command headquarters has seen the permanent embedding of senior civilian personnel within the structure, which does offer enhanced opportunities for interagency contact. However, this could actually harm coordination efforts.

A popular idiom suggests that nature abhors a vacuum—so, too, does the interagency. Deficits in interagency policy making and implementation are often filled by the interagency participant that can quickly bring sufficient assets to bear on the matter. Due to its overwhelming resources and command authorities, the Department of Defense is usually the organization that fills such deficits. There is a "tendency to default to the Department of Defense,"[21] which leads to a "Matthew Effect."[22] The effect is that "the Department of Defense undertakes what should be a civilian agency's project because the military has available resources, and in the next budget cycle the Department of Defense receives increased resources to cover its broader role, while the civilian agency that could not undertake the mission" receives similar or fewer resources compared to the prior budget cycle.[23]

A second challenge involves roles and missions for command staff. The headquarters structure has not alleviated span of control or unity of command issues impeding interagency coordination and collaboration. Senior civilian agency personnel are embedded within the command but their roles are more akin to advisors and liaisons. They have authority within the command but not with respect to their home departments and agencies. They cannot commit interagency partners to work with the military in Africa. Assigned personnel should be able to advise the AFRICOM headquarters as to how other U.S. government organizations will react to AFRICOM policy planning—hopefully steering such planning in a direction supported by the entire interagency—but they cannot force policies that are unsupported by home departments.

The next problem is that the Department of Defense may gain too much control over interagency decisions at the regional level, leading to the militarization of Africa policy. Interagency program directors should consider all policy and planning options, not those that emerge from military planning processes. Interagency and international partners should be included in strategic planning and policy development. Some of these partners may chaff against a combatant command process merely because it will attach the U.S. military to whatever policy is recommended.

An additional problem, which relates to the military's rich resource base, is the risk of mission creep. AFRICOM's primary role of supporting military training, humanitarian missions, and development programs could move, over time, toward a more traditional military combat role. This is most likely to result if civilian organizations are not sufficiently resourced to complete their assigned roles. Although General Ward "views the Department of Defense's role in Africa as part of a 'three-pronged' U.S. government approach, with DoD, through AFRICOM, taking the lead on security issues, but playing a supporting role to the Department of State, which conducts diplomacy, and USAID, which implements development programs,"[24] the question remains as to how the military's role will change when other agencies fall short.

The final problem with AFRICOM relates to the above-mentioned perception that AFRICOM will lead to the militarization of African security affairs. In addition to the problem of AFRICOM having the potential to militarize U.S. policy, other nations may seek to balance against AFRICOM by increasing their defense and military presence. Some lament that "AFRICOM is a dangerous continuation of U.S. military expansion around the globe…AFRICOM will only inflame threats against the United States, make Africa even more dependent on external powers and delay responsible African solutions to continental security issues."[25]

Conclusion

While AFRICOM offers a new mechanism for coordination, further interagency reform at the regional level is needed. When civilian missions occur in steady-state, generally secure environments, other methods of interagency integration should be explored. One option is to continue using the current NSC system. The Africa regional Policy Coordinating Committee (PCC) could create sub-PCCs in Washington for individual or similar interagency missions in Africa. These sub-PCCs would be tasked with policy formulation and close mission monitoring. Another option is to continue using the lead agency concept, but couple it with significant reforms to budgeting, resourcing, and human capital systems. These changes would serve to empower the lead agency vis-à-vis interagency counterparts involved in a specific mission. A third option is to create regional interagency coordinating mechanisms. Established with proper legislation, they could be afforded the necessary authorities and resources to enable interagency implementation of policy. With respect to each of these options, flexibility could be built into the system to afford AFRICOM the necessary level of combat command authority for military operations.

Notes

1   See studies including: The U.S. Commission on National Security/21st Century (July 1998–February 2001); Clark A. Murdock and Michèle A. Flournoy, *Beyond Goldwater Nichols Phase II Report: Defense Reform for a New Strategic Era* (CSIS, 2005); and The Project on National Security Reform (PNSR): Transforming Government for the 21st Century (2006–present).

2   Isaac Kfir, "The Challenge that is USAFRICOM," *Joint Force Quarterly*, no. 49, 2nd Quarter 2008.

3   Christopher Thompson, "The Scramble for Africa's Oil," *New Statesman*, June 18, 2007.

4   Marco Overhaus, et al, eds., "Dealing with Dependency: The European Union's Quest for a Common Energy Foreign Policy," *Foreign Policy in Dialogue*, vol. 8: no. 20, 2007.

5   Robert B. Oakley, and Michael Casey, Jr., "The Country Team: Restructuring America's First Line of Engagement." *Strategic Forum* No. 227 (Washington, D.C.: National Defense University, 2007), 3.

6   Barry Buzan, and Ole Wæver, *Regions and Powers: The Structure of International Security.* (New York, New York: Cambridge University Press, 2003), 4.

7   Ibid.

8   Ibid.

9   USACOM's maritime AOR relating to certain African islands was transferred to EUCOM through a 2000 UCP revision.

10 Ibid., 8.

11 Brett D. Schaefer and Mackenzie M. Eaglen, "U.S. Africa Command: Challenges and Opportunities," *Backgrounder* No. 2118, The Heritage Foundation, March 21, 2008, fn2.

12 Catoire, 8.

13 Daniel Volman, "Why America Wants Military HQ in Africa," *New African*, January 2008.

14 Ibid.

15 General Ward, responses to "Advanced Questions for General William E. 'Kip' Ward, U.S. Army, Nominee for Commander, U.S. Africa Command," 6.

16 Minister of Defense Brownie Samukai, quoted by Sean McFate, "U.S. Africa Command: A New Strategic Paradigm?" in *Military Review*, January/February 2008, 19.

17 Ibid., 7.

18 These include the Director for Strategy, Plans and Programs, the Director for C4 Systems, and the Director for Operations & Logistics.

19 These include the Director for Outreach, the Director for Intelligence and Knowledge Development, and the Director for Resources.

20 Biography, AMB Mary C. Yates, **http://www.africom.mil/yates.asp** (accessed April 9, 2008).

21 Richard Weitz, PNSR, "Conference Proceedings," July 25–26, 2007.

22 This is a reference to the Gospel of Matthew: "For everyone who has will be given more, and he will have an abundance. Whoever does not have, even what he has will be taken from him."

23 PNSR, "Conference Proceedings," 45.

24 Lauren Ploch, "Africa Command: U.S. Strategic Interests and the Role of the U.S. Military in Africa," Congressional Research Service, *Report for Congress*, December 7, 2007, 8.

25 Danny Glover and Nicole C. Lee, "Say No to AFRICOM," *The Nation*, November 19, 2007, 2.

Changing Face of the U.S. Military: Promoting Maritime Security in Africa

Derek S. Reveron

When President Bush announced in early 2007 that the United States would become more strategically engaged in Africa, it was through the creation of a new military command—U.S. Africa Command (AFRICOM)—and not through increasing the activities of the U.S. Agency for International Development or the State Department's Bureau of African Affairs. Yet, tellingly, this new "combatant" command is not focused on fighting wars. Rather, it is structured to promote international military partnerships. Through the creation of AFRICOM, President Bush has moved away from his observation in 2000 that the military should not engage in nation building, and instead is continuing the post–Cold War practice of using the military in nontraditional ways. Yet a key unanswered question is how the U.S. military will increasingly fill diplomatic and development roles. This chapter discusses preliminary field work of U.S. military activities in East Africa, the lessons of which continue to shape AFRICOM.

When President Bush announced in early 2007 that the United States would become more strategically engaged in Africa, it was through the creation of a new military command—U.S. Africa Command (AFRICOM)—and not through increasing the activities of the U.S. Agency for International Development or the State Department's Bureau of African Affairs. Yet, tellingly, this new "combatant" command isn't focused on fighting wars, but rather is designed to promote international military partnerships.[1] In fact, since the announcement has been made, the word "combatant" has fallen away, underscoring the emphasis this new unified command will place on non-combat functions. Through the creation of AFRICOM, President Bush has moved very far from his observation in 2000 that the military should not do nation building, and instead has continued the post–Cold War practice of using the military in nontraditional ways.

For President Bush, AFRICOM is designed "to strengthen our security cooperation with Africa to help create new opportunities to bolster the capabilities of our partners in Africa."[2] Some have interpreted the creation of this new command as recognition of the growing importance of West African oil or as preparation for a future cold war with China, but these observations fail to capture the extent to which the U.S. military has been changing from a force of confrontation to cooperation. This change is reflected in the continued evolution of language used to describe how security services are used. The War Department of World War II gave rise to the Cold War Defense Department. One might think of today's Defense Department as the Security Cooperation Department, given how much effort is now expended building the militaries of other countries, from Afghanistan to Yemen. For the U.S. military today, building and rebuilding other countries' militaries is a full-time job and occupies current thinking on ways to negate non-state actors' capabilities. The creation of AFRICOM is a logical outgrowth of this change away from confrontation to capacity building to support conflict prevention.

AFRICOM should also not be interpreted as a great change in U.S. policy as it relates to Africa; the U.S. military has been actively promoting African security for decades through three existing U.S. military commands, a 1,200-person U.S. military base in the East African country of Djibouti, and security assistance teams deployed in dozens of African capitals. Further, bilateral and multilateral military activities have occurred for decades; one case in point is the U.S. Navy's annual West African Training Cruise that began in 1978. Instead, the creation of AFRICOM signals an attempt to bureaucratically reform an antiquated command structure and provide better assistance to African countries. Instead of coordinating U.S. policy toward Africa at three geographically dispersed headquarters in Hawaii, Florida, and Germany, there is now a single command focused on Africa.[3] While some critics of the new command have characterized AFRICOM as a symbol of U.S. neocolonialism, it is likely better thought of as a tangible commitment by the United States to fulfill its national security goal of improving human security around the world. The precursor to this change was the 2005 Defense Department Directive 3000.5 that placed stability and security operations on par with major combat. With this formal acknowledgment of the Defense Department's shift from war to security cooperation, the military has evolved from being a supporting actor in the political sphere to serving as a central player.

Military Force and Diplomacy

While the State Department is America's lead foreign-policy organization, U.S. military commanders are as much policy entrepreneurs as they are war fighters, and they increasingly fulfill important diplomatic roles.[4] The Defense Department has a distinct advantage over the State Department in both size and resources, with an operating budget sixty times greater and personnel numbers that dwarf the modest size of the diplomatic corps, which is composed of 6,000 foreign service officers (FSOs). Africa Command headquarters is to be composed of about 1,200 military personnel, which vastly outnumbers the approximately eighty employees of the State Department's Africa Bureau. In East Africa, the U.S. military has over 2,000 personnel, who are primarily noncombat personnel focused on engineering and construction projects, medical and veterinary care, and providing various forms of military training. In contrast, the U.S. FSOs and development officers in the region number in the hundreds. When it comes to resources, Congress funds the military vastly better than any other foreign assistance agency, and this is likely to continue in the future.

The United States' military commands, with their forward presence, large planning staffs, and various engagement tools, are well equipped for these changing roles and increasingly welcome them. Today they routinely pursue regional-level engagement by playing host to international-security conferences, promoting military-to-military contacts, and providing American military presence, training, and equipment to nearly every country in the world. This provision of security assistance can help fledgling democracies consolidate, fragile states avoid failure, and authoritarian states liberalize.[5] Furthermore, security is essential for economic and social development.[6]

While some argue that this new role for the U.S. military reflects a desire to employ forces in new ways given the fact that the advent of a more stable international order has reduced large-scale direct military confrontations, this charge overlooks both a military's natural predisposition to eschew non-warfighting activities, the current high tempo of operational counter-insurgency, and the military's role as a tool of national power that is increasingly used in noncoercive ways. Given the very real combat demands of U.S. forces in Iraq and Afghanistan, one would actually expect to see a decline in nontraditional military activities, yet the creation of AFRICOM and the transformation of U.S. Southern Command, which operates in the Western Hemisphere, illustrate the opposite. British General Sir Rupert Smith described the change that the Defense Department is responding to, noting: "War as cognitively known to most noncombatants, war as a battle in a field between men and machinery, war as a massive deciding event in a dispute in international affairs; such war no longer exists."[7] Given the importance of this change, there is increasing demand to understand how militaries are adapting their strategies and capabilities to fulfill noncombat roles.

A key component of exporting security is security cooperation, which is the ability of militaries to interact together to build defense relationships that promote specific security interests, develop allied and friendly military capabilities for self-defense and coalition operations, and provide foreign forces peacetime and contingency access. The U.S. Navy in particular has embraced the notion of security cooperation, given its shrinking fleet and increasing global challenges. Senior Navy strategists Vice Admiral Morgan and Rear Admiral Martogolio have noted that "policing the maritime commons will require substantially more capability than the United States or any individual nation can deliver."[8] In an effort to bolster its own capacity, the United States seeks partnerships with international navies in order to create the proverbial 1,000-ship navy that can respond to piracy, smuggling, other illegal activities, and protect important sea lines of communication. And where no able partners exist, the United States will help build national capabilities. To be sure, the concept does not anticipate 1,000 ships or confine itself to Navy vessels only. In fact, the term of art has changed to "global maritime partnerships." Underlying the global maritime partnership concept is recognition that no single country can keep the oceans safe for trade and other legitimate activities, but the importance of seaborne trade, the size of the world's oceans, and globalization cannot be ignored.[9] The trend of maritime cooperation is a very large endeavor and it will take decades to judge its effect. The rest of this chapter examines this initiative in more detail; specifically, the roots of maritime cooperation in East Africa and the Southwest Indian Ocean.

East Africa and Southwest Indian Ocean Initiative

The primary military command that focuses on East Africa is Combined Joint Task Force—Horn of Africa (CJTF-HOA), which is located in Djibouti. While much external impressions of CJTF-HOA were defined by its early focus on lethal military action, the command has evolved since 2002 and is decidedly focused on building partners' capacity today. Part of the command philosophy is "do no harm."[10] CJTF-HOA's vision emphasizes the broader shift in U.S. strategic thinking from confrontation to cooperation: "CJTF-HOA is all about building friendships, forging relationships, and creating partnerships. The integration of Diplomacy, Development, and Defense efforts is essential to ensuring our success. With effective partnership, we will see increased Security, improved Stability, and strengthened Sovereignty in the Horn of Africa."[11] To be sure, CJTF-HOA does train land and maritime forces to be more effective, but it also builds schools, digs wells, and facilitates development through road building and other infrastructure projects. Since CJTF-HOA pursues a regional approach that covers thirteen countries, working with key national representatives is critical.[12] One such program is the East African Southwest Indian Ocean (EASWIO), which is focused on improving maritime safety and security from the Gulf of Aden to the Mozambique Channel.

Arguably, piracy off the Somali coast and fears of seaborne terrorism were the initial issues that brought international attention to maritime issues in Africa. Yet, it will be economic concerns that drive the improvement of national maritime capabilities, and that will keep international navies and coast guards engaged in the region for the foreseeable future. With 90 percent of the world's trade seaborne, maritime security is a key component of energy security, food security, and economic security.[13] U.S. Vice Admiral Kevin J. Cosgriff, commander of the U.S. 5th Fleet, summed up what the United States and more than twenty of its allies are attempting to do: "Even as we struggle daily against violent extremism, our maritime security operations offer tangible benefits to all entities that use the seas—and need to be able to use the seas—without risk of harassment or worse. Our power is in the capability and intent to safeguard peaceful use of waterways and the resources of the sea."[14]

Tangible benefits of strong maritime security include reducing illegal, unreported, and unregulated (IUU) fishing, which is estimated to cost African countries one billion dollars annually.[15] Other tangible benefits include improving countries' abilities to monitor their territorial waters and exclusive economic zones, developing capabilities to respond to crises at sea, and improving the state's ability to provide security. In addition to the tangible benefits, a major focus includes increasing political will to effect change. Political will is lacking for four basic reasons: lack of awareness, limited vulnerability of national governments to maritime threats, immature domestic industry to develop maritime resources, and government apathy when it comes to corruption, enforcement of maritime laws, and implementing existing international regulations.[16]

Started in 2006, EASWIO brings together many of the region's countries annually to discuss maritime issues and synchronize planning with partner countries. By hosting conferences, CJTF-HOA intends to raise awareness of maritime security issues, provide grist for national and regional maritime strategies, and work with other regional partners to improve maritime safety and security.[17] According to the head of CJTF-HOA, Rear Admiral Phil Greene, Jr., "The importance of maritime security and safety in this region is driven because of the economic challenges that the region faces. This is due to criminal activities at sea, trafficking of drugs, smuggling of illegal cargo, trafficking of people as well as armed robbery and piracy at sea."[18]

The 2006 and 2007 EASWIO Maritime Security Conferences were the primary regional maritime engagements for CJTF-HOA. The first was hosted in Antananarivo, Madagascar, in 2006. Representation was mostly military, and it focused on the need to develop maritime strategies. The second conference was hosted in Mombasa, Kenya, and featured a mix of military personnel, civilian maritime, and port security authorities. It focused on several key issues raised during ESAWIO-I, including the need to develop bilateral and multilateral collaboration on maritime security issues in the region. The 2008 conference was hosted in Djibouti with the explicit goal of producing a maritime strategy document that could be used as a template for both national and regional development for subsequent endorsement at a planned sub-ministerial meeting. Conference attendees left with a solid academic background in the strategy and methodologies necessary to conduct capabilities gap analysis and an analysis of policy stakeholders. From CJTF-HOA's perspective, EASWIO nations need to expand national strategies and remove perceived barriers to African-led solutions to security challenges in the region. Through the EASWIO process, formalizing a maritime strategy should assist in the more effective development of national-level regulatory and legal regimes.

The three conferences held to date have solidified this regional view and helped develop approaches to creating effective maritime capabilities. As a basic goal, EASWIO has the potential to lay the groundwork for a regional maritime organization that can facilitate information sharing, establish regional maritime domain awareness, and foster regional cooperation. Fundamental to this is enabling EASWIO countries to take the lead in maritime issues. International cooperation is key to the U.S. approach toward maritime safety and security. This was institutionalized at the second EASWIO conference where the decision was made to create a Maritime

Regional Center of Excellence. The center will fill many roles, including serving as a regional forum for development of policy and doctrine, hosting operational and tactical training, and promoting maritime standards and safety procedures. With the desired end goal of creating a self-sustaining institution with African instructors and administration, the center would service many countries from the region.[19] As of this writing, the center will be built in Kenya with U.S. military funds and will serve as a regional hub for military and civilians involved in maritime safety and security issues. At the 2008 conference, a participant from landlocked Uganda outlined the importance of this international approach: "It is about partnership, it is about cooperation, it is about countries pooling their resources, sharing information, and all of this is for the economic benefit for the people in this region of Africa."[20] While bilateral assistance efforts must undergird the regional approach, the regional approach sets the course and speed for countries to reach. From a U.S. perspective, assistance is not about harking back to the Cold War practice of buying influence or simply building infrastructure.[21] Instead, these programs are about creating sustainable maritime services to improve individual countries' ability to control their territory. Some African leaders object to this approach as providing conditions, but it is illustrative of the change not only in policy, but also views of the security environment. In an increasingly globalized political space, the United States and its European partners can no longer ignore instability far from their own shores that produces illegal trafficking of people, drugs, and other contraband. And with a new emphasis on linking results to strategy, programs will be monitored closely and can be cancelled if they fail to meet objectives.

Promoting cooperation also extends down into national governments. One tangible benefit of U.S. military-hosted conferences like EASWIO is increasing the dialogue between civilian and military agencies on national maritime strategies and port security operations.[22] Since security issues are no longer the exclusive realm of militaries, a major security cooperation goal is to bring together personnel from law enforcement, port authorities, think tanks, and other relevant civilian government ministries such as natural resources, customs, and finance.[23] These conferences have an explicit goal of improving interagency cooperation within respective countries and sharing knowledge across countries. For example, at the 2008 EASWIO conference, a civilian port operator from Mauritius was able to share his port's best practices with representatives from ten other countries. He explained the steps his port used to become certified under the International Ship and Port Facility Security Code (ISPS) and the international impact of becoming ISPS compliant. The example also highlights that maritime security is no longer defined at the water's edge, but begins ashore in ports, customs facilities, and warehouses.

Finally, the effort made to have experts from the region present material reinforced that the United States does not monopolize solutions to security problems. In fact, as the Director of Strategy, Plans, and Policy said during the 2008 conference, "Seeing the issues each nation is up against sets a framework for finding solutions in the future. Because of the limited resources involved, and the overlapping challenges the countries in the region encounter, if they can start thinking about working together to improve the overall security situation, this region in Africa will be one step closer to achieving the goals of the working group."

Conclusion

The CJTF-HOA in general, and the East African Southwest Indian Ocean program in particular, illustrate how the U.S. military has changed over the last two decades. With a history that is six years older than AFRICOM and a basing presence in Africa, many of the lessons of CJTF-HOA continue to inform how AFRICOM will be shaped. While there has been much symbolic resistance to the creation of AFRICOM, these concerns are not based on a critique of ongoing U.S. military activities in Africa or on the recognition of how U.S. military power is shifting from a force designed for confrontation to one being redesigned for cooperation. Instead, criticism is based on outdated thinking about U.S. foreign policy or fear that the United States will displace particular regional powers. To overcome this, AFRICOM will have to reassure key states that it seeks to serve as a catalyst for national security improvements and not fill the security void with U.S. presence. Critics must understand that there is no political will or national interest for a hegemonic presence in Africa, nor the necessary resources to establish such hegemony. While it is too soon to know if AFRICOM, CJTF-HOA, and EASWIO will be effective in the long-term, the commands must be judged by their own criteria—which are improving stability and security in Africa. These criteria will be driven more by partner countries in Africa than any external organization. At least at the command's inception, U.S. military leaders seem to understand this and have let partner countries set the pace for engagement activities.

Notes

1   "Africa Command will enhance our efforts to help bring peace and security to the people of Africa and promote our common goals of development, health, education, democracy, and economic growth in Africa," George W. Bush, The White House, "President Bush Creates a Department of Defense Unified Combatant Command for Africa," http://www.whitehouse.gov/news/releases/2007/02/20070206-3.html.

2   White House, "President Bush Creates a Department of Defense Unified Combatant Command for Africa," February 6, 2007, http://www.whitehouse.gov/news/releases/2007/02/20070206-3.html.

3   As of this writing, Egypt will remain in U.S. Central Command, so there will be technically two commands engaged in Africa. However, AFRICOM will oversee engagement activities with fifty-two of fifty-three countries.

4   See Derek S. Reveron and Judith Hicks Stiehm, eds., *Inside Defense: Understanding the 21st Century Military* (New York: Palgrave Macmillan, 2008).

5   "Security assistance refers to a group of programs by which the United States provides defense articles, military training, and other defense-related services to foreign nations by grant, loan, credit, or cash sales in furtherance of national policies and objectives." Programs include: Foreign Military Sales, Foreign Military Financing, International Military Education and Training Program, and the Economic Support Fund. See US Department of Defense, *Joint Operations*, Joint Publication 3-0, September 17, 2006, VII-7.

6   Carol Atkinson, "Constructivist Implications of Material Power: Military Engagement and the Socialization of States, 1972–2000," *International Studies Quarterly*, 50, 2006, 509–537.

7   Rupert Smith, *The Utility of Force: the Art of War in the Modern World* (New York: Vintage, 2007), 3.

8   Vice-Admiral John Morgan, Jr. and Captain Charles Martoglio, "The 1,000-Ship Navy: Global Maritime Network," U.S. Naval Institute *Proceedings* 131, November 2005, 18.

9   This is a strong underlying premise in the 2007 *Cooperative Strategy for Twenty-First Century Seapower*, www.navy.mil/maritime/MaritimeStrategy.pdf.

10   United States Central Command, "Memorandum for Combined Joint Task Force—Horn of Africa, Strategic Guidance for 2008," March 10, 2008.

11   Combined Joint Task Force—Horn of Africa, "Command Brief," May 2008.

12   This includes Comoros, Djibouti, Eritrea, Ethiopia, Kenya, Madagascar, Mauritius, Seychelles, Somalia, Sudan, Tanzania, Uganda, and Yemen.

13   The White House, *The National Strategy for Maritime Security*, (Washington: White House, September 2005), 1.

14   "Maritime Security Operations Key to Regional Stability, Security," Navy Newstand, October 11, 2007.

15   Marine Resources Assessment Group Ltd, "Review of Impacts of Illegal, Unreported and Unregulated Fishing on Developing Countries Synthesis Report," July 2005, http://www.dfid.gov.uk/pubs/files/illegal-fishing-mrag-synthesis-report.pdf.

16   Combined Joint Task Force—Horn of Africa, "Conference Report," East Africa and Southwest Indian Ocean Maritime Security Conference (EASWIO), Antananarivo, Madagascar, July 25–27, 2007.

17   It is important to point, however, that there are other national and international organizations pursuing similar goals, so it would be essential to understand the extent to which military activities are coordinated with non-military activities.

18   Scott Cohen, "*African Nations Working for Maritime Security*," June 23, 2008, http://www.hoa.centcom.mil/ArticleArchive/June2008/EASWAIO062308.asp.

19   CJTF-HOA Maritime Security Group, "Maritime Regional Center of Excellence Concept," East Africa and Southwest Indian Ocean (EASWIO) Maritime Security and Port Security Seminar, Mombasa, Kenya, September 4–7, 2007.

20   Cohen, "*African Nations*," http://www.hoa.centcom.mil/ArticleArchive/June2008/EASWAIO062308.asp. While Uganda is landlocked, it has considerable maritime issues on Lake Victoria and plans to provide coastal patrol forces for a peacekeeping deployment off the Somali coast.

21   In fact, this can be frustrating for the partner countries who expect U.S. resources to make up for national shortfalls. The United States continues to balance resource requests against what is sustainable. It is very easy to provide a country boats, but if there is no infrastructure or trained personnel to maintain the boats, the investment will fall short of expectations.

22   This also holds true from a U.S. government perspective. At the 2008 EASWIO conference, there were representatives from at least six other U.S. organizations to include Department of State, Office of Secretary of Defense, and other non-CJTF-HOA DOD components.

23   Further, with the development of national level and regional strategies, the EASWIO process gives way to civil-military discussions of strategy. While military personnel are often better positioned than civilian personnel to develop strategy, tenuous civil-military relations can prevent the necessary dialogue. Through EASWIO, CJTF-HOA brings together personnel from across the government to ensure that dialogue can produce consensus on the ways and means required for improving maritime safety and security.

Michael P. Argosino is a 2008 graduate of the Security Policy Studies Program at the Elliott School of International Affairs and a market intelligence and business strategist for a California-based startup engaged in leadership and organizational development. His professional experience includes financial, commercial, and security management. He has also consulted to the American Red Cross National Headquarters on IT systems for disaster preparedness and response.

Peng Claire Bai is a doctoral student at the Massachusetts Institute of Technology and has an MA in Security Policy Studies from George Washington University's Elliott School of International Affairs.

Lieutenant Colonel Shannon D. Beebe is the Senior Africa Analyst in the Office of United States Army Deputy Chief of Staff, Intelligence. He has been selected to be the military attaché to Angola beginning August 2009. Beebe is the recipient of an Institute of National Security Studies grant to study Environmental Security issues for AFRICOM. A conservation and environmental security expert, his research addresses the effects of conflict, the environment, and sustainability on stability, work that has brought non-traditional partners into the security dialogue. LTC Beebe is a frequent speaker at the Joint Special Operations University; the United States Foreign Service Institute; National Defense University; the Center for Strategic and International Studies; the Royal United Services Institute; and the Woodrow Wilson Center; he contributed to the Council of Foreign Relations Report, "*Climate Change and National Security: An Agenda for Action*" (by Dr. Joshua W. Busby). He was also featured in a National Geographic Television special on the environment and security in Africa. The article represents the research and opinions of the author.

Peter Clark is Managing Director of Cannon House Partners LLC., where he directs investments in emerging economies with a primary focus on Asia. He previously worked in real estate acquisition, investment, and development with the Seattle offices of Dutch investment group HAL Holding N.V and as a principal with Landstar Inc. As an analyst with the Program on Transitions to Democracy, he worked on post-cold war peace settlements. Clark has an MA in Security Policy Studies from the Elliott School of International Affairs at the George Washington University, an MBA in Finance from the Marshall School of Business at the University of Southern California, and a BA in Economics and Political Science from The Johns Hopkins University. The article represents the research and opinions of the author.

Melissa Cox-Bosse is a Joint Warfare Analyst at Science Application International Corporation supporting the Secretary of Defense and the Chief of Naval Operations Capability Analysis and Assessment Division. Ms. Cox-Bosse previously served as a Surface Warfare Officer in the United States Navy and is a veteran of Operation IRAQI FREEDOM, where she served aboard USS Philippine Sea (CG-58). Ms. Cox-Bosse led wartime joint and coalition maritime security operations in the North Arabian Gulf and is has in MA in Security Policy Studies from the George Washington University's Elliott School of International Affairs.

Appointed CENSA Executive Director in March 2008, **James T. Kirkhope** possesses over 20 years of experience delivering a broad array of consulting, training, and research projects on international affairs and homeland security. He founded both the Terrorism Studies Group and Terrorism Studies Network in 2002 and manages Kirkhope Consulting International. Mr. Kirkhope has published widely in academic journals, books, and electronic media on political violence and domestic security issues since 1989. Mr. Kirkhope's clients have included private companies, publishers, universities, think tanks, and government agencies. He has been deeply engaged in the operationalization and delivery of a variety of significant Department of Homeland Security initiatives, leading unclassified Defense Department research projects, as well as international exchange projects and international development efforts focused on conflict resolution and democracy and governance. Mr. Kirkhope holds a BA in History and Psychology from Bowling Green State University, an MA in International Affairs from The George Washington University, and an MA in Political Science from Columbia University.

Sean McFate is a senior consultant with Bearing Point. Previously, he was a Program Director at the Bipartisan Policy Center and a Program Manager for DynCorp International, where he led several African security and stabilization programs. A former Captain in the U.S. Army, he has published in Military Review, RUSI Journal, African Affairs, and the Review of African Political Economy and is a doctoral candidate at the London School of Economics.

Anthony D. McIvor is a national security subject matter expert and writer working chiefly in the civil-military relationship area. He was a principal advisor to the Deputy Chief of Naval Operations on US Maritime Strategy and advises the Marine Corps Warfighting Laboratory. He co-led the development of the "Rethinking the Principles of War" project sponsored by the Office of Force Transformation and the Secretary of the Navy and was the editor of Rethinking the Principles of War (USNI Press, 2005). Dr. McIvor is the editor of the American Intelligence Journal, a member of Executive Committee of the National Military Intelligence Association, and serves on the Intelligence Advisory Council of the American Military University. His current research is focused on the Maghreb and Sahel regions of Africa.

Sean T. Macrae is an active duty infantry Major in the United States Army. He currently serves on the Army Staff as a strategist in the Office of the Deputy Chief of Staff, Operations focused on Force Planning and Integration as well as Global Defense Posture and Realignment initiatives. He recently served as the AFRICOM and EUCOM Desk Officer for the Army Staff. He served as a Ranger Platoon Leader, Ranger Executive Officer, Battalion Plans Officer, and Airborne Company Commander in combat and peacetime with operational experience in both Iraq and Afghanistan. MAJ. Macrae earned a Bachelor of Science in Environmental Engineering from the United States Military Academy at West Point in 1999 and a Masters in Public Administration from the Harvard Kennedy School of Government in 2008. His article represents the research and opinions solely of the author.

Richard Mehring received an MA in Security Policy Studies in 2008 from the Elliott School of International Affairs at the George Washington University in Washington, DC. He received a Bachelors degree in English and writing from Houghton College in western New York. He is a native of the Washington area and lives in Silver Spring, Maryland.

John N. Paden (M.A. Oxford, Ph.D. Harvard) is Clarence Robinson Professor of International Studies at George Mason University (GMU). He is the author of fourteen books on Africa, the most recent being *Faith and Politics in Nigeria* (U.S. Institute of Peace Press, 2008.) The author has more than forty years experience observing Africa, overlapping with more than twenty-five years experience observing China. From 1981 to 1996 he served on the US-China African Studies Exchange Committee that helped to set up African studies in China. Subsequently, he was Director of the GMU summer graduate programs in Beijing in collaboration with Capital University of Economics and Business, focusing on "international commerce and policy" (1998, 1999, 2000). He has made more than a dozen trips to China and he has been Co-Director of the GMU Center for Asia Pacific Economic Cooperation (CAPEC) since 1996.

Michael Radosh is a Senior Consultant at Booz Allen Hamilton, where he has been employed since 2006. Prior to that, Mike was a Paralegal Specialist at the US Department of Justice. Mike graduated from the University of Maryland, College Park in May 2003 with a BA in Government and Politics. He received an MA in Security Policy Studies, with a concentration in East Asia and Transnational Security, from GWU in May 2008. The views and opinions expressed in his article are solely those of the author.

Derek S. Reveron is a Professor of National Security Affairs at the US Naval War College in Newport, Rhode Island. He specializes in U.S. foreign policy, military-political affairs, and intelligence. The views expressed in this chapter are his own and do not reflect any official opinion of the United States Navy; he can be reached through at **derekreveron@gmail.com**.

Angela Sapp Mancini is Managing Director and Head of Asia, Africa and Eurasia Programs at the Financial Services Volunteer Corps, a U.S.-based not-for-profit organization focused on financial sector development of emerging economies. She has worked for Deloitte and Touche LLP in San Francisco and served in various senior finance roles for private sector firms in the U.S. and Russia. She founded a weekly newspaper, *The Azeri Times*, in Azerbaijan in 1998. She holds a Bachelors of Arts degree in

Business Economics from the University of California, a Masters degree in International Affairs from Columbia University's School of International and Public Affairs, and is a licensed CPA. She is a Term Member of the Council on Foreign Relations and served as Vice Chair of CENSA (2006-2008).

Matthew A. Shabat practiced corporate and securities law before joining the Project on National Security Reform's core study team and Structure Working Group as a Research Fellow. He received a B.A. in history from Stanford University, a J.D. from the University of Pennsylvania Law School and a M.A. in Security Policy Studies from the George Washington University's Elliott School of International Affairs.

David H. Shinn is Adjunct Professor of International Affairs at the Elliott School of International Affairs at George Washington University and serves on a number of boards of non-governmental organizations. Ambassador Shinn served for thirty-seven years in the US Foreign Service with assignments at embassies in Lebanon, Kenya, Tanzania, Mauritania, Cameroon, Sudan and as ambassador to Burkina Faso and Ethiopia. An expert on the Horn of Africa, Dr. Shinn speaks at events around the world. He is the co-author of *An Historical Dictionary of Ethiopia*, has authored numerous articles and book chapters, and has recently completed a book on China-Africa relations. His research interests include China-Africa relations, East Africa and the Horn, terrorism, Islamic fundamentalism, conflict situations, U.S. policy in Africa, and the African brain drain. Dr. Shinn received his BA (1963), MA (1964), PhD (1980) from George Washington University and a certificate in African studies from Northwestern University.

Blair Sondker is a Consultant on Homeland Security and Law Enforcement programs at Detica. He is responsible for providing timely analysis of tactics, techniques, and procedures in relation to the use of improvised explosive devices (IED) by terrorists throughout the world. Additionally, he provides support to the Department of Homeland Security on various issues of terrorism and critical infrastructure protection. Mr. Sondker is also a Senior Fellow for the Terrorism Studies Group. Previously he served as the principal analyst and project lead for the Global Risk Matrix at the Terrorism

Research Center and Total Intelligence Solutions. He built and managed the creation of the Global Risk Matrix—a massive analytical product that examined eleven varieties of risk for over 200 countries. While at the Terrorism Research Center and Total Intelligence Solutions he undertook long term research projects that examined the biological and sociological characteristics of IED makers in South Asia and the Middle East. Mr. Sondker has received his Masters in International Security and his Bachelor's in Anthropology and has served as a research assistant to both the Center for Strategic and International Studies and U.S. Northern Command.

Ian Taylor is a Professor in International Relations at the University of St Andrews. His main research interests are in Africa's international relations and Chinese foreign policy. Prior to coming to St Andrews in 2004, Dr. Taylor taught African Politics for four years at the University of Botswana and has lived in China and Africa for a total of eleven years and has visited/conducted research in 29 African countries.

Robert R. Tomes is adjunct professor of security policy studies at the at the Elliott School of International Affairs at the George Washington University, Washington, DC and is a Director of CENSA. Dr. Tomes is the President of Liminal Leadership, LLC, a security and intelligence consulting firm and is also a Director of the Anna Sobol Levy Foundation. He is the author of numerous articles and book chapters as well as *US Defense Strategy from Vietnam to Operation Iraqi Freedom* (Routledge, 2007). He has a BA from the University of Iowa, an MA from Iowa State University, and a PhD in Government and Politics from the University of Maryland, College Park.

Daniel Trapp holds an MA in Security Policy Studies from the Elliott School of International Affairs at the George Washington University, where he focused on political risk and energy and a BA in International Affairs and German from Valparaiso University in Valparaiso, Indiana. Daniel is a native of Minnesota and currently resides in Washington, DC.

Joshua Aaron Vogel has worked in various political and security related positions at the Center for American Progress, the Metropolitan Airport Authority, and the Bureau of Political Military Affairs at the State Department. Currently, he is the legislative review coordinator for the Office of Enforcement and Compliance Assurance at the U.S. Environmental Protection Agency. A Phi Beta Kappa, Joshua earned a Master of Arts in Security Policy Studies at the Elliott School of International Affairs with concentrations in Homeland Security and Military History and Strategy and serves on the Board of Directors of the Ladder 23 Corporation, a non-profit philanthropic organization.

Paul D. Williams is Associate Professor in the Elliott School of International Affairs at the George Washington University, Washington, DC. His latest books are *Security Studies: An Introduction* (Routledge, 2008) and co-edited with David R. Block, *The International Politics of Mass Atrocities: The Case of Darfur* (Routledge, 2009).

Theresa Whelan is Deputy Assistant Secretary of Defense for African Affairs within the Office of the Secretary of Defense. Her office is responsible for Department of Defense policy for all of Sub-Saharan Africa. Ms. Whelan previously served as Director of the Office of African Affairs and from June 1998 to November 2000 served in the Under Secretary of Defense for Policy's Balkans Task Force as the NATO Team Chief and then as the Task Force Deputy Chief of Staff. She was also a Defense Department representative on the US negotiating team at the Kosovo Talks in Rambouillet and Paris, France. Her prior positions in the Office of the Secretary Defense include those of Senior Program Director for the US/South Africa Joint Defense Committee, Countries Director for Southern Africa and Countries Director for West Africa. From 1987 to 1991 Ms. Whelan served as Defense Intelligence Agency analyst responsible for West, Central, and East African countries. Ms. Whelan has an MA in National Security Studies from Georgetown University, an MS in National Security Strategy from the National War College, and a BA in International Relations (Russian Studies minor) from the College of William and Mary.

To Order:

**To order more copies of this book, send $27.50
(including shipping and handling) to:**

Council for Emerging National Security Affairs
Cathedral Station, P.O. Box 534
New York, NY 10025

Or visit:
http://www.censa.net

ABOUT CENSA

The Council for Emerging National Security Affairs is a non-partisan, nonprofit research organization established in 1999. Its mission is to contribute to the ongoing dialogue shaping national security policy through formal discussion series, graduate level teaching programs, and collaborative research projects leading to publications of lasting quality. CENSA's activities draw upon the talents of its mid-career membership, a diverse, international group of public sector foreign policy specialists, military officers, private sector professionals, and accomplished academics.

www.censa.net

Council for Emerging National Security Affairs